Literary Gestures

The Aesthetic in Asian American Writing

Literary Gestures

The Aesthetic in
Asian American Writing

EDITED BY
ROCÍO G. DAVIS
and
SUE-IM LEE

TEMPLE UNIVERSITY PRESS / PHILADELPHIA

Temple University Press
1601 North Broad Street
Philadelphia PA 19122
www.temple.edu/tempress

Text design by Kate Nichols

⊗ The paper used in this publication meets the requirements of the American
National Standard for Information Sciences—Permanence of Paper for Printed
Library Materials, ANSI Z39.48-1992

Library of Congress Cataloging-in-Publication Data

Literary gestures: the aesthetic in Asian American writing / Rocío G. Davis and Sue-Im
    Lee, editors.
    p. cm.
    Includes bibliographical references and index.
    ISBN 1-59213-364-9 (alk. paper)—ISBN 1-59213-365-7 (pbk. : alk. paper)
    1. American literature—Asian American authors—History and criticism.   2. Asian
Americans—Intellectual life.   3. Asian Americans in literature.   4. Aesthetics, American.
I. Davis, Rocío G.   II. Lee, Sue-Im, 1969–

PS153.A84L58   2005
810.9'895—dc22

                                                                                    2005053805

2 4 6 8 9 7 5 3 1

Contents

1

Introduction

The Aesthetic in Asian American
Literary Discourse

SUE-IM LEE

SIAN AMERICAN LITERARY SCHOLARSHIP of the late twentieth
century has struggled to negotiate a balance between the immanentist understanding of literature (as a symbolic embodiment that
bears the historical and material forces of its production) and the counter-
vailing attempt to argue that literature represents "something else"—that a
literary text is more than the sum of its identifiable (sociological, economic,
political, historical) parts. The "aesthetic" has been an indispensable banner
in projects seeking to articulate the "something else" of the literary, and this
volume contributes to that effort by demonstrating the vitality and the volatility of the "aesthetic" as it circulates in Asian American literary discourse. By
positioning issues of literary aesthetics and formal analysis at the heart of
Asian American literary studies, this volume seeks to counterbalance the
prevailing dominance of sociological and cultural materialist approaches in
Asian American literary criticism, to bring about a self-consciousness in the
multidisciplinary uses of literary texts, and ultimately, to argue the complementary possibility of a historically and materially engaged analysis that *also*
recognizes the aesthetic as a rich critical variable.

As with scholarship in many other minority literatures, the emergence
and growth of Asian American literary criticism in the larger sphere of
American literary studies has depended upon its ability to represent the
material realities of its marginalized constituents. The parallel beginnings

of Asian American Studies in the academy and of Asian American political activism in the late-1960s have meant that, by and large, Asian American literary criticism has primarily sought to "speak" the material realities of hitherto "invisible," "disenfranchised," or "silent" subjects.[1] Particularly in the last two decades, amidst the powerful influences of new historicism, poststructuralism, cultural studies, and the growing trend toward interdisciplinarity, Asian American literary criticism has become almost indistinguishable from the reading of "culture," a term most expansively understood as the material and discursive structures of organized life. In this mode of criticism, literary works have been readily examined as symbolic enactments of material forces; as exemplifications of a particular ideology, phenomenon, or a conflict; or as illustrations of the political, economic, and sociological concerns of the times.

The prevailing strength of late twentieth century Asian American literary discourse, then, lies in arguing the *constructed* nature of human organizations—the complex ways in which power operates in the formation of particularly racialized subjects called "Asian American." Although Asian American literary criticism, like other minority literature scholarship, began with race as its pivotal lens of analysis, it has moved beyond the category of race to examine other social categorizations and institutions such as gender, class, sexuality, nation, capital, labor, and globalism. Perhaps one can discern the primacy of these sociological, economic, and political concerns most readily from the titles of monographs, anthologies, and edited essay collections in Asian American literary criticism of the last two decades. Concepts that recur as a title's keyword, such as "cultural politics," "nation," "transnation," "orientalism," "resistance," or "subversion," bespeak the discipline's particularly focused energy upon such concepts.[2] Certainly, materialist and political examinations of race, gender, sexuality, and nation need not preclude or exclude the possibility of treating texts as literary objects, but just such a balance, we contend, has not been successfully maintained in the Asian American literary criticism of the last two decades. That is, Asian American literary criticism at large has been slow to extend the analysis of the constructedness of human-made categories and institutions to include the examination of Asian American literary works as aesthetic objects—objects that are constituted by and through deliberate choices in form, genres, traditions, and conventions.[3]

The aesthetic, here, signifies the *constructed* dimension of the literary, the fact that literary objects are no less human-made—no less contrived—than ideological apparatus and social institutions. While the constructed nature of race, gender, nationality, sexuality, family, colonialism, among others, have been featured in the spotlight of Asian American literary discourse, other equally constructed practices, such as formal conventions, literary devices, genre particularities, and figurative language are more likely to be left in the wings of the critical stage.

This de-emphasis of literary aesthetics is certainly not unique to the field of Asian American literary discourse. In a germinal expression against this lacuna, George Levine's introductory essay "Reclaiming the Aesthetic," in *Aesthetics and Ideology* (1994), argues the pressing necessity of keeping a critical eye on "what constitutes the 'literary'" in order to "rescue it [the literary] from its potential disappearance into culture and politics."[4] Pointing to critic Walter Benn Michaels's oft-quoted assertion—that "the only relation literature as such has to culture as such is that it is part of it"—as exemplifying a critical environment that subsumes whatever particularity literature might have to the material forces of its production, Levine faults literary approaches that are indistinguishable from studies of sociopolitical, economic, or material forces or studies of ideological demystification.[5] Reading literature as an immanent expression of material conditions and structures of power, Levine argues, denies the fact that "literature is a definable category of discourse," and an "exclusive study of it [literature] is [deemed to be] complicit with unattractive political and social positions," such as the buttressing of the patriarchal Western canon.[6] Hence, *Aesthetics and Ideology*, a critical forerunner contesting the severely diminished presence of the aesthetic in late twentieth century literary analysis, argues the necessity of exploring the concept of the aesthetic as an entity more *complex* than simply reflective, immanentist, or complicitous with dominant structures of power and institutional discourse.[7]

Levine's call to breathe new life into the aesthetic by situating it as a central player in literary analysis has been answered in numerous ways. First, a number of recent essay collections recount the intellectual genealogy of the aesthetic, demonstrating the concept's long history of usage from classical philosophy to contemporary critical theory.[8] While offering a useful overview of the aesthetic's long intellectual history, such collections also highlight the multiplicity of meaning found under the concept—how the aesthetic "stands for" numerous uses, meanings (such as beauty, pleasure, the sublime, ethics, or aestheticism) that emerged from different moments of Western literary history.

Another notable approach to the aesthetic explores the uses of the concept as the apolitical, ideologically neutral standard and determination of beauty, pleasure, ethics, or value. As Emory Elliott writes in his introduction to *Aesthetics in a Multicultural Age* (2002), a "widespread cultural discrimination" functioning through the claim of aesthetic universality has operated throughout the Anglo-American academic judgment of cultural and artistic production.[9] How does the assumption of universality affect and interact with discourses of diversity and locality, with differences of race, class, ethnicity, sexuality, and other categories of identity and artistic production? Even if we disown the universality of literary excellence and values, obviously *some* criteria of evaluation are still in place, and articulating the terms of that evaluation is a project explored through the concept of the aesthetic.[10]

A renewed emphasis on formal analysis and close reading of literature is another significant strategy in revitalizing the aesthetic, and it is this approach to which our collection most closely adheres.[11] In the same way that the above projects seek to "recuperate" or "reclaim" a place for the aesthetic, this collection shares a keen awareness that any discussion of the aesthetic must take account of the "crucial insights provided by ideological criticism and contemporary theory."[12] Far from being a call for a "return" to an uncritical appreciation of the aesthetic as the ahistorical, universal standard by which artistic production should be measured, this renewed interest is motivated by a desire to rediscover the critical power of the aesthetic in the contemporary theoretical and artistic landscape. The impressive number of scholarly projects that revolve around the aesthetic points to its revitalization in contemporary critical discourse—as a distinct mode of human expression that requires a particular analysis of its rules and traditions; as a conceptual entity that's employed for multiple and sometimes conflicting uses; and as a discourse that cannot be divorced from political discourses while not being reduced to them.

As the following essays will demonstrate, however, the revitalization of the aesthetic has distinct political and historical implications for the field of Asian American literary discourse. Like many minority discourses in the academy, Asian American Studies has its beginnings in the political activism of the 1960s, as a multidisciplinary approach devoted to the examination of the material and discursive ramifications of being particularly interpellated as "Asian American." Asian American literary criticism thus entered the academic discourse as a body of studies that attested to the public and cultural visibility of a heretofore marginalized population. The title of Elaine Kim's groundbreaking work of Asian American literary criticism—*Asian American Literature: Introduction to the Writing and Its Social Context*—exemplifies the inextricable relationship between Asian American literature and the material contexts of its production.[13] As the first comprehensive study of its kind, Kim's study approaches Asian American literary production through the history of Asian American presence in the United States, a scholarly exemplar that has deeply inflected Asian American literary discourse at large. The artistic and political modality of Asian American literary criticism demonstrates, in a meta-critical sense, what Raymond Williams calls the dual condition of "representation": there is a "degree of possible overlap between representative and representation in their political and artistic senses."[14] That is, Asian American literary criticism serves as more than a second-level "representation" of the artistic endeavors of Asian American literary production: it fundamentally functions as a discursive "representative" of Asian American subject positions, and it uses Asian American literature to expound the material, historical, political, economic, and cultural visibility of Asian American presence, legitimacy, resistance, and call to power.

The interweaving of literary analysis and sociohistorical emphasis testifies to the fact that a truly useful and responsible intellectual inquiry into the artistic production of a marginalized people cannot be divorced from questions of the material and discursive contexts within which those expressions emerged. There cannot be something called a "literary question" that remains untouched by specific historical and institutional forces, by issues of legal, social, economic, national as well as transnational concerns, sexuality, gender, religion, popular culture, and more. Interdisciplinary approaches to literature, then, have been fundamental to the rich intellectual growth of Asian American literary discourse in the late twentieth century, and they hold the ability to enliven our understanding of literary texts and their imbrication within a larger material context and within other intellectual disciplines.

Our emphasis on the aesthetic as a missing category of analysis continues the argument that Levine began earlier. Too often in interdisciplinary approaches to literary analysis, or in ideological assessments of literary works, the aesthetic becomes a conscripted agent, a transparent medium that yields a particular disciplinary "content." If the discursive "representative" strength of Asian American literary criticism emerged through its focus on historical and material specificities, it was a strength that rested on an inversely minimized role for the role of the aesthetic. Missing, then, is a consideration of how the constructed nature of the aesthetic, as a series of human-made gestures, functions as a critical variable in affecting the outcome of the analysis.

Addressing this imbalance in Asian American literary criticism is particularly urgent in order to counter the assumption in the larger academic discourse that "ethnic" interests are disparate from aesthetic interests. As Emory Elliott argues, such a demarcation was a principal part of the "culture wars" or "canon wars" of the 1980s and 1990s. Pointing to a continuation of "conservative politics" and "conservative aesthetics," Elliott identifies "a strong tendency in the arguments from the right to universalize beauty and art and to judge objects and artifacts on the basis of how they measure against the ideal. Of course, what is posited as universal and essential is nothing more than the classical Western canons of art and literature."[15] The conservative deployment of the aesthetic "implies that 'artistic merit' and 'minority writers' are mutually exclusive terms."[16] Likewise, the universal standard of aesthetic excellence enables what Abdul R. JanMohamed and David Lloyd identify as the dominant humanism's practice of ascribing "a single model of historical development within which other cultures can only be envisaged as underdeveloped, imperfect, childlike."[17] Hence, for those who wish to deploy the concept of the aesthetic as the bastion of Anglo-American cultural primacy, a distinguishing mark of ethnic minority writing may be its seeming irrelevance to aesthetic concerns. Nathaniel Mackey, contesting precisely such an ethnic-aesthetic divide in the critical reception of African American experimental poetry, writes: "Failures or refusals to acknowledge complexity among writers from socially marginalized groups, no matter how 'well-intentioned,' condescend to the work and to the writers. . . . [A]llied with such simplistic readings is the tendency to overlook variance and divergent approaches in the writing from such groups, especially to overlook writing that defies canons of accessibility."[18] Ultimately, the practice of attributing an ethnographic transparency to ethnic minority works denies these works "[t]he ability to influence the course of the medium, to *move* the medium, [and] entails an order of animacy granted only to whites when it comes to writing."[19]

Now, at the beginning of the twenty-first century, scholars and students of Asian American literature should examine their own methodological approaches to literature, and question whether their own uses of Asian American literary production have adequately contested that conservative use of the aesthetic. In examining the field's success as a discursive "representative" of "Asian America," they should be alert to the dangers of using Asian American literary production as a field of evidence from which to argue the constructed nature of racial and ethnic formations, gender and sexuality constraints, nationalist and globalist pursuits, and more. Ultimately, those concerned with Asian American literary studies need to be keenly self-conscious of the *verbs* that they employ as the agents of the critical "representative," and ask how their own use of Asian American literature as "attesting to," "exemplifying," "illustrating," or "testifying to" material and historical constraints and veiled ideologies may not adequately contest ethnographic assessments of ethnic minority literature.

Scholars of Asian American literary discourse needs to envision a more multivalent critical vocabulary, one that pursues the drama of material and discursive constructedness with a *parallel focus* on the drama of aesthetic constructedness. Put another way: What would a materialist and formalist Asian American literary criticism look like? How would an analysis of material conditions and ideological values be affected by an analysis of the literary work's use of formal strategies or figurative language? How would a consideration of a work's manipulation of genre conventions affect the kinds of conclusions one may draw regarding its race/gender/sexuality ideologies? How would an analysis alert to the way a particular Asian American literary work "talks" to other works within that genre, within literary history, within the canon, affect the overall balance of analysis? How would an analysis attuned to the significance of literary genealogy interact with the discernment of material forces at work?[20]

Consequently, our call for invigorating the place of literary aesthetics in Asian American literary studies is not a call for a disciplinary embargo, for building a conceptual fortress around literary analysis to protect it from other disciplinary incursions. Nor is our emphasis on formal analysis a return to New Criticism's valorization of a literary work's totality of design and organicity or a return to the Russian Formalists' pursuit of structural wholeness. It is a symptom of any intellectual inquiry that the subject of the inquiry tends to take on the definition that best suits the interests of that inquiry. For instance, the American New Critics or Russian Formalists did not necessarily believe that the literary had nothing to do with the historical; rather, they deemed the immanent press of the material reality to be outside the business of their study. Their particular conceptualization of the literary was then directly related to their critical practice of formalism. Similarly, cultural studies practitioners or sociological readers of literature would not deny that the literary work is an artificial construct—a set of contrivances whose strategies are traceable within the history of literary practices. Rather, it is more accurate to say that they would not deem the study of those artificial constructs to be the stuff of their immediate business. Our call for pursuing both kinds of constructedness—of human organizations and of literary practices that make up Asian American literary texts—is then a call for a complementary perspective between cultural materialist and formal modes of analysis. Ultimately, it is a call to expand the scope of our scholarly business, and in the same step, expand the subjects of our business.

This is a call that many Asian American literary artists have voiced, usually as a form of grievance, against the business of literary criticism. For instance, poet Garrett Hongo in "Asian American Literature: Questions of Identity" warns:

> [If Asian American literary critical discourse does not] produce new critical approaches and widen parochial perspectives regarding literary style, I fear there will continue to be three dominant, ideologically narrowing modes out of which critical thinking (and the construction of literary curriculum) will emerge: (1) the unconscious assumption that what is essentially Asian American is a given work's overt political stance and conformity to sociological models of the Asian American experience, (2) the related notion that a writer writes from a primary loyalty to coherent communities, and (3) vehement castigation or rude, categorical dismissal for literary qualities deemed 'assimilationist' or 'commercial.'[21]

From meta-critical scrutiny of how the aesthetic operates within Asian American literary criticism and Asian American Studies, to concentrated formal analysis of specific Asian American literary texts, the essays in this collection attempt to expand the subjects of our business by keeping critical focus upon the aesthetic. A notable characteristic of the essays collected here—in fact, a characteristic of *all* the interventions mentioned above, that seek to reinvigorate the aesthetic—is that despite their collective use of the term as the critical pivot, individual contributors do not employ the term toward the same end.

Indeed, the intellectual, not to mention the emotional, investment surrounding the term is made evident in "Is There an Asian American Aesthetic?" a transcript of a panel session called "Defining Our Culture(s), Our Selves" that took place at Hunter College in 1991.[22] The various ways that the session participants understood the question represent the multiple perspectives and interests that converge on the concept of the aesthetic: Is there a conceptual, political, or artistic practice that Asian American artists share? Is there a body of writing that can be categorized as Asian American literature by virtue of some commonality in theme and subject matter? Is the concept of an Asian American aesthetic necessary as a framing ground of scholarship and basis of critical inquiry? Does such a question seek homogeneity as a criterion of Asian American art, and if so, does the question itself foster the disciplinary ghettoization of ethnic minority art? The multiple ways of understanding and of using the aesthetic exemplify the concept's utility, but also a distrust of such a utility.[23]

The eleven original essays in this volume likewise pursue the aesthetic through different perspectives, and in the process, recall the variegated history of the word—as a criterion of taste, value, sensory judgments, beauty, pleasure, and ethics. In the process, they engage with the history of the aesthetic through diverse ways, such as the historical relationship between the aesthetic and literary canonicity, between the aesthetic and literary periodization, and between the aesthetic and genre conventions. Although the essays do not employ a single definition of the aesthetic, they do have a common meeting ground: they approach the aesthetic dimension of Asian American literary texts as a rich arena of constructedness, as a complicated maneuver of literary conventions, genres, forms, and strategies. Through concentrated literary analysis keenly attuned to the inextricability of formal issues to thematic or topical concerns, these essays contest the notion that literary texts can be read as transparent windows onto material reality. Ultimately, they argue the epistemological richness to be gained by complementing the question of "what"—what social, material, economic, historical topics the literary text addresses/examines—with the question of "how"—how the rumination of said topics are realized through a manipulation of form, convention, constraints, and literary history.

The section "Asian American Critical Discourse in Academia" includes essays demonstrating the centrality of the aesthetic in comprehending some of the major tensions in contemporary Asian American literary studies. As they reread the contested sites of Asian American literary categorization, evaluation, institutional operations, and academic relations to political activism, the essays uncover how the concept of the aesthetic is integral to the overall business of producing "knowledge" in regards to a body of literature called "Asian American" and to an institution called "Asian American Studies." Mark Chiang's "Autonomy and Representation: Aesthetics and the Crisis of Asian American Cultural Politics in the Controversy over *Blu's Hanging*" shows that two very different notions of the aesthetic currently circulate in Asian American literary discourse. Chiang historicizes the competing roles of the aesthetic by returning to the beginning days of Asian American Studies. The aesthetic, which functioned as a concept firmly bound to a localized constituent called "Asian American" and accountable to the larger political aims of the Asian American "community" in the past, has now come to function as a concept of value-free, liberatory, autonomous space of artistic and intellectual freedom as the field has expanded its institutional and academic stature. When both notions of the aesthetic vie for legitimation, they inevitably collide. Chiang highlights an instance of this strife through a reading of the controversy that surrounds the Asian American Association's 1998 Fiction Award to Lois-Ann Yamanaka's novel, a novel whose depiction of Filipino American characters was deemed reprehensibly racist by those who contested the award choice. Continuing the discussion of the aesthetic in current Asian North American scholarship, Iyko Day's "Interventing Innocence: Race, 'Resistance,' and the Asian North American Avant-Garde" argues that the field is limited in envisioning an aesthetic that best effects "resistance." Exploring the limitations of reading for ethnic minority resistance predominantly through the "social-realist" representational text, Day points to those Asian Canadian writers whose nonrepresentational, formally disjunctive works challenge the false binary between politically engaged works and formally engaged works. Day's analysis of Asian North American avant-garde examines the commodification and containment of ethnic minority literature, and critiques how Asian North American literature operates through "an economic consumer logic: the larger the reading public, the more social good."

The essays in "Aesthetics and Ethnicity" examine how the aesthetic operates in the larger environment of reception in which Asian American literary production is first and foremost an expression and an attestation of ethnic minority realities. The resulting bifurcation of "ethnic" interests from "aesthetic" interests, these essays suggest, leads to an oppressive topical paradigm as well as an oppressive formal paradigm by which Asian American literary artists are assessed. Through their analysis of specific Asian American literary texts, these essays trace a formal rebellion that literary artists stage against the constricting expectations of the ethnic/aesthetic divide. Mita Banerjee's "The Asian American in a Turtleneck: Fusing the Aesthetic and the Didactic in Maxine Hong Kingston's *Tripmaster Monkey*" offers a comparative reading of *Tripmaster Monkey* and Gerald Vizenor's writings on Ishi, a Native American historical figure who, at the hands of mainstream ethnography, comes to stand for the iconic Indian—heroic, other-worldly, and always of the lost past. When the interpellation of an ethnic other's "difference" is always locked in place, the very structures of reading and reception present an almost insurmountable challenge to the ethnic minority writer. A certain corrective imperative enters the site of literary production, then, and Banerjee identifies an "open-ended didacticism" at work in *Tripmaster Monkey* that is distinguishable from the refusal of engagement represented by Vizenor's Ishi. Similarly, Christina Mar's "The Language of Ethnicity: John Yau's Poetry and the Ethnic/Aesthetic Divide" addresses the political implications of aesthetic acts, exploring the racialized implications by which "ethnicity" is formulated in the criticism of experimental poetry. Pointing to the peculiar position that John Yau occupies in the field of language poetry, Mar traces a critical paradigm wherein the discernment of "ethnic" performance is unrelated, sometimes even oppositional, to the discernment of "aesthetic" performance. Such a paradigm continues, Mar argues, the "official diversity" strategy of multiculturalism, a conceptualization of diversity that does not threaten the myth of American national wholeness. Hence Mar's formal analysis of John Yau's poetry simultaneously highlights the poems' political engagement with the logic of American national wholeness.

The following two essays in particular explore the affective power of the aesthetic to invoke concepts such as beauty, justice, and ethics. Their formally attuned analysis connects the aesthetic experience and the power of that experience to invoke a political engagement. Patricia Chu's "'A Flame against a Sleeping Lake of Petrol': Form and the Sympathetic Witness in Selvadurai's *Funny Boy* and Ondaatje's *Anil's Ghost*" examines how two Sri Lankan Canadian novelists, Shyam Selvadurai and Michael Ondaatje, skillfully manipulate the bildungsroman convention, as well as well-known plot configurations and tensions, to elicit sympathy and identification and to heighten the individual text's specific material concerns. Chu highlights the explicit invocation of the aesthetic in these texts as a function of truth and justice (in *Funny Boy*) and of empathy and compassionate witness (in *Anil's Ghost*). Gita Rajan's "Poignant Pleasures: Feminist Ethics as Aesthetics in Jhumpa Lahiri and Anita Rao Badami" continues to examine the relationship between aesthetics and ethics, particularly between aesthetics and feminist ethics. Tracing the formal strategies by which Anita Rao Badami's novel *A Hero's Walk* and Jhumpa Lahiri's short story, "When Mr. Pirzada Came to Dine," represent trauma and tragedy, Rajan argues that a strategy of "beguiling banality" prompts the reader to consider the ethical ramifications of the plot events. Such an aesthetic of "poignant pleasure," Rajan argues, is suggestive of an "ethical realism" that implicates the reader in the consequences of failing to act ethically; furthermore, the ethical function of the aesthetic in these works highlights the inevitable limit of liberal generosity across "first world" and "third world" divide.

The contributions in "Intertexts: Asian American Writing and Literary Movements" examine the concept of aesthetics at the intersection of Asian American literature and literary periodization and canonicity. They examine how canonical periodization, categorization, and identification affects the reading, teaching, and criticism of ethnic minority literature. Josephine Nock-Hee Park's "'A Loose Horse': Asian American Poetry and the Aesthetics of the Ideogram" situates contemporary Asian American poetry at the convergence of two competing paradigms—of the canonical influence of modernism and the discourse of orientalism. Park begins with a strong salvo: "Asian American poets have a singular plight: they write within the constraints of an American poetry indelibly marked by orientalism."

Exploring the racial reductivism and essentialism of "the Chinese ideogram" in Anglo-American Imagism, Park asks: how do contemporary Asian American poets formally and topically engage with this history? In what ways may they write themselves within as well as against the tradition of Imagism? Park offers a formally attuned analysis of Ho Hon Leung's poems to highlight a strategy of simultaneously addressing and interrogating the orientalist use of Chinese writing in Imagist poetry. Likewise, Donatella Izzo's "'A New Rule for the Imagination': Rewriting Modernism in *Bone*" questions the hierarchical top-down operations of canonical influence. Crucial to dismantling the role of the Western literary canon as the measure of aesthetic standard, Izzo argues, is a heightened recognition and assessment of Asian American literary works as complex formal performances. Putting Fae Myenne Ng's *Bone* in dialogue with key Anglo-American modernist texts such as *The Great Gatsby*, Izzo discerns a "self-aware rewriting of modernism" in *Bone*, a rewriting that consciously invokes and adapts modernist literary strategies and motifs. Izzo pursues an understanding of the canon as a flexible entity in living dialogue with Asian American literature.

The section "Rewriting Form, Reading for New Expression" highlights the formal innovations in contemporary Asian American literary works, while continuing to examine the larger concerns common to the essays—the aesthetic/ethnic divide, the politically charged environment of reception, various conceptualization of Asian American "resistance," the link between Asian American literature and multiculturalism, the tension between ethnic minority writing and the primacy of the canon, and the function of the aesthetic as the definitive category of evaluation. Rocío Davis's "Performing Dialogic Subjectivities: The Aesthetic Project of Autobiographical Collaboration in *Days and Nights in Calcutta*" engages the political implications of formally manipulating the conventions of autobiography. A collaborative autobiography like *Days and Nights in Calcutta*, Davis argues, presents a challenge to the literary tradition of autobiography; it also participates in the dismantling of the autonomous, monologic subjectivity that scholars of feminist, postcolonial, and ethnic minority studies problematize. By tracing the literary deviations in collaborative life telling, Davis connects formal innovations to political challenges to ideas of nation, national identity, and ethnic affiliation.

Celestine Woo's "Bicultural World Creation: Laurence Yep, Cynthia Kadohata, and Asian American Fantasy" introduces the contributions of Asian American writers to the genre of fantasy. The literary tradition of fantasy has been dominated by, and identified with, Anglo-American practitioners (C. S. Lewis or J.R.R. Tolkien) almost exclusively, an identification that results in an inhospitable environment for interventions by ethnic minority writers. Drawing a parallel between the formal conventions of world-creation in fantasy and the "bicultural world creations" that Laurence Yep and Cynthia Kadohata offer, Woo invites us to appreciate the formal innovations in their works as carefully inflected expressions of material concerns. Such "innovative synthesis of the wonder of world-creation and the allegorical representation of Asian American experience," then, disrupts the identification of fantasy as a racially "white" aesthetic tradition. Kimberly Jew's "Dismantling the Realist Character in Velina Hasu Houston's *Tea* and David Henry Hwang's *FOB*" identifies Asian American contributions in the field of experimental theater. While a realist aesthetic has dominated Asian American theater, Jew argues, the appeal to identification with the characters on stage has risked the reification of a fixed, knowable entity called "Asian American character." Jew points to the plays of Hwang and Houston as Asian American exemplars of the non-realist dramaturgical tradition such as surrealism and expressionism. As models for an aesthetic of the "true unreal," Jew argues, these playwrights suggest a reformulation of the process by which Asian American characters are performed.

As the essays centrally position the aesthetic in their analysis of Asian American literature, they highlight the particular tension points that recur in the larger conversation of the aesthetic. For instance, what is the relationship between the "aesthetic" and the "literary"? Just as the essays engage in particular dimensions of the aesthetic (as a criterion of taste, value, sensory judgments, beauty, pleasure, and ethics), they envision variable relationships between the two terms—the aesthetic and the literary as interchangeable notions, the aesthetic as a perennial constitution of the literary, or the literary as a particular instantiation of the aesthetic. Rather than announcing a single, fixed relationship between the two key terms, the essays demonstrate something more fruitful: the "aesthetic" and the "literary" are inextricable pursuits, and the two terms, whose meanings are in constant flux, must be understood in a relational manner informed by the specific context of the discussion. The various theoretical approaches represented by the essays invite another productive question: What is the particular strength of each critical approach in recentering the aesthetic? Not only does this volume rearticulate the advantages of the formal criticism, but it also reintroduces the possibilities of genre criticism, reader-response criticism, and psychoanalytic criticism. An ongoing speculation on the unique strengths and particular implications of each theoretical approach will no doubt enhance the centrality of the aesthetic in literary studies. Questions such as these point to the necessarily limited parameters of this volume: at the same time, they underscore the collection's scholarly contribution as an open conversation on critical strategies.

As these contributions reevaluate contemporary Asian American literary discourse through the pivotal lens of the aesthetic, they dismantle the seemingly inverse and seemingly exclusive relationship between ethnic minority literary production and the concerns of the aesthetic. They enact the very fact that the study of the aesthetic is *not* a non-Asian American activity. At the same time, they reinforce the argument that the critical enterprise surrounding the aesthetic can never be divorced from the concerns of history, from the disparities of institutional and material power, and from the ramifications of ethnic minority literary production. In the process, they rescue the aesthetic from critical exile as a tired concept lacking any power of affect and save it from becoming a transparent tool wielded in the service of political directives, specific ideologies, or the machinations of capital.

Ultimately, the aesthetic in the recent critical environment may still seem a concept in need of perennial rescue: witness the critical titles on the aesthetic, mentioned above, such as "Return of the Aesthetic," "Reclaiming the Aesthetic," and "Revenge of the Aesthetic." Each act declaring the return of the aesthetic—in which we include the present volume—contests the appropriation of the aesthetic as an unwitting tool or as a subject of sinecure. By asserting an active role for the aesthetic, and by emphasizing the constructedness of the aesthetic, this volume hopes to animate Asian American literary discourse in an unique way—toward a critical venture that examines the constructed nature of literary forms, genres, and gestures as deliberately as it examines the constructed nature of human organizations.

Part I

*Asian American Critical Discourse
in Academia*

2

Autonomy and Representation

*Aesthetics and the Crisis of Asian American
Cultural Politics in the Controversy over* Blu's Hanging

MARK CHIANG

T ITS ANNUAL CONVENTION IN 1998, held in Honolulu, Hawaiʻi,
the Association for Asian American Studies (AAAS) presented a
Fiction Award to Lois-Ann Yamanaka for her novel, *Blu's Hanging*.
Immediately following the presentation, though, a resolution was introduced
to rescind the award, based on the charge that Yamanaka's work contains
stereotypical or racist depictions of Filipinos. The Honolulu convention was
perhaps the most tumultuous in the short history of the AAAS (which was
founded in 1979). The atmosphere was highly charged and many had a sense
that the events taking place could mean the end of the Association. During
a special emergency plenary session, supporters and critics of Yamanaka
read statements followed by a general discussion. At the presentation of the
award itself, three Filipina students from the high school where Yamanaka
teaches writing accepted the award on her behalf while many members of
the audience, wearing black armbands, stood up and turned their backs to
the stage. The vote was conducted by secret ballot, and the resolution passed
by the vote of 91 to 55. The award was withdrawn.

In the wake of these events, their lessons remain unclear. My argument
here is that the conflicts over *Blu's Hanging* were so traumatic precisely
because they brought to the surface a number of contradictions in the critical
orthodoxy of Asian American literary studies and called into question some
of the most basic assumptions of the field. The protests against the Fiction

Award sought to raise questions concerning the marginalization of Filipino Americans in the AAAS and in the field of Asian American Studies, and they did prompt the Association to make efforts to redress those problems. The pressing cultural questions raised by the controversy, though, have largely been ignored. In taking up the call to rethink the question of aesthetics, I want to suggest that the intractability of the issues raised by the protests over *Blu's Hanging* are closely connected to the neglect of aesthetics in Asian American literary studies. While many Asian Americanist critics have employed various kinds of formal analysis and "close reading" as part of their method, I would agree with Sue-Im Lee that literary aesthetics has been a "missing category" in Asian American literary discourse.[1] I want to approach aesthetics, though, as the question of the categorical construction of literature as a distinct kind of writing. In other words, political criticism in Asian American literary studies has tended to discount the specificity of the literary to the extent that the field now has no account of why people continue to perceive literature as *different* from other kinds of writing. To simply say that they should not see it as different is to ignore the entire apparatus by which that perception is reproduced.

The conflicts over *Blu's Hanging* hinged importantly on the question of the book's status as literature, and it was in this juncture, it seems to me, that Asian American literary theory faltered. Faced with the question of what it means that a *literary* text was being charged with racial stereotyping, the field has had no response, either affirmative or negative, except for a rather surprising recourse to conventional liberal axioms of artistic value. Is it possible to see in the *Blu's Hanging* episode something else besides an affirmation of the transcendence of "literature" or evidence of its essential fraudulence? In this essay, I want to focus specifically on the issues concerning culture and literature that were brought up by these events. In particular, I want to investigate how those who defended the choice of the award committee employed a discourse of artistic freedom and literary value in order to counter the charges of racism. Such a ready adoption of dominant liberal notions of the aesthetic as a domain apart from politics seemed to sit uneasily with the socially conscious traditions of Asian American cultural production.

The category of the aesthetic is a crucial site of philosophical inquiry in the development of modernity because it speaks, among other things, to the constitution of the individual and the formation of a liberal democratic society predicated upon the ethical subject. As various critics have demonstrated, the concept of the aesthetic emerges out of discourses of politics and economics in the eighteenth century, and only subsequently became separate and indeed opposed to those other spheres of social activity.[2] While the aesthetic is now primarily associated with the emergence of an autonomous sphere of culture, it also provided a discourse in which to articulate ideas of autonomy that have been fundamental to the political philosophy of bourgeois liberalism, as in the separation of spheres, as well as of the autonomous, self-directed subject. In this historical context, it makes a certain sense that the heated political conflicts over the award should have been translated into the language of the aesthetic and of culture. It is my contention that many of the underlying political antagonisms had precisely to do with the question of autonomy and that the neglect of aesthetics in Asian American literary studies is tied to the evasion of this issue. The problem, I argue, is that one of the basic premises of a great deal of Asian American cultural politics consists of a rejection of autonomy at the critical/theoretical level even as the field at the institutional level engages in a number of practices that seek to protect or expand its autonomy. This is the fundamental contradiction that is concealed in the realm of the aesthetic.

The controversy over *Blu's Hanging* was actually the culmination of a long-standing protest against the portrayal of Filipinos in Yamanaka's writing that began with the publication of her first book, *Saturday Night at the Pahala Theatre*.[3] Several of the poems in that book feature what many saw as stereotypical descriptions of Filipinos as sexual predators, although the speakers of the poems are adolescent girls, a fact that led some to claim that they were unreliable voices. When *Saturday Night* won the AAAS literary award in 1994, protests were raised, but there was no concerted effort to block the award. When Yamanaka's next book, *Wild Meat and the Bully Burgers*, was again given an AAAS award in 1997, however, the level of dissent was raised to a higher pitch. The Board of the Association responded by deciding to withdraw the award, and no award was given that year. As a result of the furor over that action, however, the Board later decided to adopt a policy stating that it could not interfere with the decisions of the award committees. This policy was immediately put to the test when the following year's literary award committee again voted to give first prize to Yamanaka's third book, *Blu's Hanging*.

The debate over *Blu's Hanging* in particular came to revolve around one character in the book, Uncle Paulo, a young Filipino man who sexually abuses his adolescent nieces and rapes the narrator's brother, Blu, in the climactic moment of the book. A major part of the interpretive disputes had to do with context, since the protesters pointed to the fact that the racist nature of the depictions of Filipinos took on a heightened significance in the context of the history of interethnic relations in Hawai`i. The figure of Uncle Paulo seemed to recall too clearly extant stereotypes of Filipinos as rapists and perverts. These stereotypes derived from the plantation history when Filipino men were imported as labor, resulting in large communities of single men. As competition for other ethnic groups in the plantation system, antagonism toward the economic threat of Filipino labor often expressed itself through stereotypes of sexual deviance. Filipino Americans remain a disadvantaged group in Hawai`i, in contrast to Japanese Americans, who have the highest socioeconomic status and the most positions of political and economic power.[4] These ethnic hierarchies further magnify Yamanaka's representations of Filipinos since it is Japanese Americans (among others) who have had the power to perpetuate stereotypes of Filipinos, and not the reverse. In addition, the fact that the vast majority of scholars in the AAAS are from the continental United States, and that none of the award committees that have given Yamanaka the award have ever had a scholar from Hawai`i, raises questions about the discrepant attitudes and perceptions of those from the continent as opposed to Hawai`i.[5]

One reason that this controversy seems significant is that it produced an intense public debate in Hawai`i that made culture matter and that empowered many people to feel a sense of ownership over it. There were a continual stream of articles on Yamanaka leading up to the convention, and the affair lingered in the media for quite a while afterward. If this was the case, then it seems more surprising that the episode should have generated so little discussion in academic publications since making culture matter and political empowerment are the avowed goals of so much political criticism. In fact, the mutual incomprehension of all sides in this conflict simply demonstrates the distance between academia and the actual struggles that occur in the political field. It is the extension of this distance, however, which is precisely the aim in the construction of autonomy, a fact that is somewhat at odds with the repeated claim of political engagement in so much literary theory and criticism. In this regard, the conflicts over the Fiction Award are an important test case for any theoretical model of Asian American literature or culture that claims to have a political import, and they offer a crucial instance for the translation of theory into practice.

I. Autonomy and Aesthetic Value

Given the voluminous public discourse concerning the controversy, it is difficult to provide an effective mapping of all of the positions that were taken. I shall not attempt to do so here. Instead, I want to focus upon the award itself in order to elucidate the particular interests that were invested in defending it. In this section, I examine specific responses to the protests by Asian

AUTONOMY AND REPRESENTATION / 21

American writers and by the Board of the AAAS. Racism is an issue that seems quantifiable in terms of various forms of social inequality, but what constitutes racism in the domain of culture and how is it redressed? Insofar as the issue of racism became centered upon the Fiction Award, it had necessarily to undergo a certain process of translation. Certainly no one stood up to defend Yamanaka's right to produce racist or stereotypical representations of Filipinos. What accounts, then, for the tremendous resistance put up by Asian American writers and the AAAS to the revocation of the award? As the responses of both groups demonstrate, they interpreted the charge of racism primarily as a threat to their autonomy. The award effectively served as the hinge that connected the kinds of issues that the protestors wanted to talk about with the forms of value that the writers and the AAAS tried to defend. In a sense, the protest exceeded the parameters of its initial impulse because in seeking to raise questions of social inequity within the context of culture, the protestors were forced to engage with many of the defenses that have been developed to protect the autonomy of culture.

I begin with the group whose own material interests were most directly affected by the motion to rescind the award, that is, Asian American writers. The primary document of their response was a petition drafted by the Japanese American writer David Mura that was widely circulated over e-mail and signed by almost 80 Asian American writers and other artists. The petition begins by protesting the withdrawal of the award the previous year and urging the AAAS to stand behind its award committee. It then goes on to express these points:

2. I am concerned too with a reading of Yamanaka's work which ignores or misreads the way a fictional character or narrator functions in a literary work.

3. I also wish to reaffirm that writers often must, by the nature of their enterprise, upset and question prevailing views, evoke extreme and visceral reactions, and write in ways where ambiguity and complexity take precedence over "political correctness" or safe and comforting portraits of the world, our community, or the individuals who reside there.

4. I am also concerned with the way the AAAS has sometimes seemed to organize "witch hunts" against various writers. This is not to say that writers should be immune from criticism. Indeed, criticism is a necessary part of the creation of a literary culture. Perhaps, though, it might be helpful for people to look into the mechanism and psychological reasons why those within a community wish to tear someone from the community apart once they have become successful.

The question of racism, in this response, is almost inseparable from the possible withdrawal of the award because both issues speak to the legitimate definition of literary value, which, as Bourdieu argues, is the fundamental stake of competition in the autonomous literary field. A large part of the interest of this document is how it reveals internal contradictions in certain notions of the function of art. For example, the assertion in the second point that some interpretations result from ignorance does not quite align with the suggestion in the third point that the task of the writer is to provoke a reaction irregardless of what that reaction might be. It is the last point, however, that seems most telling. While conceding that criticism is a "necessary" part of the creative process, the section goes on to attribute criticism to jealousy and the "wish to tear someone from the community apart once they have become successful." The rather hysterical quality of this accusation reveals more about the writers' interests and anxieties than anything having to do with the protests.

The writers' statement, moreover, indicts the Association as a whole, despite the fact that the Board of the AAAS sought to uphold the choice of the award committee. Responding to the protests in a statement published in the newsletter of the AAAS, the Board defended its actions in these terms:

> The decision not to overturn the 1998 fiction award . . . stemmed from our belief that the autonomy of the book award committees is central to the integrity of the book awarding process. This policy of non-interference is consistent with that of most other professional academic associations. . . . Our stance was not meant to protect any single author but to ensure that all of us (especially junior scholars) will have due process free of interference if and when our work is considered for an award in the future.[6]

The issue of autonomy is explicitly posed here, but the question is how the Board defines what constitutes autonomy. First, I want to ask what it means that the Board chose to adopt a policy of non-interference in the decisions of its award committees. Who, or what, does this really protect? While the threat of undue influence upon the committees is a serious one, the integrity it protects is primarily that of the judges, and not of the candidates for the award, since there is in fact no check upon the biases of the judges. The fundamental assumption of the entire process is that, left to themselves, the judges' decision will be fair and objective, and the only thing that would distort this process is political pressure. This type of reasoning, however, naturalizes the impartiality of the evaluations that are made inside the committee, the effect of which is to erase whatever politics are operating on the inside by externalizing political pressure as something that only comes from out-side. What autonomy protects, therefore, are the organization's policies and procedures, as well as the institutional structures of the academy as a whole.

In their response to the protesters, for example, the award committee acknowledged the lack of consensus as to the value of the book, but they asserted this argument as a reason to let the award stand:

> [T]here is no clear critical consensus among Asian American readers of the value of Yamanaka's artistic work or her representations of Filipino Americans and other ethnic groups. Yet despite this lack of consensus, Yamanaka's detractors demand that the Fiction Award Committee as well as the AAAS Board withdraw its support of *Blu's Hanging* for this year's prize as part of their ongoing belief that Yamanaka's work is not only dangerous but also needs to be censored and unacknowledged by Asian American critics.[7]

One might well ask whether the lack of consensus would not be an equally valid reason to overturn the award. Is there another work on which there would be consensus? No effort was made to explore this option. There is a curious logic at work here in which the opinions of a minority can only be overturned by a clear consensus. What is elided here as elsewhere in the committee's statement are the disparities of power underlying all relations of representation. That is, given the lack of consensus, the only thing that confers superiority upon the judgment of the award committee is their institutional sanction as representatives. This authority has nothing to do with consensus or the approval of the membership to begin with (or rather, consent is presumed as a condition of membership in the association).

If the reason to let the Fiction Award stand is to protect the legitimacy of the AAAS, the question that many asked is why the AAAS, as an aca-demic organization, gives awards for literature in the first place when the only other awards they give are for academic work. I have already suggested that one function of culture is that it constitutes a site for the imaginary resolution of real material contradictions, but the other function, I would argue, is that of institutional legitimation. That is, in its allegiance to art, the AAAS demonstrates its adherence to the disinterestedness and universality of the aesthetic that is the philosophical basis for rational objectivity (not to mention citizenship). The Fiction Award also presents a clear instance of the process of reciprocal legitimation between Asian American intellectuals and Asian American cultural producers. In promoting Asian American writers, the AAAS can extract some of the symbolic capital of writers who have been "consecrated" by the dominant autonomous literary field.[8] In return, they provide the stamp of the "community" as further recognition. The protests over *Blu's Hanging* disrupted this entire cycle of mutual recognition and capital accumulation.

To return to the writers' complaint against the AAAS, if criticism motivated by jealousy is not a legitimate part of the creative process, what is acceptable, it seems, is formal criticism. Asian American literary studies, however, have mostly been opposed to formal criticism. Thus the conflict over the award exposed the tension between writers and critics; that is, the interest of the academic field in linking an autonomous aesthetic to an oppositional politics runs counter to the interests of writers, who do not want to be evaluated according to political criteria. The issue here is not that writers refuse to be political. Rather, the threat that politics poses to art is that it undermines the autonomy of the field by forcing it to submit to external values and standards instead of the criteria that are entirely determined by artists themselves, that is, formal criteria. Politics intrudes into the autonomous literary field as a dangerous site of heteronomy, one that jeopardizes the integrity of the boundaries of the field by ceding control over the legitimate definition of literature to *critics*. The opposition between politics and culture, then, is not simply a mystification of bourgeois ideology, but the site of real material investments in the reproduction of the autonomous literary field, as well as of academic literary criticism.

II. Historical Transformations of Asian American Literary Studies

The *Blu's Hanging* controversy presents an important test case that highlights certain contradictions in the relation of culture to politics in Asian American Studies. In order to understand how these contradictions arose, we need to situate the controversy in the context of the historical transformations in the underlying cultural politics that define the field. I identify three basic paradigms of the relation between culture and politics in Asian American literary studies. Emerging out of the Asian American political movements of the 1960s, Asian American Studies began as a component of the Ethnic Studies Departments that were first institutionalized at University of California–Berkeley and San Francisco State as a result of the Third World Strike. One of the basic axioms of Asian American Studies that has remained fairly constant is the understanding that culture is political. The only question, then, is how is it political? One of the basic problems with this equation is that it tends simply to collapse culture into politics, so that aesthetic questions are conflated with political positions. In order to trace the history of Asian American literary studies, we need to separate the two for analytical purposes. In this way, it becomes apparent that while the political goals of an Asian American cultural studies have remained somewhat constant (at least in its stated aims), the aesthetic theories underlying them have entirely reversed themselves.

To put the question in somewhat different terms, how did Asian American literary studies go from an aesthetics that was defined by *No-No Boy* to one that was defined by *Dictee*?[9] It is striking that this seismic shift in the normative aesthetics of the field occurred virtually without controversy, in contrast to the much more visible debates over questions of nationalism and transnationalism. From the crude realism of Okada to the high modernism of Cha, it is not difficult to perceive an almost direct correlation between the trajectory of aesthetic values and the degree of institutionalization of the field, but this does not tell us much about how the two are articulated. For example, the claims for *Dictee* that are elaborated in the essays in *Writing Nation, Writing Self* are very much anti-canonical and opposed to conservative celebrations of high art.[10] Nevertheless, these political claims are derived from a text that throughout the 1980s was perceived by the entire field as being fundamentally opposed to the political and cultural values espoused by Asian American Studies and the Asian American movement. What happens to that earlier politics when it becomes articulated through a previously antithetical set of texts? Underlying current conceptions of the field is an implicit periodization of Asian American literary studies that stems from the 1960s to the present.[11] The evolution of literary theory has been linked to a historical account of the fragmentation of the Asian American community. The *Blu's Hanging* incident, in contrast, precisely calls into question the *telos* of this historical account by demonstrating how "earlier" forms of culture and identity politics have not been superseded.

The study of Asian American literature began within the framework of identity politics and cultural nationalism, which in most academic accounts is identified primarily with the work of the *Aiiieeeee!* editors.[12] The function of culture in this context lay in the elaboration of a singular Asian American identity and consciousness that would help to promote political unity among a population divided along ethnic and other lines. Within Asian American Studies, cultural nationalism has been criticized for various forms of racial, gender, sexual, and class essentialism. Much of this anti-essentialist critique was also linked to a critique of a cultural nationalist aesthetics that took *No-No Boy* as its exemplary text because it advocated a referential mimetic realism. That is, literature was political because it reflected the world, hence the text had a direct impact on the way that readers perceived reality. The images in Asian American literary texts were representations of Asian American people, so literature had a responsibility to present Asian Americans in ways that countered their general negative depiction in American society. This is the aesthetics of stereotypes and positive images that informed the protests against *Blu's Hanging*.

A cultural nationalist perspective also informs the first book of Asian American literary criticism, written by Elaine Kim, although Kim does not explicitly articulate such an aesthetic, and is careful to assert the importance of both formalist and contextualizing readings of Asian American literature.[13] Nevertheless, she chooses to perform the latter because of the necessity of providing basic contextual information so that the literature will not be misunderstood. Sau-ling Wong, in contrast, provides the former in her theory of an Asian American textual coalition. Wong proposes a different relation between culture and society, suggesting that:

> students of Asian American literature tend to be united by a desire to ensure that voices of Asian Americans are heard and to make known the richness of and complexity of Asian American writing. Just as the Asian American ethnic group is a political coalition, Asian American literature may be thought of as an emergent and evolving textual coalition, whose interests it is the business of a professional coalition of Asian American critics to promote.[14]

There is an entire theory of culture and politics encapsulated here that requires greater elaboration, but we might say initially that the relation between the two is more allegorical than mimetic. Or rather, it is a relation of symbolic representation, that is, the task of Asian American writers is not to produce positive representations, but to become successful representatives. The community that critics represent, consequently, is not Asian Americans in general, but Asian American writers specifically. There are a number of important turns here, but they are all linked to the division that Wong opens up between literature (and literary studies) and politics. Writers are no longer responsible for directly producing politics, but for achieving recognition in the dominant literary field.

While I agree with the proposition that the aesthetic needs to be brought back into Asian American literary and cultural studies, I think it is imperative that this cannot be a return to any manifestly traditional conception of the aesthetic.[15] In the Introduction, Lee argues that Asian American literary discourse "needs to envision a more multivalent critical vocabulary, one that pursues the drama of material and discursive constructedness with a *parallel focus* on the drama of aesthetic constructedness." One caveat I have about this formulation is its insistence upon the "parallel focus," for this raises again the question of articulation. Instead of a history or sociology *and* an aesthetics, my position is that we need a history and sociology *of* the aesthetic. Here the monumental work of Bourdieu seems essential for any attempt to rethink the aesthetic. One of the things that Bourdieu's analysis offers is the possibility of overcoming the antagonism between immanent and formal analysis, in that the value of the literary work is the product of a structure of perceptions that is only constituted insofar as an entire group of people—writers, critics, publishers, readers—come to subscribe to a belief in that value.[16] The question is what relation Asian American critics and writers have to this process of value production in the dominant literary field. Although Lee echoes many in her view that Asian American literary studies is perhaps too dominated by sociohistorical approaches, historical and sociological readings in Asian American literary criticism have generally tended to be posed against "aesthetic" ones. One has either political readings that dissolve the specificity of the cultural, or aestheticist readings that include historical context only in order to illuminate the aesthetic value of the literary text.

It is in this conjuncture that the work of Lisa Lowe became so influential. What Lowe proposes in *Immigrant Acts* is a theoretical model that can potentially resolve the tension between Kim's cultural nationalist politics and Wong's aestheticist criticism. Lowe's work is oriented around several fundamental questions. How does one produce a non-essentialist model of either Asian Americans or of Asian American literature while still retaining an oppositional politics? How does one reconcile formal concerns with a politicized reading of literature? What Lowe brought to these questions was a Marxist ideology critique. It is ideology henceforward that connects culture to society. One problem with the reception of a cultural studies paradigm in the American academy is that it is a rather different thing to talk about the ideological work of culture (in the sense of a way of life) than about the ideological work of literature (or culture in the rather narrower sense of aesthetic practices).[17] The difference inheres in the relative autonomy of the cultural field from political and economic determinations, and what tends to drop out in such a move is precisely the aesthetic, by which I mean not the special or distinctive qualities of the literary work but the historical development of the cultural field that produces those qualities in the first place.

Lowe, however, explicitly rejects the idea that Asian American literature can be incorporated into the autonomous literary field. In contrast to conceptions of "high art" as a domain outside of instrumentalized culture, Lowe argues that Asian American culture refuses assimilation into modern institutions: "Asian American cultural forms neither seek to reconcile constituencies to idealized forms of community or subjectivity, nor propose those forms as 'art' that resides in an autonomous domain outside of mass society and popular practices."[18] The repetition of "form" here raises certain questions. While not referring specifically to literary forms, Lowe's analyses in the book are almost entirely concerned with the ideology of form and not content.[19] Nevertheless, the political valence of Asian American culture is entirely dependent upon its not being "literature." The problem is whether form has any meaning, ideological or otherwise, outside of the field of autonomous literature. Lowe argues that it does, for instance, in the signal example of the realist developmental narrative, which she sees as the formal site of production of the bourgeois ethical subject.

The issue becomes a bit clearer when we compare Lowe's version of the critique of realism with another similar one by Shelley Wong. It was the work of Shelley Wong and Lowe on *Dictee* that was largely responsible for the major critical revaluation of that text in Asian American literary studies, one that amounted to a virtual epistemic shift in the field.[20] While Wong concedes that the use of realist forms by Asian American writers of a previous generation responded to certain political necessities, she argues that demographic shifts in the Asian American community over the course of the 1970s and 1980s meant that racial identity could no longer be the sole index of an oppositional politics. As a result of immigration reform in 1965, the Asian American community subsequently became much more ethnically diverse. The impact of new social movements further fractured the Asian American coalition by calling attention to gender and sexual hierarchies, and the rise of a significant Asian American professional and technical class meant growing class divisions. All of these factors, and others, have created multiple political antagonisms within the Asian American population. "It is within this moment of tension," Wong claims, "when the politics of identity confronts a politics of difference that a space can be found in which to read *Dictee*."[21]

What is noticeably absent from the list of contextual forces shaping the moment of *Dictee's* revaluation is the growing institutionalization of Asian American literary studies. Asian American Studies faced hostile institutional environments throughout the 1980s and fought simply to maintain itself. In the late 1980s and early 1990s, a new surge of graduate students entered the field. Having been trained in traditional disciplines and without a mass movement behind them, they began to propel the field in the direction of institutional regularization and absorption. As a result of its greater academic respectability, and driven by student activism, more Asian American Studies programs began to be established around the country. Although Wong and Lowe both argue that *Dictee* cannot be construed as an autonomous text, the question remains of what it means that the kind of oppositional politics artic-ulated through *Dictee* can only, it seems, be read within texts that otherwise look very much like texts of the autonomous literary field. Against the realist aesthetics of earlier Asian American writing, recent Asian American liter-ature achieves its subversive effects through complex and elaborate formal structures. Is the valorization of formal complexity driven by new political imperatives, or does it respond to the institutional demand (of academic literary studies) for literary texts that will allow critics to produce more so-phisticated theoretical readings?

The rejection of autonomy reiterates the opposition between autonomy and politics, but the *Blu's Hanging* incident, I contend, demonstrates that politics and autonomy are not necessarily opposed. Indeed, one might say that it is the very autonomy of *Dictee* that allows it to be political in the juncture described by Shelley Wong. What needs to be specified, though, is the kind of politics at stake. In the case of *Dictee*, the theoretical revaluation of Asian American cultural politics occurs at the conjunction of two dis-continuous political fields, that of politics proper, or the political sphere of civil society, and "aesthetics," which is a metonym for the field of academic politics. The yoking of an oppositional politics with aesthetic autonomy is the manifestation of the effort to combine the original political commit-ment of Asian American Studies to the Asian American community with the struggle for greater institutional legitimacy. The problem, however, is that in order to accomplish the latter objective, Asian American Studies as an academic field needed to achieve greater autonomy, which meant that it had to distance itself *from* the community.[22] While Asian American Studies always recognized the need for autonomy from the educational institution, the changing political atmosphere of the 1970s and 1980s meant that com-munity demands for "practical" scholarship became an enormous obstacle to academic legitimacy.[23] The introduction of *Dictee* into the Asian American literary field was one of the signal moments in the gradual disengagement of Asian American Studies from community politics, but this necessitated the rearticulation of political commitment, hence the turn from realist represen-tation to a cultural politics of ideological subversion.

III. Autonomy, Aesthetics and Decontextualization

We can now situate the *Blu's Hanging* controversy in the larger trajectory of Asian American Studies. The protests over the Fiction Award, we might say, are the manifestation of the repressed contradictions in the aesthetic politics of the field. Despite Lowe's claim that Asian American culture does not "seek to reconcile constituencies to idealized forms of community or subjectivity," it is difficult not to see the AAAS Fiction Award as doing precisely that. The aesthetic names the site where autonomy and representation collide, and it is in the field of culture that the AAAS has sought to resolve this contradiction. If a unitary political representation of the Asian American community is no longer possible, then the project of unifying the community must be displaced into the realm of culture, taking the form of aesthetic or symbolic representation. This is, however, precisely the hegemonic function of canonical literature against which the revaluation of *Dictee* is posed. The shift from a cultural politics of realism to a politics of post-structuralist ideology critique putatively opposes the canonical function of literature, but then how do we account for the institutional investment in the Fiction Award? While Asian American literary studies are marked by a theoretical critique of the aesthetic, Asian American politics retains some fairly conservative notions of aesthetic value. As became evident in the conflicts over the award, this contradiction was managed through the division of the imagined community into an outside of politics and an inside of culture. That is, the ethnic community's relation to the dominant culture is defined by politics while the space inside the ethnic community is constituted as a space of culture.

The shift from a realist to an ideological criticism constitutes an implicit narrative of development of Asian American literary studies but it has been naturalized simply as the product of historical necessity rather than as a strategic response to institutional imperatives. The *Blu's Hanging* episode, however, challenges that narrative because the protests arise as an atavistic eruption out of a cultural nationalist past that history has supposedly consigned to the ash heap. In order to grasp their dynamics, however, we have to step outside of the academic orthodoxy that opposes an anti-essentialist politics of difference to an essentialist identity politics. If the antagonism between writers and critics expressed itself in terms of the opposition between art and politics, the two groups were nevertheless aligned in terms of their common stake in maintaining a structure of autonomy that insulated them both from the institutions of the dominant culture *as well as* from the ethnic community. In their demand for accountability, then, the protests necessarily had to position themselves against autonomy.

What purposes might a theory of aesthetics serve in this conjuncture? By foregrounding it as a discourse of autonomy, aesthetics might serve as an important site for debates about the meaning of autonomy in Asian

American Studies. Rather than remaining in the political unconscious of the field, I think we need a critical analysis of the structures of autonomy that surround the work of academics and cultural producers. There is no doubt that autonomy is an important historical achievement of the bourgeoise in its struggles for hegemony, but in the current moment, effective intellectual work requires a much more detailed understanding of the truly liberatory, as well truly disabling, features of the structures that uphold the autonomy of culture and of the educational institution. The conflicts over *Blu's Hanging* reveal fundamental contradictions between political engagement and the defense of autonomy. The AAAS proved to be profoundly vulnerable because it had no coherent account of either of its primary goals, and more important, little sense of the tremendous tension between them.

All this may seem rather far afield from the realm of literary studies, which is the problem that the "return to aesthetics" sought to address. In the last part of this essay, though, let me try to sketch what a critique of autonomy might look like in a literary analysis, and where else to begin but with *Blu's Hanging*? With regard to literature, it seems crucial to recall that the flip side of autonomy is decontextualization; that is, culture was only constituted as a separate domain by gradually undergoing a process of alienation from the various social functions that it formerly served. The contemporary notion of literature as consisting primarily of fictional narratives is a fairly recent historical development, and what much historicist analysis fails to consider is the process whereby history becomes divorced from literature in the first place, such that it needs consequently to be "restored" to the text by the literary critic. The category of "fiction" is one end-product of this historical evolution, and the only thing that constitutes fiction as such is its opposition to fact. In turning fact into fiction, literature engages in a process of decontextualization that abstracts "stories" from "history." One question for Asian American literary studies is what relation writers establish to this obligatory process of abstraction.

The corollary to this question is to ask what relation critics bear to that process. The conspicuous lack of scholarly commentary on this entire affair seems to signal a certain difficulty in figuring out how one exactly talks about the controversy within the norms and protocols of academic literary studies. Turning to the scant handful of articles that have reached publication, what we can see is that in bringing these events into academic discourse, several of the articles not only do not contest the process of decontextualization, but actually advance that process. *The Journal of Asian American Studies*, for example, recently published an article on *Blu's Hanging* by Crystal Parikh in which she declares, "I am bringing together the literary 'reading of' the novel and the political 'taking sides' in the debate. In so doing, I hope to confuse and transgress the disciplinary lines between the 'real' material politics of race as they are lived in Hawaiʻi and the 'representational' work of literary and academic production."[24] Despite this promising announcement, the reader is surprised to discover that there is no further mention of any of the extratextual events in the rest of the essay. Parikh offers a theory of "racial melancholia" as a "necessary alternative perspective" on the award controversy, but her essay provides not so much an alternative as an erasure.[25] Since there is almost no discussion of the conflicts, her analysis is only an alternative in the sense of being entirely separate from the actual events.[26]

In her article, Parikh compares *Blu's Hanging* with *Rolling the R's*, by R. Zamora Linmark, arguing that Uncle Paulo, the Filipino rapist in *Blu's Hanging*, stands as the figure of everything that must be excluded in the constitution of the Asian American subject, while *Rolling the R's*, in contrast, does not allow us to forget. I would agree with this in general terms, but let me take the argument one step further. Both *Blu's Hanging* and *Rolling the R's* are marked by a keen sense of the costs resulting from the decontextualization that must be enacted in order to be perceived as literature. I would argue that the latter, though, exerts a much greater resistance to literary abstraction than the former.[27] At the same time, the investment of Linmark's characters in the 1970s pop culture that surrounds them ensures that the book's fragmented narrative style cannot be subsumed under the category of high art in the same way that a text like *Dictee* can. These characters bring the kind of sustained attention that properly belongs to high art to their discussions of *Charlie's Angels*, disrupting the usual appropriative strategies of autonomous art toward mass culture, which is to say, a patronizing mimicry that masquerades as *homage* or the absorption of pop cultural elements within formal complexity.

This is not to say that *Rolling the R's* does not decontextualize its narrative. Of course it does; it is still literature after all. The point is that it continually seeks ways of interfering with the process of decontextualization in order to generate friction, not fiction. Emblematic of this effort is the last section of the book, a fifth grade book report on Judy Blume by Katherine Katrina-Trina Cruz, which is simply given to us with no narrative frame whatsoever. Here *Rolling the R's* offers an interpretive paradigm that is relentlessly localizing rather than universalizing, and it is one model for what an aesthetic analysis in Asian American cultural studies might look like. In order to read the book report, one has to ask not "what does it say?" but "what does it do?" Katrina is not at all interested in the *meaning* of the book; interpretation is entirely irrelevant here. Rather, she performs the kind of reading that so many of us find irritating in our students; she identifies with the characters and relates them to her life. In particular, the report features an extended comparison between the relationship of the two main characters in the book and Katrina's relationship with "Erwin Castillo, star quarterback for the undefeated Farrington Govs," with a special emphasis on the quality of the sex in each relationship.[28]

The report finally concludes with this rather startling pronouncement:

> I recommend this book for you especially, Mrs. Takemoto, cuz you might learn a thing or two about love and the painful truth that nothing last forever, not even love. I know you know and everybody know that your husband stay screwing my mother. That's how come you hate my guts so much. [...] But that's beside the point. What I trying for say is the same thing that my mother tell me everytime about me and Erwin. She tell me that if Erwin no love me no more, I should tell him to fuck off, that I should move on with my life, cuz I only going be miserable the whole time I stay hanging on to him. I say the same thing to you, Mrs. Takemoto. Why hang around somebody when he like you out of his sight? You only wasting your time.[29]

What would it mean to understand this as the main point of the reading offered in the report? This is a canny strategic reading, but what is the strategy? In extracting the moral for Mrs. Takemoto, the report discloses its own interests in advancing a certain interpretation. Subsequently, however, it takes a surprising turn. It may appear that Katrina's advice is motivated simply by a desire to see her mother and Mr. Takemoto together, except that Katrina also seems to be making a concerted effort to go beyond her own self-interest in order to assess what is in *Mrs. Takemoto's* best interests. Katrina is, in other words, engaging in an exercise of disinterested judgment, and is this not fundamentally the function of the aesthetic in Kant? The ability to exercise disinterested judgment is what allows one access to the universality that is the precondition of ethical subjectivity and citizenship, but this is not the kind of universality that is recognizable as such anywhere in American culture, as the title of the chapter—"F for Book Report"—reminds us.

Needless to say, this kind of reading is almost entirely antithetical to the criticism that is produced by academic literary studies, but instead of simply assuming the distance between these two modes of reading, an aesthetic analysis can begin to investigate the structures that produce and sustain that distance, which is an index of the degree of autonomy of the institution and the field. The question of aesthetics in Asian American literary studies, then, might be construed as the collision of these two antithetical modes of reading, an autonomous and a heteronomous one. An aesthetic analysis that can begin to bridge this gap might lead to a transformative critique of autonomy. What Asian American studies needs at this moment is a thorough assessment of how the forms and structures of autonomy either advance or impede the field's political and institutional aims.

3

Interventing Innocence: Race, "Resistance," and the Asian North American Avant-Garde

IYKO DAY

> *it marks what I can only call 'the end of innocence'*
> —STUART HALL, "NEW ETHNICITIES"[1]

OR SOME TIME it has been a critical commonplace to appeal to the various tropes of resistance in cultural texts. In a 1988 essay Meaghan Morris characterizes the discourse of resistance as the "banality" of cultural studies, calling into question the disarticulation of consumption from relations of production through the idealization of an all-knowing but nevertheless consuming subject of abjection.[2] John Guillory refers to this discourse as a form of "voluntarism" that encourages "a descent from the rigor of analysis to the rhetoric of praise or blame and thus links voluntaristic discourse to an even less credible moralism."[3] Not only in cultural studies, the discourse of resistance is the legitimating principle for the justification of many forms of academic study across the humanities. In every pocket of culture, from South Asian hip hop to Filipina debuts, cultural insurrections are brought to light to reveal paths to political redemption. The result for Morris, remarking rather cynically, is that "I get the feeling that somewhere in some English publisher's vault there is a master-disk from which thousands of the same article about pleasure, resistance, and the politics of consumption are being run off under different names with minor variations."[4]

Asian American criticism has seen its fair share of both resistance and accommodation. In his recent book Viet Nguyen examines the way Asian American criticism falls into a binarized activity of locating either the resistance of "bad subjects" or the accommodation of "model minority" subjects.

Poem from *Waitng for Saskatchewan* (Winnipeg, Manitoba: Turnstone Press,1985). Used by permission of Fred Wah.

One of his principal critiques is directed at the way Asian American resistance to capitalist exploitation develops from a negotiation with and accumulation of symbolic capital surrounding Asian American racial identity. While an Asian American strategic essentialism and valorization of the "bad subject" is necessary for political mobilization in the short term, he concludes, "In the long term, however, the inaccuracy that is inherent in the discourse of the bad subject prevents Asian American intellectuals from recognizing the ability of late capitalism to transform Asian American racial identity into a commodity and Asian America into a niche market for that commodity."[5] This essay takes up this problem of resistance, whose sedimentation in academia has the potential to fetishize a delimited form of racial identity, by examining its discursive function in a broadened "Asian North American" literary field that encompasses both Asian Canadian and Asian American texts, especially as it applies to the development of an Asian North American avant-garde. The main questions I ask are as follows: what are the consequences of an overdetermined discourse of resistance in the expanded field of Asian North American literary studies?[6] Which texts stand in as what Nguyen calls the resistant "bad subject" or the accommodating "model minority"? Further, how does the integration of Asian American and Asian Canadian texts under the "Asian North American" umbrella term affect the development of an avant-garde political project? In order to answer these questions I plan to examine how a discourse of resistance constrains the visibility of certain Asian Canadian avant-garde writers.

To be clear, the purpose of this essay is not to reject the act of resistance itself; rather, it is to propose that oppositionality has been discursively constituted in Asian America on different terms than in Canada, thereby limiting the visibility of Asian Canadian cultural projects. In particular, for writers of colour in Canada, the history of legislated multiculturalism has generated cultural responses that differ from those that emerged out of civil rights activism and Asian American cultural nationalism in the US. In order to illustrate this erasure of Asian Canadian forms of opposition, I focus on the disappearance of renown Asian Canadian writer Fred Wah from an expanded Asian North American context. Considering the many books of poetry, critical essays, and prose-poetic "bio-text" that comprise Wah's oeuvre, not to mention the *Tish* poetry newsletter he cofounded in Canada in the 1960s and the prestigious Governor General's award he won in 1991, I find mysterious the virtual absence, or vanishing, of his avant-garde poetics in emergent discussions of "Asian North American" writing. This exposes, perhaps, the problem non-referential, non-representative, avant-gardist writing by Asian Canadians poses for Asian North American literary criticism. Equally curious is the seeming indifference to Wah's Chinese-Canadian racial difference in avant-garde critical quarters, suggesting, on the other hand, the problem race poses for the delineation of the "avant-garde."[7] I trace this double erasure of Fred Wah to conflicting paradigms of resistance constructed broadly on an opposition between the popular—what Pierre Bourdieu refers to as "heteronomy"—and the unpopular—what he calls "autonomy." By relying on the broad terms of the popular and the unpopular, I suggest only that formal strategies are often linked to the size and composition of a given work's audience.

Exploring the terms of Fred Wah's erasure, I will argue that the discourse of "resistance" functions as a form of symbolic capital in the context of Pierre Bourdieu's delineation of the field of cultural production. It attempts to transcend the gendered antinomies emanating from the masculinist construction of resistance value; between the resistant and the accommodationist, the political and the merely aesthetic, the materialist and the abstract, and the democratic and the elitist by examining the national contexts out of which certain formal strategies emerge. At the same time it is concerned to clear a space for a more serious and sustained inquiry into the Asian North American avant-garde of which I include Wah. He and other members of a predominantly western Canadian group of Asian Canadian writers, such as Roy Kiyooka, Roy Miki, Mark Nakada, and Rita Wong, collectively register decades of engagement with the assimilating role of national culture, articulated through disjunctive formal strategies which warrants serious investigation. Jeff Derksen describes some of this work as "unrecognizable" insofar as it attempts to escape absorption into the neo-liberal and race commodifying logic of legislated multiculturalism in Canada that celebrates a managed form of "diversity" while obfuscating the systemic nature of racism. As I will attempt to demonstrate, these "unrecognizable texts"[8] frustrate both dominant conceptions of resistance in Asian America as well as in a predominantly white avant-garde. Beyond the conflicting claims associated with national minority literatures and the avant-garde, moreover, I suggest that there is evidence of a certain tension between Marxist and deconstructive approaches to the politics of minority representation that also thwart the development of an Asian North American avant-garde.

This theoretical rift between Marxist and deconstructive critical approaches, which comes to light in the context of defining oppositionality, renders an Asian North American avant-garde in a perpetually nascent state. With a few well-known exceptions such as Theresa Cha, Li-Young Lee, and John Yau,[9] it appears that formally experimental Asian North American writers are not easily incorporated into the historical materialist emphasis of Asian American literary criticism. Alternatively, discourse-driven theories that assert the mediation of all experience through the thoroughly unstable coordinates of language enable a predominantly white avant-garde movement such as the "Language school" for instance, to envision itself as *more* resistant because of its opposition to the fetishization of personal experience narrated through conventional modes of communication they claim are symptomatic of capitalism. This movement,[10] whose radical language politics first emerged in response to Vietnam War and gained prominence in academia through the deconstructive turn, remains influential in the avant-garde literary scene, performing their resistance in language with an eager dispensation and criticism of a (white) authorial subject position represented by the lyric "I"—a normative identity that writers of colour do not have access to, let alone can dispense with. The Language school, paralleling a minority literature framework, also incorporates the discourse of social and cultural marginality to advance the radical theoretical positions in its essays and poetry, while nevertheless delimiting, as Timothy Yu observes, Language poetry "as a gender- and class-specific writing *distinct from* the writing undertaken by women or 'minority' writers."[11] Their ability to be both marginal and subjectless relies on an unspoken ideology of "literary Darwinism," a concept Jeff Derksen uses to describe a gendered and racial split between the avant-garde, "which is historically viewed as white and male—and so-called 'ethnic' writing that is characterized by narrative expectations that emergent 'ethnic voices' must first tell their stories in a recognizable way in order to inhabit a subjectivity that has been denied them."[12] Indeed, Ron Silliman, a key figure of the Language school claims that challenges to the naturalized construction of the autonomous subject is reserved principally for "white male heterosexuals" since they have historically been the subjects of history and can therefore condemn a subject position they firmly occupy.[13] I will attempt to counter this developmental view of Asian North American writing in my reading of Fred Wah's poetry in the latter part of this essay.

To locate an avant-garde movement in Canada by focusing on writers and critics who blur the genres of theoretical and creative writing is to offer a different starting point on a growing discourse surrounding "Asian Canadian" writing. Despite a perception that Asian Canadian writing has only "recently" arrived vis-à-vis a more established Asian American literary tradition, Canadian writers of Asian descent have written and mobilized around race for decades. In recognition of the important cultural work that precedes the more recent academic inauguration of an "Asian Canadian" category,[14] therefore, I would like to suggest that there is no "innocent" origin from which this writing emerges. In this section I provide a brief genealogy of Asian

Canadian criticism in order to highlight some of the tensions in the politics
of representation introduced by the naming of "Asian Canadian" that reveal
contrasting views on the relationship between form and social structure. By
focusing briefly on the complexities of the Asian Canadian field, we are prepared to understand the further intricacies introduced by a larger and more
inclusive Asian North American term.

After a long labor that began in the 1960s with the Asian Canadian
Writers Workshop, the "protracted birth"[15] of Asian Canadian writing, categorized as such, was revitalized by Roy Miki's important conference paper
"Asiancy: Making Space for Asian Canadian Writing"[16] delivered in 1993 at
the Association for Asian American Studies conference. While Miki's paper
is often cited as inaugurating the institutionalized academic study of Asian
Canadian literature, what is equally important is its call for a radical politics
of "deterritorialization," adopting Gilles Deleuze and Felix Guattari's term,
to challenge the assimilating role of Canadian multiculturalism for writers of
color. One of the major developments of the Asian Canadian renaissance has
been in the increased examination of the historical and literary relationship
of Asian Canadian to Asian American literature.[17] These discussions have
led to the attendant birth of the term "Asian North American," in recognition
of the important Asian Canadians texts which have hitherto "passed" as
Asian American. For example, in Marie Lo's critique of Asian American
literary studies, she examines the way Asian Canadian texts have historically
been appropriated as a necessary "Other" in the cultural nationalist project
of claiming America[18] by focusing on Asian Canadian border-crossing texts
by writers such as the Eaton sisters, Joy Kogawa, and SKY Lee. Donald
Goellnicht further highlights the positive influence of Asian American Studies and seeks an Asian North American coalition that would put necessary
pressure on a stagnant Canadian academic culture that defends a form of
race-evasiveness and perpetuates the "disavowal or deferral in dealing with
'race' as a cultural category." Various critics have also highlighted the insur-
gent potential of Asian Canadian literature in relation to Asian American and
mainstream Canadian contexts through an expanded Asian North American
framework.

Meanwhile, Roy Miki reveals a strong skepticism of the value of the
pan-ethnic designator, wary of "Asian Canadian" absorption and containment into national culture. He writes, "Such a reification process . . . could
inflict a form of critical and institutional 'branding' that replays the function of a 'brand name' in commodity capitalism—the curious inversion of
a 'branding' through a re-racialization process."[19] In another article, critical
of mainstream reading practices that constrain the potential value of "Asian
Canadian" literature, Miki warns that "in this compromised situation, the

scene of reading Asian Canadian has the potential to become the 'seen' of reading,"[20] as "other" objects of knowledge [are] splayed out for neo-liberal consumption. A common thread in Miki's work, therefore, is his acute awareness of and struggle against the "over-determined commodification of difference in the service of the same."[21]

What we find in the foregoing brief survey of criticism are somewhat contradictory engagements: an expansionist "Asian North American" movement on one hand, and a critical hesitation and reflection of the limits of "Asian Canadian" representation by Miki on the other. This tension represents a larger struggle in the politics of representation; between the political urgency to gain visibility and the imminent commodification and containment of that visibility within national culture. Given the insidious role of Canadian legislated multiculturalism to manage and commodify difference "in the service of the same," we can contextualize Miki's promotion of a formal and critical strategy of *unrecognizability* to thwart the commodifying gaze of national culture. But how do we situate this politics of "unrecognizability" in an Asian North American framework, given the dominant influence of Asian America whose foundational theories of breaking silence and indivisible subjectivity[22] constrain the visibility of experimental writers? Furthermore, the appropriation of "marginality" by a traditionally white avant-garde also functions to legitimize a form of resistance that is the exclusive province of normative subjects of history. The question is how to claim a political avant-garde for Asian North America that does not further circumscribe oppositionality.

If an Asian Canadian avant-garde project such as Fred Wah's remains invisible because of its disarticulation from a dominant Asian American politics of representation *and* a racially-(un)marked avant-garde project, can we locate the general structural coordinates that account for his lack of visibility? In order to explore this question, I draw on the work of Pierre Bourdieu to map out the contest for artistic legitimacy in the field of cultural production, of which Asian American literature and the avant-garde represent two in a wide array of positions in the field.

In Bourdieu's examination of the field of cultural production, he takes an external perspective to investigate the role of symbolic objects, such as visual art and literature, in the reproduction of structural inequality. For instance, Randal Johnson calls attention to the importance Bourdieu places on art and cultural consumption by explaining that "although they do not create or cause class divisions and inequalities, art and cultural consumption are predisposed, consciously and deliberately or not, to fulfill a social function of legitimating social differences and thus contribute to the process of social reproduction."[23] Bourdieu is particularly interested in this field[24] because it represents an "economic field reversed" insofar as it tends to place greater symbolic value on cultural objects that maintain the greatest distance from the logic of the market economy, the main determinant of social hierarchization. In other words, a kind of "pure" or "disinterested" art that abides by an ethos of "art for art's sake" is often attributed greater value than art from an unrestricted "public" or popular field of production because the former shuns the calculated, functional logic of the economy and aspires to a creative realm that supposedly exists beyond market or material demands (which are seen to compromise creative freedom). As Bourdieu explains, "the specificity of the literary and artistic field is defined by the fact that the more autonomous it is, i.e., the more completely it fulfills its own logic as a field, the more it tends to suspend or reverse the dominant principle of [economic] hierarchization."[25] Artists that appear disinterested in popularity or unaffected by market constraints therefore abide by the historically dominant logic of the field. Here we should pause to note various ways to interpret Bourdieu's concept of "autonomy." On one hand, its value appears constructed out of social, historical, and political transcendence; however, it is also possible to view it as a kind of "interested disinterestedness" in challenging and contradicting the logic of market demand. However, Bourdieu would most likely situate Asian American literature at the heteronomous or popular pole of the field of cultural production insofar as it is tied to and often held accountable to community interests.

One of the effects of this opposition between the two fields of production, between the restricted and unpopular position of high art and the unrestricted position of popular art, is the fetishization of form in the former and content in the latter. But it is not simply a fetishization of content over form that restricts the expansion of the Asian North American canon or the traditional parameters of the avant-garde. Rather, it is my claim that it is through a broader fetishization of resistance that exists in these fields. Viet Nguyen explains of the Asian American context, "value is determined not by financial capital but, in this case, by a symbolic capital that derives its worth from the idea of political resistance and social change."[26] In other words, because an Asian North American body of literature is principally situated at the heteronomous, non-restricted pole in the field of cultural production, its interest in instilling social change by affecting a *popular* consciousness regarding Asian Americans becomes a legitimating principle of resistance. This principle of resistance is frustrated by those artists such as Wah, whose work is often without recognizable markers of race, ethnicity, or class, and seems to be situated in the autonomous or restricted pole of cultural production insofar as his work is neither "popular" given its level of formal difficulty which limits its audience nor transparently clear in terms of the political interests at stake in his writing. But what is important to recognize is that work such as Wah's *also* frustrates the principle of resistance advocated by an avant-garde project such as the Language school. Despite his disjunctive formal style, Wah nevertheless commits to an author-situated rather than subjectless exploration of race, ethnicity, and class experience within and through language. Alternatively, given its anti-commodificatory oppositional stance, Bourdieu would probably situate the Language school, which eschews popular or conventional "expressive" modes in order to effect a discursive challenge to what they view as the commodification of language in late capitalism, at the *autonomous* pole in the field of cultural production. Therefore, at the level of consumption, Wah is situated somewhere in-between a heteronomous principle of resistance and an autonomous principle of resistance. In order to make him visible in an Asian North American framework I think we need to replace the discourse of resistance, which is often exercised by delimiting value to a particular content and/or form, with articulatory politics that seek to connect both popular and unpopular strategies to address issues of inequality that arise in a multiplicity of national and transnational contexts. In other words, we need to problematize the dichotomization of the popular and unpopular in delimiting resistance because contemporary local and global realities require articulated strategies to produce alternative knowledges to challenge the many forces that project what Gramsci refers to as "common sense."[27]

The features of accessibility that are often characteristic of cultural production found at the unrestricted heteronomous pole are often mapped onto the genre of realism, features which are often absent in experimental or otherwise non-representative writing–particularly experimental poetry–revealing a dichotomy in the Asian American field: the accessibility of prose fiction versus the difficulty of poetry, and by extension, the social and political nature of fiction versus the private and individual nature of poetry. Noting the existence of such a formal opposition between poetry and prose, for instance, Juliana Chang observes a "critical perception that poetry is to prose precisely as the private and individual are to the public and the social, and that the poetic therefore has less social relevance."[28] Of course these distinctions are oversimplified and fail to take account for the many works that transcend crude generic divisions between prose and poetry, as well as the number of authors who write in more than one genre. Nevertheless this reductionism has been highly effective in making an oppositional virtue of the related terms of *accessibility* and *authenticity*. In other words, the popularity of prose, which is arguably the most "accessible" literary form, is legitimated through an economic consumer logic: the larger the reading public, the more social good. And to add the stamp of authenticity onto this consumer logic, the larger the reading public has access to "authentic" narratives of the oppressed, the more social good will come of the politically urgent need to "set the record straight." The value placed on mimetic representation serves as a legitimating principle in the field of Asian American literature and illuminates a particular relationship between form and its perceived social function.

Since oppositionality based on accessibility of the popular in a dominant Asian American field makes it difficult to clear a space for Wah's poetry in an expanded Asian North American context, we can explore further his lack of fit in the less popular oppositional project represented by a literary avant-garde such as the Language school. The Language school serves as a useful corollary to Wah since the Black Mountain poetics in which he was trained was an important precursor to Language poetics and much of his work reveals similar concerns with language. Since the 1980s, the Language school has become virtually synonymous with innovation in its questioning of historical agency and linguistic subjectivity and its rejection of the conventions of narrative. Disposing of functionality for the *materiality* of language, therefore, Language poetry attempts to transform the hegemonic role of language in national culture. As Language poet Bruce Andrews explains of the basic contours of Language practice in "Poetry as Explanation, Poetry as Praxis" under the sub-heading "I GET IMPATIENT": "Conventionally, radical dissent & 'politics' in writing would be measured in terms of communication & concrete effects on an audience,"[29] but "such conventionally progressive literature fails to self-examine writing & its medium, language."[30] He proposes instead "writing as politics, not writing about politics."[31] Similarly, in "Aesthetic Tendency and the Politics of Poetry: A Manifesto," Language poets Ron Silliman, Carla Harryman, Lyn Hejinian, Steve Benson, Bob Perelman, and Barrett Watten elucidate further a claim that the expressivist poetic tradition is responsible for making poetry "nice but irrelevant"[32] which they challenge by looking toward "analogies between the structure of language and social reality"[33] as an explicitly *social* movement. By rejecting the genre of "realism" in particular, a genre that Silliman refers to as "the illusion of reality in capitalist thought"[34] these poets intend to corrupt and thus decommodify language in poetry in such a way that will lead to social justice and freedom. Silliman also adds that poetry's transformative potential is rooted in its "historical standing as the first of the language arts . . . yield[ing] less to (and resisted more) [to] capitalist transformation"[35] being the only genre where narrative justifications are unnecessary and unconventional spellings are customary.

As we noted earlier, the properties of the Language school are in many ways situated within Bourdieu's definition of "cultural autonomy," which he identifies as constituting the legitimating principal of the cultural field. Despite the Language school's radical and anti-capitalist oppositional claims, its experimental forms are clearly distanced from the popular logic that dominates the heteronomous pole in the field of cultural production. In other words, Language poetry, in its rejection of expression and many other "communicative" forms of discourse, is tied to the autonomous pole where formal experimentation, defamiliarization, and rejection of a stable lyric "I" are regarded as a more serious obstructions to capitalism.

The Language school, however, recirculates a problematic elitism in its anti-capitalist claims. While the desire to maintain a distance from the logic of the capitalist economy is meant to register as an anti-capitalist cultural tactic, strategies associated with the restricted or autonomous field nevertheless invest in, trade in, and profit from a different but equally important *cultural* and *symbolic* economy. While these terms are related, symbolic capital emphasizes a kind of prestige or honor that comes with being a talented violinist, for instance. Cultural capital, however, is usually tied to educational credentials in the form of an academic degree. For many, it is the cultural capital of the degree that serves to substantiate the symbolic capital of one's talents. While experimental poetry may be less subject to commodification, it is the limited access to cultural capital—usually linked to race, gender, and class—that, as I will argue below, maintains problematically its position in the restricted "autonomous" field.

The main problem with the critique of popular genres such as realism which, as the Language school suggests, contributes to social normalization through the fetishization of referentiality in language and alienating other aspects of signification, is that it fails to consider the historical development of the anti-commodification position in the art world. Embedded in this anti-economic position and construction of "autonomy" are genealogical traces of cultural elitism based on the historical accumulation of symbolic capital through differential consumption patterns. Although critiques of elitism are often disregarded as "anti-intellectualist" projections, its development has a material basis.

For Bourdieu, elitism functions as a form of "distinction" premised on the inequality of access to cultural goods. He traces the development of cultural autonomization—or the way certain arts became cut off from the logic of the economic world—in his essay, "The Market of Symbolic Goods." In this essay he explains how in the Middle Ages, part of the Renaissance, and throughout the French classical age, intellectual and artistic life was dominated by "external sources of legitimacy,"[36] meaning that art was largely under the control of aristocratic and ecclesiastical tutelage. When art became progressively freed from this supervision, artists became freer in the sense that they were able to create art that could be autonomous from the mandates of church or state. As Bourdieu explains, "The end of dependence on a patron or collector and, more generally, the ending of the dependence upon direct commissions, with the development of an impersonal market, tends to increase the liberty of writers and artists."[37] This was, however, a *relative* autonomy insofar as art became more subject to the impersonal forces of the market, which made artists entrenched in a form of demand "that necessarily lags behind the supply of the [art] commodity"[38] evident in sales figures and exercised by publishers, theater managers, and art dealers. No longer constrained by patronage, all artists for a time became "autonomous" or free agents, which meant that the public now had much greater access to high cultural products *because* of its commodification, particularly the literary arts. This process of facilitating democratic access through the transition of art into a commodity emphasized however the tremendous power of non-producing consumers to drive demand and determine artistic value through that demand. In a seeming twist of fate, therefore, certain artists began to realize that the market actually became a liability to the very autonomy it was supposed to enable. As John Guillory explains, "These cultural producers seem to have acknowledged very early what Bourdieu calls their 'structural domination' by the market, the fact that they had exchanged one master for another."[39] In response to this false autonomy produced by the market was the emergence of the "field of restricted production" in which artists could produce for other artists in a sphere outside of market demands.

The major tension between the unpopular or autonomous and popular or heteronomous poles in the field of cultural production is with respect to the difference of consumption, both which rely for their definition on objective structures that limit or facilitate access to goods, services, and power—particularly through education. What is interesting about literary arts, therefore, is that the mode of consumption demanded by the field of restricted production "offered to the dominant classes a more reliable means of restricting access to the work of art than the mechanism of price itself."[40] In other words, the restricted field assumed a mode of consumption that required a specific kind of knowledge associated with educational institutions.

Bourdieu explains this dynamic as follows:

> While consumption in the field of large-scale cultural production is more or less independent of the educational level of consumers (which is quite understandable since the system tends to adjust to the level of demand), works of restricted art owe their specifically cultural rarity to the rarity of the instruments with which they may be deciphered. This rarity is a function of the *unequal distribution of the conditions underlying the acquisition of the specifically aesthetic disposition and of the codes indispensable to the deciphering of the works belonging to the field of restricted production.*[41] (emphasis added)

Therefore, the restricted field of cultural production determines cultural value not in terms of market demand but rather in terms of its distance from that demand, defining itself through the terms of an "aesthetic disposition." While it seems on the surface that the restricted field of production offers a more "pure" method of determining cultural value, Bourdieu's main point is that the aesthetic disposition required to assess works in the field of restricted production—generally the disposition of artists themselves—is dependent on a relatively exclusive kind of knowledge. Historically, the aesthetic disposition had the added effect of permitting, as Guillory explains, "the dominant classes' perception of their real freedom from economic necessity to be conflated with the cultural producers' claim to have *freed themselves* from determination by the market."[42] Thus we witness the way cultural distinction or elitism emerged first out of a separation then conflation of cultural and material capital, which is the context from which the anti-economic critique of the popular is born.

To sum up the foregoing section, what is most problematic about the unpopular autonomous field is not necessarily its desire to maintain a distance from market demands or to determine artistic value outside of book sales; rather, it is that the status of cultural products has been historically overdetermined by *limited access* to those products. Distinction, or cultural capital, is produced precisely out of the inequality of access to different kinds of cultural goods. Therefore, my point is that the appeal to autonomous production, as a more politically resistant alternative to "realism" or the popular makes the reading of "resistance" available only to those with an unequally distributed cultural capital. It is this delimiting of resistance to the field of restricted production that nevertheless enables a traditionally white male avant-garde to assert its detachment from not only market relations but gender, race, and class relations as well. Paradoxically, this autonomy from outward constraints registers as the surplus of resistance potential.

If neither a heteronomous popular or an autonomous or unpopular avant-garde can offer a coherent formulation for resistance that can make room for a disjunctive poet like Fred Wah, where do we go from here? To answer this question I would like to return once again to Miki's call for a radical politics of "deterritorialization." In Gilles Deleuze and Felix Guattari's far-ranging critique of Western metaphysics, capitalism, and Oedipal myth, they affirm the possibility of a world without hierarchy and dialectical opposition by scrambling or *deterritorializing* all social, cultural, and political codes.[43] I propose that we think of deterritorialization not in terms of disarticulation but rather as articulation: to rearticulate Marxism's materialism and deconstruction's textualism in order to connect the political goals surrounding both popular and unpopular literatures as a first step in redistributing access to cultural works and employing them in the critique of national and transnational systems of oppression. I make this proposition based on the observation that Language poetics, with its fundamental concern over the materiality of language and rejection of meaning often attract post-structuralist theorizing, while ethnic minority writing is often subject to substantive contextualization via Marxist historical materialism, of which a significant objective is to reveal the many contradictions of Western modernity that shape the conditions of production imbedded in the text.

In order to examine this mode of critical deterritorialization, how can we integrate Marxism and deconstruction in a reading of Wah? From a post-structuralist standpoint, textuality is a process that undermines the underlying binaries and logics of Western ideology and metaphysics. Through the logic of the supplement, which continually upsets the criteria through which the text and its subjects make sense of themselves, textuality can be considered oppositional insofar as it exposes the inability of Western ideology to stabilize meaning and value. In contrast, Marxism is focused less on exposing the inherent instability of Western metaphysics than on throwing light onto the shadows hiding the history and politics that have been repressed in the text. Marxist literary criticism directs its attention on re-contextualizing literature and politics by emphasizing the material, economic, and ideological forces that shape the conditions of its production. As Michael Greer outlines, "post-structuralism's project is to demonstrate the interplay of textuality, subjectivity, and ideology, while Marxism sees itself as reinserting texts into the material networks of power and exchange by which they are determined".[44]

Although there is no easy synthesis of these approaches, we might begin to locate their interdependence within a larger critique of globalization. Jeff Derksen makes this important observation of the theoretical exigencies of our current historical moment:

> Cultural studies, economic analysis, Marxism, postmodernist thought, post-colonialism, socialist feminism, etc., become constituent tools and positions in the critique of globalization rather than their own semi-autonomous standpoint theories. Following the necessary critique and resistance of grand narratives by poststructuralism (in the aesthetic field), postcolonialism (in the social field) and postmodernism (in the cultural field), the critique of globalism emerges as the encompassing contestatory discourse of and for this moment.[45]

In this context we can see how these approaches implicitly and explicitly articulate in their desire to expose how capitalism's expropriation of surplus labor depends on the grand narratives of modernity—of progress, of racial superiority, of scientific positivism, for example—to justify the imperialist expansion of markets. A brief look at Fred Wah's work in the concluding section gives us an opportunity to consider the interdependence of concerns associated with Marxism and deconstruction out of which his poetry arises.

During a conversation with bp Nichol in 1977, Fred Wah discusses his search for a "middle voice" that was introduced to him by Charles Olson while he was a student of Olson's graduate poetics program at SUNY-Buffalo in the 1960s. Wah explains that the middle voice is simultaneously active and passive, eliminating a clear subject or object: "Like I could say, 'I floating' rather than 'I float,' which is too direct. A condition . . . 'I floating' . . . if I could state that. I work toward that."[46] Wah's emphasis on the middle voice and "trans," the latter he refers to as a poetic process that enables him "to go to something existing between it and the language or having a language happen between I and it that leads to other things,"[47] illuminates his interest in the objective and subjective conditions of language. What underlies this brief view into his poetic strategies is, among other things, the deflection of a coherent or autonomous self. For Wah, language both embodies and is embodied: he produces language as much as it produces him. Far from "breaking the silence" by claiming voice or epistemic privilege, Wah's poetics contradict altogether the availability of a stable lyric "I."

This formulation shares much with Foucault in the way that it displaces the authoritative position of the writing subject and reveals instead how the subject is produced *within* discourse. Wah's liminal poetics also hint at his suspicion toward the relation between narrative and national culture, a suspicion also held by the Language school that we have already examined. For

Wah, the concerns of Russian formalist Victor Schlovsky to employ strategies of defamiliarization or "making strange" are a key aspect of his work which are often invoked in his critical essays and poetry. In his recent collection of essays, *Faking It: Poetics and Hybridity*, Wah refers to Schlovsky's articulation of the properties and effects that distinguish poetic language: "The purpose of art is to impart the sensation of things as they are perceived and not as they are known. The technique of art is to make objects 'unfamiliar,' to make forms difficult, to increase the difficulty and length of perception because the process of perception is an aesthetic end in itself and must be prolonged."[48] Wah incorporates this notion of "making strange" in what he refers to as an "alienethnic" poetic stance that involves "defamiliarization, deconstruction, displacement, negative capability, or nonnarrative, not knowing, indeterminacy, silence, distortion, parataxis, non-referentiality, dictation, ambiguity, disfunctioning, fragmentation, undecidability, Differenzqualitat, departure, derivation, opposition, divergence, alter-native, and on and on."[49] But this formal desire does not arise to simply privilege the artfulness of the object; rather, it is the form that itself becomes the object and in doing so rearticulates and/or displaces the racialized subject of the poem. As Derksen points out, Wah's poetics go beyond Schlovsky insofar as they are one of "situatedness and rearticulation [which] would not again try to make the stone stony in an attempted return of our multinational sense . . . but would articulate links that are deflected within social relations and dearticulate other links that give the appearance of a social totality."[50] We can briefly consider some of these elements at work in the following poem that appears in his book of poetry *Waiting for Saskatchewan*:

> Relation speaks. Tree talks hierarchy loop subject returns.
> Knowledge a bag of things to be changed later to
> knowledge. Statement of instructions horoscope Wah
> language reads reading out of order in order to speak to
> itself feed picked up lists family and complete branches/
> worlds end there.[51]

At first glance, there is nothing in this poem that overtly betrays Wah's Chinese Canadian or working-class background. Indeed, there is very little that points to a human subject of the poem if we notice that there is no clear subject controlling the action: "Relation *speaks*"; "Tree *talks*"; "Statement of instructions *horoscope* Wah"; "Language *reads*" (italics added). Not only does it displace a clear subject, but it also rejects a narrative teleology. Rather, the poem is more circular and even tautologous as "knowledge a bag of things to be changed later to knowledge" and "language reads reading out of order in order to speak to itself." But as Wah has written elsewhere, "because we do not know does not mean we are lost. Something that is strangely familiar, not quite what we expect, but familiar, is present."[52] The deferral of subjectivity and linearity in this poem perhaps comments on properties of language that constantly displace and reorganize. To this extent, we can perhaps agree that this poem is about language. But not just any language: the "statement of instruction," the "knowledge a bag of things," and the "lists" suggest systems that organize language and bodies. These systems are set in relation to "Wah," the name and the poet who is "horoscop[ed]" by expectations that those systems produce. Therefore, the Chinese Canadian, working-class identity is constituted as "Wah" and the "family" in relation to these systems of language and power that converge to construct an idea of national progress, producing contradictory forces that recruit foreign labor and racialize Chinese immigrants through head taxes and exclusion laws. It is a system that Wah exposes as neither arbitrary nor neutral but rather racially determined and self-serving: "to speak to itself," changing knowledge "later to knowledge." What seems to be present in this poem is precisely the tension and negotiation between the freedom and constraints of language in the production of social order. It is precisely the "relation" of discourse and power that "speaks."

There is no question that this poem disrupts narrative expectations of ethnic voice and demonstrates the tactics of deterritorialized writing that Miki calls for by refusing to submit to the multicultural gaze—refusing to be commodified as an ethnic object of knowledge. In order to read Wah without evacuating the political and the social registers of his poetry, we must therefore take into account his social location and see his poem as both a response to that location and constitutive of new positions within ideology. To this extent, this writing is grounded by the specific material conditions of Canada—where legislated multiculturalism functions to homogenize ethnic difference into a quintessential "Canadian condition"—but also plays a constitutive role by repositioning, rearticulating the racial subject in language, and calling into question the neutrality of knowledge and truth. It is writing that does not escape ideology but rather repositions itself against the system that seeks to suture its subjects into a multiculturally homogenous and celebratory national universal. Derksen refers to this kind of writing as "antisystemic," as "writing that "consciously counters a system that seeks to interpellate a subject within a particular field of relations."[53] Of course, this is not the only way in which articulation can occur: the Asian North American avant-garde is one out of many potential discourses that help to rearticulate local and global politics.

   In the end there is no oppositional victory for the popular or the unpopular. There is no ideological outside for which either can project its oppositionality. By considering the disappearances of Fred Wah, this essay has attempted to push Asian North American criticism to go beyond a discourse that delimits resistance toward a consideration of an articulatory poetics and politics that reveal, in different degrees, the material and textual negotiation of the subject in ideology.[54]

Part II

Aesthetics and Ethnicity

4

The Asian American
in a Turtleneck

*Fusing the Aesthetic and the Didactic in Maxine
Hong Kingston's* Tripmaster Monkey

MITA BANERJEE

I PROPOSE TO READ THE DEVELOPMENT of the field of Asian
American Studies from its beginnings to its present articulation through
the tension between the aesthetic and the didactic. This tension, I sug-
gest, can be mapped onto the fictional difference between Maxine Hong
Kingston's earlier novel *The Woman Warrior* and her subsequent narrative
Tripmaster Monkey, which appeared almost ten years later. I will argue that
Tripmaster Monkey employs a *form* hitherto absent from Asian American
literature as well as the theoretical discussion surrounding this literature.
Tripmaster Monkey can be read as an instance of what I would call "open-
ended didacticism." Both the strength and the pitfalls of this concept, I will
suggest, are inherent in its fusion of apparent paradoxes. While didacticism
logically presupposes closure or clear-cut definitions, Kingston's narrative
upsets this very logic. The structure of my paper arises from this paradox.
I will situate *Tripmaster Monkey* in relation to literary theories that explore
either the notion of open-endedness (especially the work of Native American
writer and critic Gerald Vizenor) or that of didacticism (particularly with regard to the Asian American theorist and writer Frank Chin). None of these
theoretical approaches, however, considers the fusion of the didactic and the
open-ended exhibited in *Tripmaster Monkey*'s paradoxical form. Following
Vizenor, I suggest that the mainstream projection of "ethnic" difference can
be resisted only through an emphasis on the fundamental open-endedness of

culture that is now no longer understood as mere cultural *difference*. Maxine Hong Kingston's aesthetic politics in *Tripmaster Monkey*, I suggest, are exemplary of this very open-endedness.

The connection between Kingston's work and that of Gerald Vizenor has been emphasized by John Lowe, who writes, "Kingston's [*Tripmaster Monkey*] is, I believe, indebted to the achievements of her colleagues, especially Vizenor." [1] While Lowe stresses the (postmodernist) tricksterism in which Vizenor's *Griever: An American Monkey King in China* and Kingston's *Tripmaster Monkey* converge, my emphasis on Wittman's didacticism would stress the difference between the two texts. While Vizenor's fiction and theory is opposed to any notion of closure, I would propose that the didactic element of Kingston's narrative to some extent reintroduces such closure.

The question I address is thus significant for both Asian American Studies specifically and minority politics as such. How, through what aesthetic politics or form, can a mainstream be resisted that is certain of the fact that the Other can be *known*? The dilemma is in fact that between education and representation: in order to convince the mainstream of the shortcomings of its own categories, its perception or rather, "invention" of ethnicity, the ethnic subject needs to convey a difference that is recognizably "ethnic." Through such a representation, however, the minority subject at once confirms—in spite of itself—the knowability of ethnicity. The key question is thus whether the didactic can be reconciled with an open-ended inscription of ethnic subjectivity. It is in this paradoxical fusion, I will propose in the following, in which Maxine Hong Kingston's narrative aesthetics in *Tripmaster Monkey* engage. It is significant, however, that *Tripmaster Monkey* has not met with as much critical success as, for instance, Kingston's earlier text, *The Woman Warrior*. The question I would like to raise is whether this lack of critical success may be due to the fact that the aesthetic and the didactic do not mix. Significantly, Kingston stages, within the pages of *Tripmaster Monkey*, an Asian American play that is characterized by precisely such a mixture. And this play is received, by the mainstream critics described by the narrative, only with ridicule. From the point of view of these fictional critics at least, open-endedness does not work, especially when blended with didacticism. The paradox is this: Kingston's fictional playwright, Wittman Ah Sing, tries to resist Orientalist perceptions of Asian American art by returning the clichés to those who perpetrate them. When he realizes that white critics do not get the point, however, he goes on to *explain* his open-ended aesthetics.

Open-ended Performances: Postasian Warriors in Turtleneck Sweaters

It is this dilemma between an absence of closure and the possibility of a didactic counter-representation that may be at the heart of the shift from Maxine Hong Kingston's earlier novel *The Woman Warrior* to *Tripmaster Monkey*. The latter novel has been read by many as a complete departure from her earlier aesthetic politics and, significantly, perhaps her literary success. For *The Woman Warrior* revolves around, not so much a refusal to define a Chinese American predicament or identity as the impossibility of doing so. As the novel's protagonist puts it, "What is Chinese tradition and what is in the movies?"[2] Crucially, the Chinese American subject is unable to determine what about herself is "Chinese," what is simply a matter of personal predilection, and what is a self-image resulting from mainstream projections of Chineseness. In this dilemma, the autofictional Maxine converges with Wittman Ah Sing in *Tripmaster Monkey*, who wonders whether his personal likes or dislikes are culturally occasioned or are just that—personal: "The reason he didn't like going to football games was the same reason he didn't like going to the theater: he wanted to be playing. Does his inability at cheers have to do with being Chinese?"[3] The construction of "Asianness" by the dominant society has made the Asian American unreadable to himself. In an Asian American variation of what W.E.B. Du Bois, in an African American context, has called "double consciousness," Wittman sees himself through mainstream eyes. As the "cultural" is thus overdetermined, Wittman can no longer distinguish between the culturally occasioned and the idiosyncratic. In its "talking back" to the mainstream's assumption of cultural difference, I propose, that Kingston's narrative politics embraces the idiosyncratic. The idiosyncratic is also a marker of an open-ended definition of the "ethnic self." Yet, it is significant that *Tripmaster Monkey*, unlike Kingston's earlier narrative, does not let this open-endedness speak for itself. Instead, Wittman goes on to explain its function. In *Tripmaster Monkey*, open-ended aesthetics come with a glossary. The politics of an oppositional, deliberately idiosyncratic Asian American style are mirrored, within Kingston's narrative, by Wittman's staging of a weeklong play. This syncretic performance, I propose, is indicative of an alternative, Chinese American aesthetics. The play mirrors the cultural politics of the narrative itself. Moreover, the double frame of a theatrical performance within a literary narrative enables Kingston to comment on the politics of the *reception* of Chinese American art.

The interminable duration of the play is mirrored by the endless number of characters. Wittman informs one of the actors that his choice of roles is infinite:

> And/or you could play Liu Tang. . . . And or Tuan Ching Chu, the Gold-haired Dog, who wins from a Tartar prince a wonder horse named White Jade That Shines in the Night. And/or Doctor Huang Pu Tuan, Uncle Purple beard, a horse vet and a horse thief, the last outlaw to join the community. . . . These were not Caucasians; a Chinese can look like anything. (274–75)

This passage points to the interminable and unintelligible connections that are the hallmark of Wittman's theatrical poetics. For Wittman's audience as well as the reader of *Tripmaster Monkey*, it is impossible to keep the characters apart: Tuan Ching Chu blurs into the Tartar prince who blurs into his own horse. My point is, then, that this blurring of one character into another is the cultural principle of the ethnic open-endedness put on stage, and I will attempt to show that the aesthetic practice of Wittman's cultural theory fails. Nobody likes, or even understands, his play. It is here that didacticism comes in: Wittman must explain his play because his open-ended aesthetics fail to speak for themselves.

Wittman's play inscribes a postmodern politics of resistance in the open-endedness of cultural difference. He vows the play will contain everything. Even as his props are tokens of a clichéd Asianness, they also testify to the fact that the cliché veils an infinite wealth of meaning. For the "Asian" props employed by the playwright testify to an appropriation, by Asian Americans themselves, of "ethnic" chic: They appropriate the decontextualized cliché of Asianness (such as a Buddha backscratcher) and turn the Oriental-ist simulation back on those who believe in it: "A backscratcher from a Singapore sling, a paper umbrella from an aloha mai tai, a Buddha bottle with head that unscrews—make something of it. Use it. From these chicken scraps and dog scraps, learn what a Chinese-American is made up of" (277).

As playwright, Wittman refuses to distinguish between the marginal and the dominant. It is here that the interwovenness of the "cultural" and the "idiosyncratic" recur, which make up Wittman's open-ended definition of cultural difference. Asian American subjectivity, the play suggests, is formed out of all these discursive elements. By refusing to separate the trivial from the significant, Wittman stages a play that will be too complex to be understood in cultural clichés. He gives a Western audience the "hard hearing" of an ethnicity that cannot be grasped in preconceived terms:

We keep the men's Chinese names, we keep the women's names untrans-
lated too, no more Pearl Buck Peony Plum Blossom haolefied missionary
names. No more accessible girls and unspeakable men. . . . Let the gringo
Anglos do some hard hearing for a change. (138)

The play's aesthetics, then, are the theatrical equivalent of "hard hearing." And it is here that the question of reception comes in. The unsuspecting
mainstream audience is bombarded with aesthetics that mix the cliché with
the irreducibly personal that, given the individual histories it is predicated
on, cannot really be decoded by the observer. Clichés are fused with oppositional Asian American counter-narratives to the extent that it is impossible
to determine where the distorted mirroring of Orientalist expectations ends
and where the counter-narrative begins. The "hard hearing" of Wittman's
open-ended theatrical poetics are characterized by the fact that they are
impossible to decode: for any decoding will once again yield the idea of
a fixed, definable Asian American subject. And it is this definability that
Wittman's play contests. Wittman's aesthetics are thus in fact their own undoing: they are "hard hearing" to the extent that they cannot be understood
at all. In the multiplicity of characters and motifs, the play deconstructs itself. The only counterbalance to such theatrical self-deconstruction, then,
is the playwright's didacticism: it is he who mediates between the trivial and
the culturally significant and, through this didactic mediation, reintroduces
a hierarchy after all. Wittman's didacticism is the safety net ameliorating the
excessive open-endedness of his theatrical tour de force.

This open-ended tour de force of Wittman's theatrical poetics, in turn,
is inseparable from the poetics of *Tripmaster Monkey* itself. To a certain
extent, the play is the narrative. Wittman's project parallels the narrative's
own cultural politics. Significantly, then, both Wittman's play and *Tripmaster
Monkey* have met with adverse criticism. My claim is that this criticism is
due to the fact that both play and narrative push the envelope of how much
an aesthetic text can hold. This practice of pushing the envelope, in turn,
arises from the attempt on the part of the artist to strain the limits of what
Asian Americanness is, resisting facile ethnic categories or markers.

Importantly, reviews of *Tripmaster Monkey* center on critics' impression
of Wittman's play. These reviewers, Diane Simmons emphasizes, describe
the play (and hence implicitly also the story of *Tripmaster Monkey*) as:

exhausting. . . . The myths and sagas are particularly tiring. Wittman loves to
tell lengthy stories that possess the grandiosity and the meandering formless-
ness common to folk legends. . . . After a while the merest mention of Liu Pei
or Sun Wu Kong, the Monkey King, is enough to make our eyes glaze over.[4]

It is at this point that I would like to superimpose on Wittman's art that of another cultural performer whose open-ended politics of resistance have been described by Gerald Vizenor. Like Wittman, Ishi—a native man who was discovered by anthropologists in Northern California and paraded as "the last of his tribe"—is called upon to represent an entire community. Like Wittman, Ishi, too, resorts to aesthetics that are open-ended. Crucially, the anthropologists' reaction to Ishi's storytelling is the same as the critics' reaction to Wittman's weeklong play: their eyes glaze over. Both Wittman and Ishi, through their open-ended (or, from the mainstream's point of view, never-ending) performance, stress the fact that ethnicity does not fit in a nutshell. Like the play's content, Ishi's story has to be told in one sitting. Cultural performance, in both cases, taxes the mainstream listener's attention to an almost unbearable extent. This taxing is itself a deconstruction of the ethnographic assumption: While the ethnographer wants to finish his recording and go home, the resisting subject requires him to be *part* of the lived performance of culture. Ishi and Wittman, on the other hand, tell their listeners that there is no culture to record, only to experience. Vizenor writes about Ishi, "His stories must have come from visual memories, and he should be honored for more than his stories, his humor, and survivance: he should be honored because he never learned how to slow his stories down to be written and recorded."[5]

Similarly, the cultural hybridity of Wittman's play, which draws on Western and Chinese sources simultaneously is disregarded by mainstream reviewers. What Wittman has to find is that the reviewer-as-ethnographer goes on to *simulate* the picture he could not have taken at the performance. Having come to record the Other and having found that there was no Otherness to record, the ethnographer made a recording anyway. Where Wittman wants to stage theater, then, the critic's recorder records a multiculturalist spectacle, in an echo of Richard Fung's assertion, "Ballet is art, Chinese classical dance is multiculturalism."[6] The reviews, then, repeat the "obvious"—Chinese "authenticity"—without being aware of the hybrid cultural reality explored by the play. The reviewers experience Wittman's art as profoundly "Chinese." Wittman is adamant about the fact that the review of his play could have been written without the reviewer's having seen the play, and perhaps was:

You like the review? . . . "Sweet and sour." Quit clapping. Stop it. What's to cheer about? You like being compared to Rice Krispies? Cut it out. Let me show you, you've been insulted. They sent their food critics. They wrote us up like they were tasting Chinese food. Rice, get it? . . . That's like saying LeRoi Jones is as good as a watermelon. (*Tripmaster*: 307)

This passage may also testify to the impotence of an open-ended aesthetics. The critic as ethnographer goes to a Chinese *American* play to record *Chinese* cultural difference. Despite the play's aesthetic resistance to this ethnographic gaze, the critic goes on to record what was not there in the play: a cultural difference devoid of hybridity. It is this record of exoticism that Gerald Vizenor deconstructs with regard to Ishi. Ishi turns the photograph against the photographer, turns the ethnographic document against those who recorded it. Ishi's photographers, like Wittman's critics, record ultimate Otherness. And yet, seen from an alternative Asian American/Native American perspective, they are seen to be left with an empty picture frame. The photographer, like Wittman's critic, is left with a "fugitive pose." Vizenor states, "the fugitive poses of the *indian* other, outside the case of technologies and social functions of photographic representations, are simulations of severance, not the pictures or stories of native survivance."[7] It is in their recording "fugitive poses" that the photographer/critic as ethnographer are unable to capture the postasian subject, to paraphrase Vizenor, which is at the heart of Wittman's open-ended aesthetics.

The Politics of Reception

Crucially, the fictionalized reviews of Wittman's play can be seen as a fictional answer to the *orientalizing* reception of Kingston's novel *The Woman Warrior*. In this sense, *Tripmaster Monkey* can be seen to comment on the reception of the author's earlier narrative. The crux at the heart of the reception of *The Woman Warrior* was precisely that a mainstream public on the lookout for exoticism saw an Other presence where there was in fact only provisionality and performance. The "Chinese" woman, to paraphrase Vizenor, is the absence of *The Woman Warrior*; she is precisely the pose the novel set out to deconstruct. Chinese Americanness, Kingston asserts in this first fictional narrative, can be grasped only in the performance: it can never be fixed into definition. The answer of where the "Chinese" element begins and where the "American" ends—with personal idiosyncrasies in the middle—cannot be determined. It is to resist projections of definition, of closure, that the novel sets out.

It is significant for the purpose of my argument that in her reaction to such Orientalizing reactions to *The Woman Warrior*, Kingston insists on a politics of plainness—which in turn is a hallmark of the postasian, open-ended politics of Wittman's play. The play can hence be read as the fictionalized reaction of Kingston's initial reaction to the exoticizing reviews of *The Woman*

Warrior. Like Wittman in his didactic stage directions and his rant against his play's reviewers, Kingston *comments* on the reviews of *The Woman Warrior*. It is in this commenting that the shift from the earlier to the later novel can be seen. In *The Woman Warrior*, Kingston had trusted an open-ended aesthetics to speak for itself. In *Tripmaster Monkey*, and through Wittman's play, Kingston supplies both the open-ended aesthetics *and* the glossary explaining its open-endedness, thereby striving to preclude Orientalist misreadings. According to Diane Simmons:

> Most critics loved the book [*The Woman Warrior*]. But this did not stop them, as Kingston saw to her dismay, from reading it through a haze of cultural and racial stereotypes. In an essay entitled "Cultural Mis-Readings by American Reviewers," Kingston responded to those who both loved the book and at the same time missed its point, those who had read in the light of their own fantasies of China and the Chinese.[8]

For my purposes here, it is critical that Kingston calls for an acknowledgment of the fact that Chinese Americanness can be recognizable without having closure. It is a culture that is different from the mainstream, yet whose difference must not be *misrecognized* as being clearly circumscribed. By commenting on the reviews, Kingston *didactically* calls for a recognition of the open-endedness that is also inscribed in her fiction: She emphasizes the need for an open-ended didacticism. The reviewers' reactions criticized by Kingston, then, parallels the reaction of reviewers to Wittman's play within the narrative of *Tripmaster Monkey*. There is a parallel between Kingston's above comments and the literary politics of her novel.

At the same time, Kingston is aware of the parameters that shape the mainstream's reception of her novel. The writer's own racial features determine the audience's expectations of cultural closure *within* the text. In order to upset such closure, Kingston strives to undermine the racialized perception of her own body. Yet, like Wittman's fictional politics of resistance, Kingston's deconstruction of her own image—and, implicitly, the image of her fictional narrative—fails. The Asian American writer *deconstructs* the pose by wearing a plain black turtleneck for the photograph. There is no exoticism here. Kingston proposes that through her book, she wanted to counter:

> the stereotype of the exotic, inscrutable, mysterious oriental.... Pridefully enough, I believed that I had written with such power that the reality and humanity of my characters would bust through any stereotypes of them. Simple-mindedly, I wore a sweat-shirt for the dust-jacket photo, to deny the exotic. I had not calculated how blinding stereotyping is, how stupefying.[9]

What is devastating is precisely that the *ethnographic* gaze of the main-stream sees "Chineseness" wherever it looks. The mainstream is unaware that this politics of seeing is never neutral: the pose is its own fiction. In a magical sleight of hand, the mainstream sees traditional Chinese dress where there is only a black turtleneck sweater. Kingston's despair over this flawed vision parallels that of her fictional character, Wittman Ah Sing: "'Take me, for example. I'm common ordinary. Plain black sweater. Blue jeans. Tennis shoes ordinaire. Clean soo mun shaven. What's so exotic? My hair's too long, huh? Is that it? It's the hair?'" (*Tripmaster* 308). Wittman parodically resists the white gaze's obsession with racial markers by opting for a bodily characteristic that has nothing to do with race. He proceeds to get rid of his exoticism by cutting his hair. Once again, there is a striking parallel to Ishi. Where Ishi sets out to deconstruct the frame by posing for the pictures in his overalls, the photographer insists that authentic difference requires the Indian to show his bare chest. Vizenor notes:

"He was to be photographed in a garment of skins, and when the dressing for the aboriginal part began he refused to remove his overalls," reported Mary Ashe Miller in the *San Francisco Call*. "He say he not see any other people go without them," said the tribal translator Sam Batwi, "and he say he never take them off no more."[10]

Ishi's overalls, then, parallel Wittman's plain black turtleneck and Maxine Hong Kingston's sweatshirt worn for a jacket photograph of her book. While the "ethnics" insist on their sameness, the mainstream public "records" their exoticism.

Even as the plot of *Tripmaster Monkey* is hardly about clothing style, I propose that the marginal idea of attire is an indication of the cultural politics of the novel as a whole. The novel is in fact a narrative about an open-ended performance staged by a Chinese American playwright dressed, like Maxine Hong Kingston herself when she posed for the dust-jacket photograph of *The Woman Warrior*, in a sweatshirt, in plain American clothing. By draw-ing attention to his own "plain black sweater," Wittman drives home the compatibility of ethnicity with plain Americanness. The Chinese American playwright is thus an embodiment of his own open-ended, postasian play: there is no determining where the "Asian" ends and the "American" begins. This clothing style is paralleled by his cultural politics, his desire to become an Asian American beatnik. Beat poets, then, do not have a monopoly on the clothing of the American avant-garde. Jack Kerouac's legitimate love of football, which the mainstream denies, to the likes of Wittman, converges with the beat poet's American lifestyle, which, I would imply here, includes clothing styles. In Kerouac's poems, we encounter only the stereotypical—and stereotypically short—"Chinaman." This is a representation with which Wittman takes issue:

> If King Kerouac, King of the Beats, were walking here tonight, he'd see Wittman and think, "Twinkling little Chinese." . . . Big football player white all-American Jock Kerouac. . . . I call into question your naming of me. . . . You tell people by their jobs. And by their race. And the wrong race at that. . . . I'm the American here. . . . Just for that, I showed you, I grew to six feet tall. May still be growing. (*Tripmaster* 69–70)

Kerouac's poetics preclude the very possibility of a Chinese American beatnik like Wittman. What is significant is that Wittman exposes even the *counterculture* of the Beats as flawed in its vision of ethnicity. As an Asian American beatnik, Wittman reads American canonical art through the marginal figure of the "Chinaman" whom this art excludes. It is at this point that the significance of the playwright's name needs to be considered. For while Wittman, like his American Renaissance counterpart, "sings America," the reviewers hear a *Chinese* song. Like Ginsberg's model, Wittman's paragon, too, is Walt Whitman, the *American* poet. *Tripmaster Monkey*, then, provides us with cultural complexity and the "hard hearing" (138) of listening to a Chinese American poet in a black turtleneck reciting Jack Kerouac and, by impersonating him, setting the record of misrepresentation straight. Like the Beats, Wittman's politics of style imply a form of cultural open-endedness. What I am interested in is thus much more than a politics of leisure wear. I am concerned with the politics of cultural representation that the "plain black sweater" or sweatshirt implies. This politics of cultural representation is at once a form of self-representation.

What *Tripmaster Monkey* dramatizes is the awareness by the author (not simply the narrator) of the exoticist mode through which her narrative might be received by a mainstream keen on an absolute Otherness. Significantly, Kingston resists what Graham Huggan has called the "postcolonial exotic" by de-emphasizing this difference in both personal and fictional terms.[11] Her effort to determine the reception of the dust-jacket photograph, then, parallels her inability to determine the reception of her fictional narrative. As Sämi Ludwig has emphasized, Kingston's attempt to control the reception of *The Woman Warrior* failed:

> [I]t seems symptomatic to me that critics are less infatuated with Kingston's second autobiography and even more at a loss with *Tripmaster Monkey*, a book in which Kingston tries more actively to control the Western discourse rather than merely allude to it.[12]

The key moment in the shift to her subsequent novel *Tripmaster Monkey*, I would suggest, is that *Tripmaster Monkey* implies an impossibility to treat this failure with nonchalance. As Ludwig goes on to say, "What we have in *Tripmaster Monkey* is a way of writing that is still very dense, very allusive, . . . but at the same time also very referential in its comments on the extrafictional world, and at times very clear and even polemical in the way it comments on reality."[13] The key difference between Vizenor's Ishi and Maxine Hong Kingston's fictional rejoinder to ethnographic literary criticism through *Tripmaster Monkey* lies in the concept of overt resistance: "Ishi smiled, shrugged his shoulders, and looked past the camera, over the borders of a covetous civilization, into the distance. The witnesses and nervous photographers, he might have wondered, were lost and lonesome in their own technical activities."[14] Where Ishi smiles, then, Wittman comments. If Vizenor's 'postindian warriors' serenely ignore the fact that the mainstream does not get the (anti-ethnographic) point, Kingston's protagonist Wittman Ah Sing—whose name is, of course, itself a marker of cultural hybridity—cannot do so. Instead, he resorts to didacticism.

Fusion: Toward a Didactic Aesthetics

The formal novelty introduced by *Tripmaster Monkey* is that it *explains* the quality of cultural open-endedness inscribed by its narrative style. Aesthetic form, in this sense, is not trusted to be self-explanatory. Rather, *Tripmaster Monkey* provides both the text and the "footnotes" within its narrative form. It fuses open-ended cultural definition with a didacticism explaining this open-endedness. *Tripmaster Monkey*, then, is both a fictional text and a self-conscious manual that instructs the (mainstream) reader about how to *read* this text. The narrative fuses the aesthetic and the didactical. Like Kingston herself, Wittman has given up hope that the performance will be self-evident. Annoyed at the reviewers who saw his play as quintessentially "Chinese," Wittman informs them of the cultural hybridity of his art: "I'm having to give instruction. There is no East here. West is meeting West. This was all West. This is The Journey *In* the West. I am so fucking offended" (308). Because Wittman explains the narrative form of his play, he is not confident that its open-ended aesthetics will speak for itself. Wittman is and is not, to adapt Vizenor's phrase, a "postasian warrior." If Vizenor's "postindian warriors" proclaim the impossibility of cultural closure, Wittman's postasian politics resist closure in the representation of Asian Americanness and then go on to *explain* to a bewildered mainstream why this closure has to remain absent. If this didacticism is seen to be synonymous with representational closure, Wittman's performance does and does not have closure. His "instruction" of a tired mainstream audience having been made to sit through his play is key to Kingston's form of open-ended didacticism. Wittman's disappointment about the reception of his play (which mirrors Kingston's own disappointment about the reception of *The Woman Warrior*) may lead us to understand the need for didacticism. Didacticism is born of the despair that the reader simply does not get the point: that there *is* not Otherness to be seen, even if the Asian American subject agreed to take *off* the sweater.

Tripmaster Monkey, then, can be seen as an attempt to fuse what Dorothy Wang has called an "undercover Asian" (Wittman is, indeed, wearing an inconspicuous black sweater) *and* a recognizable representation of what it means to be Asian American. Wang's call for reading the language poetry of John Yau as Asian American (rather than merely postmodern) converges with Lisa Lowe's call for an acceptance of the heterogeneity of Asian American experience and hence cultural production. Wang emphasizes:

> Those who insist on seeing [Yau] as another "experimental" writer because his work taps explicitly into "avant-garde" American and European traditions and overtly foregrounds technique have been oblivious to the effects of his social, political, and cultural positioning as an Asian American subject/writer and the manner in which his poetry confronts the issues of assimilation, history, racism, and linguistic displacement—not thematically, straight on, but by means of mirrors.[15]

The politics of what Wang calls an "undercover Asian," then, converge with the plain black sweater worn by Wittman. Yau is both an Asian American poet and an eccentric in a turtleneck. Similarly, Wittman Ah Sing testifies to the fact that one can be both avant-garde and recognizably—even *didactically*—Asian American. While in Yau's work, however, the avant-garde precedes the explicitly Asian American,[16] *Tripmaster Monkey* fuses both phases into a single narrative—a narrative, however, that has been said by literary critics to have failed. The following statement of Wittman's is programmatic for an open-ended didacticism as such: "To entertain and educate the solitaries that make up a community, the play will be a combination revue-lecture" (288). A revue and a lecture, incidentally, do not mix. Inscribing resistance through (the) aesthetic form (of a revue) alone, this phrase implies, will not quite suffice. Aesthetic form needs to be explained through a didacticism that is curiously at odds with the open-endedness, the vitality of this form.

The question is thus whether the politics of "undercover" Asian Americanness are incommensurable with the oppositional (and hence potentially didactic) Asian American politics originally suggested by Elaine Kim more than twenty years ago. As Kim argued in her groundbreaking study of Asian American literature, which can be seen to have sparked off the development of Asian American Studies as a whole, such representation was itself based on a *correction* of mainstream assumptions. By restoring the sociological context of these works of fiction, Kim sought to insure that they would never again be read in exoticist terms.

Yet, there is a paradox in this approach. For to provide a sociological background may be to invite an ethnographic reading. There is thus a need to fuse the sociological with the open-ended. This open-endedness, in turn, counters the mainstream's tokenizing of Asian American subjects. As is implied by the very title of her study, *Asian American Literature: An Introduction to the Writings and Their Social Context*, Kim sets out to resist this ethnographic reading not by dismissing the sociological altogether, but by setting the record of *misreading* straight. As Kim puts it, "For Asian American writers, the task is to contribute to the total image and identity of America by depicting their own experience and by defining their own humanity as part of the composite image of the American people."[17] Stressing the social context from which these Asian American texts emerge, then, can be implicitly didactical. I would like to argue that *Tripmaster Monkey* fuses Kim's correction of misrepresentation with Lisa Lowe's famous statement that Asian Americanness consists in its heterogeneity and multiplicity, not its clear definitions: "Rather than considering 'Asian American identity' as a fixed, established 'given,' perhaps we can consider instead 'Asian American cultural practices' that produce identity."[18] The reference, as Vizenor writes, is in the performance.[19] As Lowe's observation suggests, then, the tension between homogeneity and multiplicity, between didactic representation and an absence of closure, is at the core of the Asian American debate. Lowe's stress on multiplicity and the open-endedness of cultural performance can be said to parallel Vizenor's postindian politics. What *Tripmaster Monkey* proposes, on the other hand, is a perhaps impossible fusion of recognizability and open-endedness.

Yet, the crux at the heart of this fusion is that in *literary* terms, this project seems to have failed. *Tripmaster Monkey* has not met with the success with which Kingston's earlier novel *The Woman Warrior* was received. Does this failure mean that the aesthetic or open-ended and the didactic do not mix? I would like to suggest that this question might be explored less in literary terms than in terms of political agendas. For if the field of Asian American Studies has reinvented itself through its departure from the cultural nationalist politics of Frank Chin,[20] in *Tripmaster Monkey*, Kingston pays homage to her own fiercest critic, Chin himself. As Simmons points out, "it is suggested [by many critics] that Wittman, with his angry response to racism and his verbal fireworks, is a portrait of Kingston's nemesis, playwright Frank Chin."[21] While Kingston herself has suspended this question of influence by observing that "many men have claimed to [*sic*] the inspiration for Wittman,"[22] Wittman Ah Sing does seem to resemble the very man who accused Kingston's earlier narrative of *distorting* Chinese tradition. According to Sämi Ludwig, "Sensing the non-Chinese elements in *The Woman Warrior*, [some critics] have called her a 'traitor' because she would tamper with the 'original' form of the legends, an act that Frank Chin labels a 'violation of history and fact.'"[23]

What does it mean, then, this unexpected, sympathetic return to what has come to be known as Chin's prescriptivism? According to this prescriptivism, the Chinese American subject had to fulfill certain criteria. As Elaine Kim puts it, "The ideal was male, heterosexual, Chinese or Japanese American, and English-speaking. The center of Chinese America was San Francisco or New York Chinatown."[24] The narrator's following remark to Wittman, I would like to suggest, can be read in more than just playful terms: "Dear American monkey, don't be afraid. Here, let us tweak your ear, and kiss your other ear" (340). Crucially, this passage can be read as Kingston's endorsement of Chin's *prescriptivism*. Yet, it is significant that this endorsement is only a partial one. Wittman complies with Chin's criteria of Chinese *Americanness*, yet his compliance is by no means a schematic one. Rather, the prescriptivism is deprived of its potentially oppressive and heterogenizing edge because Kingston *contextualizes* the need for its emergence. I would thus like to contrast Chin's cultural nationalist didacticism with the open-ended didacticism that emerges in *Tripmaster Monkey*. Frustrated by an American mainstream that does not get subtle points, Wittman opts for a didacticism that is prescriptive in its preclusion of exoticizing reviews.

As I have tried to suggest, an emphasis on form can locate insights into the politics of Asian American resistance to an "exoticizing" mainstream gaze that mere attention to plot would not have yielded. Moreover, an analysis of narrative strategies alone would not be able to point to reasons for the failure of *Tripmaster Monkey* assumed by literary critics. Following Sämi Ludwig's cue, I have argued that an emphasis on the form of open-ended didacticism may explain the narrative's critical failure. This formal possibility is absent from a theoretical debate that, as I have tried to show, posits open-ended aesthetics and didactical rhetoric as irreconcilable opposites.

To oppose an exoticist gaze, I have suggested, the Asian American sub-ject advocates a politics of plainness. Yet, where does the sameness of the Asian American in a turtleneck leave the ethnic component? I join Vizenor's postindian warriors in the claim that this ethnic reference can only be in the performance. Kingston's fictional texts—and Asian American literature as such—can be the only answer to what it means to be Asian American. By relating Kingston's open-ended, didactic aesthetics to Vizenor's postmod-ern politics, my project situates itself among a growing number of studies (such as Vijay Prashad's recent *Everybody Was Kung Fu Fighting*)[25] calling for inter-ethnic comparison. In this vein, Asian American Studies, a field that has been criticized for a lack of "theory" as opposed to literary accounts, may open up not only to theory, but to *ethnic* theory specifically.

Despite this locating of convergences, however, I have also voiced slight disagreement with Vizenor's unprovisional postmodernism. For I believe that if the only strategy of Asian American resistance to mainstream projections of "Asianness" is a playful one, mainstream newspapers may continue to send their food critics to Asian American plays. Despite the mixed reviews of Kingston's novel *Tripmaster Monkey*, this narrative may be an attempt to fuse what has been regarded by current literary theory as incompatible. In its dismissal of cultural nationalist didacticism such as Frank Chin, Asian American theory seems to have dispensed with the didactic altogether, a trend that Kingston's novel reverses by introducing a didacticism of a more open-ended kind. As *Tripmaster Monkey* attests, there may come a time in Asian American studies when a synthesis between the field's earlier and its later developments will seem fruitful: a time that, intriguingly, *Tripmaster Monkey* can be seen to anticipate. In its fictional framework, Maxine Hong Kingston and Frank Chin sit down to discuss whether staging a weeklong play is the only way to drive home the fact that Asian American identity will always be open-ended.

5

The Language of Ethnicity

John Yau's Poetry and the Ethnic/Aesthetic Divide

CHRISTINA MAR

"THERE WAS NO INDICATION," writes Marjorie Perloff of John Yau's early career, "that the poet is in fact Chinese-American."[1] In its earlier stages, Yau's poetry, Perloff's statement suggests, doesn't readily fit into any simplified conceptualization of ethnic poetry. Yet Timothy Yu has argued that "Perloff's doubt about Yau's Chinese American-ness can thus be seen as a crucial effect of Yau's work: the nagging sense that we do not know what it means to be 'Chinese' anymore, even as we are constantly reminded of it's centrality."[2] Indeed, Yau's work causes traditional assumptions of what ethnic poetry is to fray at their seams. This essay seeks to interrogate such underlying assumptions that inform the way ethnic poetry has been and continues to be constituted. Ethnic writing is often, though certainly not always, associated with what is considered at the present moment to be the regressive beliefs in the existence of the unified subject capable of being represented in language and able to act as representative of an ethnic community to which it seamlessly "belongs." Furthermore, ethnic poetry is often constituted in a disabling opposition to poetry that is

Excerpts from "Ten Songs"; "E Pluribus Unum"; "The Reading of an Ever-Changing Tale"; "You Must Remember"; "Avenue of the Americans" used by permission of the poet. John Yau is a poet, fiction writer, and critic, whose most recent book is *Borrowed Love Poems* (Penguin, 2002). He is an Assistant Professor of Critical Studies at the Mason Gross School of the Arts (Rutgers University).

engaged in the politics of aesthetic innovation by resisting representation and refusing the tyranny of the signified. In short, ethnic poetry is understood to focus primarily on social reality and is thus disinterested in artifice. Though many critical race theorists continue to address the ever-shifting meanings of ethnicity and race within contemporary discourse, the category of ethnic writing remains rather rigidly defined, especially by mainstream criticism. Does the ossification of the category of "ethnic writing" constitute the death knell of a once resistant, now appropriated cultural practice? Or rather, is the assumed rigidity of ethnic writing by major voices in mainstream criticism more symptomatic of traditional assumptions that prescribe what ethnic and racial identifications mean and how they can be imagined?

In order to address these questions, I begin with a look at Perloff's formulation of ethnic poetry. In her article "Postmodernism/Fin de Siecle: Defining 'Difference' in Late Twentieth-century Poetics," Perloff traces the various formulations of postmodernism in her response to the suggestion by several critics that postmodernism's sun has set. Postmodernism's privileging of difference, she suggests, has lead to a "bland diversity" and thus a general neglect of innovative poetry.[3] In addressing the current state of postmodernism, or, as she would have it, the current states of postmodernisms, Perloff laments this "marginalization of poetry" in favor of theory on the one hand and multiculturalism's "bland diversity" on the other. Perloff goes on to argue that ethnic poetry slavishly follows a "neoromantic" model "whose tacit assumption that the lyric is a univocal and authentic form of self-expression seems oddly out of key with the discourses of the 1990's in which it is implicated."[4] Employing the category of ethnic writing does, in fact, seem to risk co-optation by prevailing ideology.

Yet attending to the seeming overrepresentation of ethnic writing without an eye toward social ramifications precludes the needed analysis of the institutional structures that have made such "authentic" representations compulsory. Benjamin Saenz, who Perloff describes as a young Chicano poet, is rather unfortunately called upon to demonstrate the plague of neoromanticism from which ethnic poetry supposedly suffers. Perloff characterizes ethnic poetry as univocal and predicated upon the notion of the "authentic." Because of this dependency on the authentic, she concludes that ethnic poetry also commits what she calls the synecdochic fallacy where, in this particular instance, the voice of one author is falsely assumed to represent the "true" subjectivity of an entire ethnic group.[5] Although Saenz's poem, "The Willow," peppered with lines such as "I loved a tree in my boyhood," is perhaps less than innovative and fairly characterized as neoromantic, the fact that it functions in Perloff's argument as illustrative of all ethnic poetry betrays her own dependency upon the synecdochic fallacy that she elsewhere critiques. Counterpoised to Saenz in Perloff's argument stands Alfred Arteaga, a poet who Perloff praises for his complex treatment of a subject formed in the intersections of multiple ideological forces. Rather than calling into question her own reductive characterization of ethnic poetry, Perloff argues that categorizing Arteaga's poetry as "Chicano" would mean eclipsing "the important differences between it and the neoromantic model" characterized by Saenz's "The Willow."[6] While we might argue that the use of synecdoche is a necessary aspect of critical engagements with aesthetic movements, it is only through her problematic use of Saenz's "neoromantic" poetry synecdochically to represent the entirety of ethnic poetry that Perloff is able to attack what she considers ethnic poetry's naïve treatment of the subject. In short, she does not allow for the multiple states of ethnic writing that she demands be recognized of postmodernism. Her argument depends upon the assumption that ethnic writing necessarily purports to represent the "authentic" voice of a group. Perloff asserts it is the resistance to adequate criticism of ethnic poetry and the failure of cliché-ridden ethnic poetry *as poetry* that causes the marginalization of poetry. But other critics identify a very different difficulty. Juliana Chang notes the preference of the publishing world for the "literal" rather than the "literary" when it comes to ethnic writing.[7] It is this refusal to address the full complexity of ethnic writing by some publishers and mainstream critics that facilitates the marginalization of poetry and eclipses the heterogeneity of ethnic texts.

This function of what Charles Bernstein has called "official diversity" and its threat of assimilating aesthetic practices can only be fully understood by noting that, in addition to appealing to an idealized notion of American culture and restoring a notion of a universal aesthetic standard, such assumptions also create the image of a racially inclusive America that seeks to foreclose any discussion of the very (reductive) terms of that inclusion. For example, we have witnessed multiculturalism's appropriation in mainstream American culture. Mainstream multiculturalism deploys representations of various ethnic groups as equal participants in the "great experiment" in order to maintain the status quo through the elision of actual structural inequities experienced by marginalized groups in the United States. Such representations are dependent upon essentialized notions of ethnic groups that can be manipulated in order to cast racial and ethnic identity as a difference readily absorbed under national identity (what Paul Gilroy calls the notion of "'separate but equal' cultures")—the *pluribus* that constitutes the *unum* of the U.S. nation.[8] It is, however paradoxically, through the recognition of racial and ethnic difference in this way that the mechanisms producing the current myth of national wholeness render invisible alternative aesthetic practices. In addition, this myth performs an inoculation against any exposure of the embeddedness of race and ethnicity as a means by which to hierarchically organize groups at the structural as well as the ideological levels of the nation. The hegemonic nation's wielding of ethnic identity in this way also legitimates claims that minorities have not only gained equality but have taken center stage in the national drama, causing their marginalization to be interpreted as a result not of the exclusionary practices of the nation but rather of their own failure to be "proper" U.S. citizens.

The point at issue here is whether ethnic writing should indeed be understood as a category based primarily on formal properties or a self-consciously provisional political category designed to re-center our focus on the margins of U.S. national cultural production. George Uba's "Versions of Identity in Post-Activist Asian American Poetry," importantly places Yau in the context of Asian American poetry. But for Uba, the linchpin of this association is not a necessary stabilization of identity. He writes, "Yau posits a world in which the unstable traces of identity threaten to dissolve as quickly as they appear."[9] Futhermore, Uba's discussion suggests if we examine writers following the activist mode like Janice Mirikitani, who seek to "'unmask' poetry by removing it from the elitist academy,"[10] or other contemporary writers like Marilyn Chin or David Mura, for whom "conceiving identity is only possible by foregrounding its partialities," the contours of Asian American poetry are drastically changed.[11] Because this heterogeneity apparent in Uba's argument is erased in mainstream multiculturalism, the immanent necessity of maintaining the category of ethnic poetry remains unconsidered. Critiques that focus solely on ethnic poetry's seeming lack of aesthetic innovation fail to recognize the implication of controlling national ideologies in formulating and maintaining the link between articulations of ethnic identity and notions of authenticity. They implicitly subscribe to such neo-conservative assumptions about ethnic identification and authenticity that underwrite mainstream multiculturalism while disagreeing with the resultant representative multiculturalism itself.

Similar to Arteaga, who Perloff praises, much of Yau's poetry interrogates the complex function of language in the formation of the subject at the site of multiple and competing ideological forces. Nonetheless, I will resist "rescuing" Yau from the clutches of ethnic poetry in order to illuminate how his poetry is able to respond to a number of political exigencies, including the politics of ethnic representation and the politics of aesthetic practice. Of the critics who have addressed Yau's writing, none have been able to easily situate him within a particular tradition. For example, some of his poems heavily employ narrative and contain, however ambivalently, a speaking "I." Others can be situated within the tradition of language poetry, which rejects narrativity and the presence of a speaking subject. The difficulty of situating Yau in any particular tradition testifies to the importance of context in formulating resistances in his work. As there is for Yau no single totalizing ideology, there can be no singular response or intervention.

Several of Yau's poems can be associated with language writing, as they call our attention to the very processes of language whereby meaning is produced. The difficulty of producing meaning and the impossibility to render "truth" through language is clearly registered in his poem "Ten Songs":

> Making the trying something that would find its sense
> Sensing the making trying to find something it says
> Saying the finding is there to find is making it make sense
> Making it make sense is finding something to say
> Something to say is finding a lens to sense the making
> Something making the making something something else[12]

As language poetry will do, this poem renders any hermeneutic approach impotent, suggesting that meaning is not there for the "finding" or inherent to language itself, but is constructed via an ideological grid or "lens" through which we make it "make sense." Our syntactical lenses are brought in and mostly out of focus as the poem toys with the multiple functions of verbals as adjectives, adverbs, and nouns. While the verbal tags of the first three lines cited here invite comparison between lines, they are also the central cause for the instability of meaning in the poem and render comparison virtually impossible. The "sense" or meaning of the poem proves indistinguishable from our own "sense" or experience of it, so that we are implicated in the production of the meaning of the text. Depending on the lens employed in the reading of the poem, the meaning of the poem changes so that one poem becomes "ten songs."

The last line of Yau's poem, "Something making the making something something else," further offers a certain potential for subversion residing in the tension between the "something making" and the "making something." Of course, we might propose several readings of what these "somethings" are—a potentially dizzying task—but what I wish to focus on at this juncture is this important presence of an identifiable tension, suggesting, at the very least, the location of more than one site of power. Were the line to read as follows: "something making something something else" (instead of "something making the *making* something something else), the poem would ultimately leave us with an apparently single vector of totalizing power such that the first something (x) acts upon the second something (y) in order to transform it into "something else," as x's constitutive outside. In this case, the power of x is made manifest only through the subordination and manipulation of y as its Other. Yet, Yau's poem also reminds us that, as a necessary outside, y is always already inside, structuring as it is structured, productive of tensions and ruptures; y is not simply something made or transformed into something else but is also a "*making* something" [italics mine].

Focusing on "Ten Songs" and others of Yau's poems that bear the marks of language poetry ("Nasty Orders Pacify Queen," "Mon Alias, Mona Lisa") would suggest a general distrust of language to engage with social "reality" outside of language. But "Ten Songs," which was earlier collected in *Sometimes* (1979), appears among several other poems that do not launch such a staunch attack on the structures of language. "E Pluribus Unum" engages social reality by contrasting the glorified unity of the masculine civil realm with the banal details of the feminine private realm and its kitchens with "linoleum floor[s]" and "scuffed roses."[13] "The End of Summer" employs the speaking subject while simultaneously interrogating its authority by giving us a speaker who reveals "I was not born either/so I do not know the whole story."[14] And there are never "whole stories" for Yau, nor are there master narratives. Accordingly, contextualizing "Ten Songs" within Yau's overall project necessitates contextualizing challenges to traditional language by way of formal innovation among other forms of intervention. For Yau, the intervention enacted by work attending primarily to signifiers is useful only when placed in conversation with other interventions attempting to address the specific social and historical conditions that make the relation between certain signifiers and their signifieds more difficult to denaturalize (such is the case with ethnicity and its supposed signified: authenticity).

Even when there is a much more traditional use of language in his poems, Yau's critique of its structures and their relation to identity remains a central concern. Yau's "You Must Remember" participates in conventional syntax and uses concrete diction in a manner that invites criticism of its very usage. Remembering is the subject of this poem, but Yau's poem engages the act of remembering in a very different sense than poems in an autobiographical or confessional mode. Remembering here is hardly an act of personal will, the steeling of the mind against the ravages of time. The series of commands to remember draw attention to the rules that dictate remembering in the first place, making us aware of how the very concept of memory hinges upon capitulation to the fiction of the unified subject that sutures discontinuous moments by way of the conventions of time, of history, of identity. As such, the autobiographical "I" is again absent here, replaced by an insistent "you" who "must remember." The repetitive use of the possessive pronoun "your" in the poem is accordingly nothing if not ironic; the "you" of this poem has no ownership, for "your" is used only to formulate commands for what to do with "your hands" and "your head."

> YOU MUST REMEMBER
>
> not to mumble
> not to mangle
> the words
>
> you are holding
> in your hands
> in your head

The charges in the poem sound like a series of instructions that might be given in an elementary school or perhaps even a prison (the two can be so easily confused). The subject is bombarded with commands that *must* be remembered (the "or else!" that seems to finish the phrase is deafeningly silent here). Any differences, preferences, or tastes of the subject are inconsequential, as the subject is expected to "swallow" without question whatever is placed on "plate or page."

> You must remember
> to deliver your head
> to the auditorium
>
> where it will be mounted
> along with the others
> your hands and head
>
> going together
> to the auditorium
> where someone
>
> maybe more than one
> is waiting for you
> to deliver your voice
>
> mangled as
> it was
> formed[15]

Even what sounds like democratic inclusion, an opportunity for the subject to "deliver" its voice and speak, proves to be part and parcel of its marginalization. Instead, the subject is asked to deliver, in the sense of a relinquishment, the voice; thus, the privileged tool of democratic representation proves a tool of hegemonic occlusion.

Certainly, the impossibility to render the "truth" of the self in language presents even greater problems when that self is meant to act as representative of a larger constituency, as it does in mainstream multiculturalism. There is a jostling of body and mind, between the consumption of bread and of words in "You Must Remember" as well. At the poem's start, the "head" paired with "hands" and made to consume what appears on "plate or page" synecdochically signifies the body, but it also metonymically signifies the mind, the Cartesian self, made to partake in the logic of language, of "words/mounted on the page." But the drawing together of the two, body and mind, in the word "head" is not simply an example of word-play cleverly troubling a key schism of Western philosophy. While we should question such a duality, for many marginalized groups the trouble lies with a too ready conflation of body with mind or self. In the poem, body and mind are increasingly drawn together as similarly produced by and thus subject to dominant discourse. In this production, bodies are signifiers of the subjects that ostensibly reside within them, and for bodies marked as gendered, raced, disabled, etc., the body is *believed* to delimit a type of mind or self. It is thus that mainstream multiculturalism strictly delineates "authentic" representation for the marginalized, who are ostensibly in closer proximity to the body, the signified, or the "real." The body, Yau's poem suggests, is not the locus of subjectivity but a product served up for consumption so that the subject's head is "sitting on/the plate," a frighteningly morbid multiculturalism.

The syntactical conventionality of "You Must Remember" is in stark contrast to the linguistic indeterminacy at the foreground in "Ten Songs." In "You Must Remember," there is an apparently arbitrary disruption of the six imbedded sentences, marked by their capitalized "You," into verse paragraphs. Paragraph breaks occur without regard to syntactical completion, mirroring the pervasive threat of bodily and psychological dismemberment. "You Must Remember" initially seems to mark a single trajectory of power in language, as an unnamed authority dictates what must be remembered. Yet amidst this fragmentation lies the possibility of poetic cohesion, of re-membering. Though syntax remains identifiable, its arbitrary fragmentation makes poetic free verse possible. No longer a function of thematic coherency, the paragraphs foreground a coherency of sound in light rhymes such as "mounted" and "head," in near rhymes such as "auditorium" and "someone," and in parallel stress contours and alliteration found in words such as "mumble" and "mangle." The title itself, in order to act as the poem's title, must battle with its other role as the beginning of the poem's first syntactical sequence so that poetic consonance rivals linguistic coherency. Under the threat of fragmentation, this poetic consonance becomes a form of intervention. Revolution is not an option here. But resistance is. The linear logic governing language is not overturned; however, it is held somewhat at bay—its power mitigated by other systems of coherency and meaning. And yet these alternative systems remain embedded in conventional syntax and implicated in traditional language. It is this deep sense of implication in the violence of ideological regimes paired with an incomplete identification with any single regime that Yau's poetry avoids absolute absorption into their mechanisms.

In this sense, "Avenue of Americans" is notable because it fairly clearly engages the question of Asian American national identity yet is highly fragmented. Indeed, the poem first appears in *Broken Off by the Music* (1981) with much fewer line breaks than appear in its later version in *Radiant Silhouette* (1989). These proliferating line breaks indicate a desire to foreground fragmentation in Asian American identification. If we place Yau's work in the context of Asian American history, it's difficult not to notice how the poem parodies the passage of the immigrant subject into full-fledged citizenship. Such heightened fragmentation when engaging with Asian American history intimates ambivalence about the accessibility of history, reveals a desire to expose how the polysemous events of history are homogenized according to the needs of the national narrative, and suggests the repression of alternative histories. The poem employs the image of the monkey (the not-quite human) as a metaphor for the immigrant subject (the not-quite citizen):

> The audience cheers as the monkey correctly
> identifies their desire by curling his lips
> around the statue of a cigarette.[16]

From this perspective, the monkey as immigrant is suggestive, on the one hand, of a rather silly but trainable creature who, like the monkey in the above passage that "correctly identifies" the audience's desire, can be forced to "monkey" or mimic the values of the American mainstream. Yet on the other hand, the image of the monkey intimates a more dangerous side to the foreign Other, a side that threatens racial and thereby national purity. The monkey evidences the sense of fear surrounding the "hordes" of "uncivilized" Asian immigrants that began arriving in the United States in large numbers during the middle of the nineteenth century.

With regard to Asian American literary tradition, the monkey functions as a trickster figure borrowed from the Chinese oral tradition that was set down in novel form under the name that translates to *The Journey West* and has been multiply reconfigured in an Asian American context, Maxine Hong Kingston's *Tripmaster Monkey* being the most widely known. In this sense, the monkey signifies transcendent genius that enables survival in an antagonistic foreign land. "Curling his lips around the statue of a cigarette," the monkey seems to be kissing what is a degraded image of the Statue of Liberty. The statue is described as bearing a "permanent shrug," suggesting that the "Mother of Exiles" is a neglectful mother at best. The monkey as metaphor for the identity of the immigrant or hyphenated subject evinces such a subject's contradictory hailing by multiple ideological systems that characterize it simultaneously as transcendent and degenerate.

"Avenue of Americans" also situates the poem geographically in New York City, a city frequently invoked as a microcosm of America. The reference to the Statue of Liberty as "the statue of a cigarette" and the suggestion of immigrants in the image of "monkeys" who arrange "themselves in alphabetical order" both intimate a radical deflation of signs of national identity and culture. With the line "Stretching from knee to shiny knee" in the first paragraph, the poem rewrites the line "from sea to shining sea" taken from the patriotic song "America the Beautiful." Such patriotic tunes play a special role in evoking the subject's identification with the nation. Benedict Anderson's discussion of national anthems illuminates this phenomenon:

> There is a special kind of contemporaneous community which language alone suggests—above all in the form of poetry and songs. Take national anthems, for example, sung on national holidays. No matter how banal the words and mediocre the tunes, there is in this singing an experience of simultaneity. At precisely such moments, people wholly unknown to each other utter the same verses to the same melody. The image: unisonance.[17]

By fostering such an idealized fantasy of the nation as undifferentiated and lacking nothing, national anthems contain within them the mechanisms for their own undoing. The call to identify with the nation's absolute purity through the coincidence of the individual voice with that of the national body in singing a patriotic tune also causes what might otherwise be seen as an innocuous slip of the tongue or minor misremembering of the language to shatter utterly the illusion of national wholeness and arrest the flow of the national narrative, a bildungsroman of coerced assimilation.

The use of pastiche in this way not only deflates the idealized grandeur of the nation, but it also undermines any sense of a single totalizing ideology. The words to patriotic tunes such as "America the Beautiful" might be counted among those that the subject was earlier told it "must remember." Improperly reciting the song reveals its speaker to be inappropriately interpellated, perhaps not constituting a revolutionary refusal that breaks free of the established order, but a refusal to identify according to the demands of the hegemonic nation nonetheless. While the subject may be hailed as a national subject, there is no guarantee that that hailing is singular or totalizing, as the poems notes a "response is not necessarily an answer." Althusser discusses these "bad subjects" who, in contrast to those that "work themselves" by properly identifying with the state, instead "provoke the intervention of one of the detachments of the (repressive) State apparatus."[18] By appropriating the language meant to foster fantasies of national unity and rewriting it in order to undermine the imagined coherency of the nation, Yau's work constitutes an aesthetic of resistance. In her discussion of the concept of "disidentification" in Asian American cultural production, Lisa Lowe locates such a resistant aesthetic practice:

> Disidentification expresses a space in which alienations, in the cultural, political, and economic senses, can be rearticulated in oppositional forms. But disidentification does not merely entail the formation of oppositional identities against the call to identification with the national state. On the contrary, it allows for the exploration of alternative political and cultural subjectivities that emerge within the continuing effects of displacement.[19]

Disidentification combines the negative project of refusing to identify according to the call of the nation with the positive project of creating subjectivities born of the recognized scission that exists between the actual experiences of the disenfranchised minority citizen-subject and the juridical promise of entitlements accorded the citizen under U.S. liberal political theory.

Importantly, New York's Avenue of Americas has become "Avenue of Americans," and the poem's degraded signs of national culture suggest the gaps between the idealized nation (America) and the way it is received by the subjects meant to identify with it (Americans). Even language meant to be wholly deterministic is subject to mutations that cannot be anticipated. The unifying message that America's goodness will be crowned by "brotherhood from sea to shining sea" could easily be understood by the non-native speaker as spanning the much smaller distance of "knee to shiny knee." These unanticipated alterations turn our attention to examine more closely the question of audience and reception. While the poem signifies multiply depending on its audience, it remains skeptical of the possibility to forecast its reception. This skepticism is apparent in the following lines:

> The woman skidded to a halt when she saw a monkey
> climb onto her windshield with a letter clamped
>> firmly in his mouth
>> . . .
> Inside the letter was a map of the highway
> leading to the correct audience[20]

A letter requires an address, an intended audience, in order to be delivered, but in this case the letter (also the building block of words) is in the possession of a monkey (also mon/key or single solution), an unreliable messenger to be certain. Complicating matters further, the "map of the highway/leading to the correct audience" is contained in this letter that won't be arriving anywhere in particular. Just what sense will be made of the letter and its map by the audience who receives it remains unknown. The issue of audience reception is additionally troubled by cultural difference, especially given the context of a city of ethnic enclaves (e.g., Little Italy, Chinatown) where "each street is named after a country/that does not return its mail." Context's importance is further foregrounded by the poem's posed question and its "answers":

> But whose angel was sitting on the smiling monkey's shoulder?

> His hand held all the answers to some of the questions
> I learned to accommodate your doubts by lying

Indenting the lines that follow the question creates an expectation of an answer, and the response is actually a clear one. It is a simple sentence with a subject, verb, object, and modifiers that "go together." In this sense, the response itself adheres to conventional structures of language. It's just not an answer to the question posed, though it wryly contains, quite literally, "all the answers." Through the context of its tension with the question, the response is denaturalized and resists the very logic of question and answer. The poem then offers the following revision:

> His answers held hands with some of the questions
> I learned to accommodate myself by doubting my own lies

The above lines still follow traditional syntax; the source of language's denaturalization stems from the incongruity of signifieds. The difficulty of reaching a particular audience and the impossibility of delimiting that audience's interpretation does not, however, indicate a radical decontextualization in favor of a retreat into formalism. Issues of context and audience matter even though they can be unpredictable. The challenge to traditional language and to official culture, it becomes evident, has many fronts depending on context.

And one of these contexts registered in "Avenue of Americans," I argue, is the current elision of particular difference within ethnic groups in favor of an uncritical celebration of difference on the multicultural stage. What is paramount to note at this juncture is the reward of U.S. citizenship as delineated in the speaker's description:

> The echo of the president's smile is carried from promise to promise.
> The boy hides the answers in his mouth, his elbows scratching his knees.
> If he is lucky, amnesia will be his reward.

The speaker locates a rather unusual reward for citizenship: amnesia. In order for the nation to promise all of its citizens equal rights, the very notion of citizenry as defined by liberal political theory necessarily depends upon the ability of the subject to shed its material difference and particular interests in order to be abstracted into citizenship. Accordingly, the will of the individual is subordinated to the general or sovereign will in favor of the common good. Citizenship defined as such depends upon a certain loss of self; however, because the notion of the abstract citizen actually assumes a propertied, white, male, heterosexual subject, this loss for the minority subject (as well as for women, homosexuals, and the poor) is much more than a shedding of personal preferences that stem from individual will; it is an erasure of entire histories of unequal power relations, preclusion from the full rights of citizenship, and denied access to resources that these groups have faced.[21] Forgetting then proves to be the means by which the minority subject is able to imagine itself as represented under the signs of the nation. Lauren Berlant identifies this phenomenon in which memory is lost in order facilitate identification with the nation, calling it "paramnesia." According to Berlant, paramnesia serves as a "substitution for traumatic loss or unrepresentable contradiction that marks its own contingency or fictiveness while also radiating the authority of insider knowledge that all euphemisms posses."[22] This unrepresentable contradiction in terms of the U.S. nation resides in the nation's juridical promise to secure the rights of all of its citizenry, while its functional conceptualization of the citizen precludes the possibility for the nation to represent the minority subject.

The waking woman referred to twice in "Avenue of Americans" underscores the desire to break the flow of the national narrative, encouraging disidentification by pointing to the rupture between the (American) dream-state and the immigrant subject's actual experience within the United States:

> She woke up, remembering the miles of empty sky
> unfurling from banner to banner
> . . . . . .
> She woke up and was rewarded
> with questions leading to questions

The first description of the woman's waking suggests the lingering memory of the dream-state where a cloudless, empty sky signifies the expansive potential afforded by the American dream; yet the belief in the dream is not without consequences. Berlant interrogates the dependency of the American dream on the notion of the citizen as "unmarked," offering the analysis:

> It is a story that addresses the fear of being stuck and reduced to a type, a redemptive story pinning its hope on class mobility. Yet this promise is voiced in the language of unconflicted personhood: to be an American in this view would be to inhabit a secure space liberated from identities and structures that seem to constrain what a person can do in history.[23]

The mobility that underpins the American dream is sharply contrasted with the world in which the dreamer finds herself upon waking, a bounded world where she is interrogated "with questions leading to questions." In order for the dream to survive according to Berlant, "the concretely unequal forms and norms of national life must be suppressed, minimized, or made to seem exceptional, not general to the population," like the immigrant boy described in "Avenue of Americans" who is forced to suppress or hide "the answers in his mouth." "See no evil, hear no evil, speak no evil" becomes the mantra that lulls the minority subject into the American dream-state. Only the white, male, heterosexual citizen—for whom the centrality of his identity, his assumed normalcy, and his ascendancy to the seat of the universal allows him to be extrapolated into asomatous citizenship—proves able to achieve the disembodiment that coincides with the prerequisites of the dream. The woman, minority, or homosexual subject's historically different relationship to the national body precludes abstraction into citizenship. Thus, the relationship to the dream for the embodied citizen is one of alienation rather than acceptance, so that to believe in the dream is to unwittingly accept the terms of one's own exclusion from it.

The fear that ethnic poetry ushers in a return to essentialism corresponds to the fear of "being stuck and reduced to a type" that Berlant locates as the impetus to identify with the American dream. To call for the excision of writing manifesting a complex treatment of the subject from the category of ethnic poetry is to suggest that "good" American poetry like "good" American citizenship is contingent upon the ability to inhabit—to use Berlant's phrasing—"a secure space liberated from identities and structures that seem to constrain what a person can do in history." The importance of ethnic and other naming within the context of U.S. national discourse resides in the fact that, inasmuch as we might argue that all subjects are characterized by heterogeneity, all differences are not equal under Old Glory. Such an extraction of writing like Yau's from ethnic writing because it engages in a complex articulation of difference would ultimately discount the import of racial and ethnic difference in structuring inequities in the nation. Furthermore, naming the work of writers like Yau as ethnic texts would be to recognize their contribution in performing the important task of challenging dominant society's articulation of minority identities. Rearticulating the meaning of ethnic identity in this way both offers an alternative view of what the subject that identifies as such can do and calls attention to the weight that ethnic and racial signifiers already bear in organizing the nation.

Yau's poetry participates, however paradoxically, in the simultaneous deployment of identity politics and the poststructural politics of difference, so that "getting ethnic" with John Yau means getting keyed into language play and vice versa. His writing should not be understood as an attempt at dialectical synthesis, for, though his work does bring together disparate perspectives, it is designed to resist ideas that privilege homogeneity, unity, and assimilation. Rather, his poetry fosters the tension surrounding the ever-present "something else," which, in its broadest definition, is a conceptualization of meaning, in the Derridean sense, that is always deferred, always residing elsewhere. In terms of identity, this important "something else" of Yau's poetry signifies a subject that, even when speaking for and about "itself," is continually displaced from the "self" about whom it claims to speak. Denying the ethnic integrant of Yau's work would threaten to expropriate it from its position at the vanguard of U.S. national discourse on citizenship and would foster the currently popular belief that to claim ethnic identity is refuse to the possibilities of movement and "progress" that shedding such identifications would afford. If Perloff is right when she states that Yau's later engagement with ethnic identity signifies a shift from his earlier work, which betrays nothing "that the poet is *in fact* Chinese-American," [italics mine] then this shift illustrates not Yau's capitulation to official culture but the heterogeneity of ethnic poetry.[24] Thus, the contours and modes of ethnic identification do not necessarily illustrate the prepackaged "fact" of ethnic identity. The dialogic relationship between an assertion of ethnic/racial identification and an insistence on difference manifest in Yau's poetry resists the possibility of otherness to become what Homi Bhabha warns us against: "the point of equivalence" in a system of differences (where differences in ethnicity, gender, sexuality, etc. can be equated with idiosyncratic differences of taste and personal preference).[25] Neither does it allow ethnic identity to be treated as an inherent, essential, or immobile condition—either version of which the controlling ideology of the nation stands ready to absorb.[26]

6

"A Flame against a Sleeping Lake of Petrol"

Form and the Sympathetic Witness in Selvadurai's
Funny Boy *and Ondaatje's* Anil's Ghost

PATRICIA P. CHU

> No more would I step out of that room and make my way . . . to the
> altar, a creature beautiful and adored, the personification of all
> that was good and perfect in the world.
>
> —FUNNY BOY, 39

> American movies, English books—remember how they all end?
> . . . The American or the Englishman gets on a plane or leaves. . . .
> It's probably the history of the last two hundred years of Western
> political writing.
>
> —ANIL'S GHOST, 285–6

Funny Boy and the Sympathetic Reader

THIS ESSAY ASKS how the formal conventions of the classic realist novel relate to its thematic and ideological concerns in Shyam Selvadurai's *Funny Boy* and Michael Ondaatje's *Anil's Ghost,* two novels written by Sri Lankan-Canadians, set in Sri Lanka in 1977–83 and 1992, respectively, and explicitly concerned with portraying violent political turmoil and its effects on ordinary people.[1] Though set outside North America and unconcerned with U.S. or Canadian relations with Asian countries or people, these texts share with Asian North American texts the drive to interpellate the reader as a sympathetic observer of social injustices.

Shyam Selvadurai's *Funny Boy* depicts the maturation of its narrator, Arjun Chelvaratnam, within a middle-class Tamil family during a period of increasing civil disturbances and publicly sanctioned anti-Tamil discrimination and violence. A series of searing epiphanies mark the title character's growing awareness of his double minority status as a Tamil and a homosexual. A classic realist novel, *Funny Boy* interpellates the reader as an ally of Arjie, the boy protagonist and the adult narrator, as he witnesses the failures of his family, school, and country. To amplify its hailing of the reader as a sympathetic middle-class witness, *Funny Boy* uses a range of devices intrinsic to classic realist fiction, including the narrator's signifying on the trope of the domestic *heroine*; the lyric epiphany stating the theme; the star-crossed love plot; the training of the reader's sympathy from lesser to greater shock; and colonial intertexts that interpellate the reader as knowing, tasteful, kind, and just. These familiarizing elements position the reader to accept Arjie as the ideal Althusserian "subject" of the realist novel, one who both identifies as a national subject and holds an exemplary subject position with which the reader is pressed to identify; thus *Funny Boy* expands the subject of the realist novel to include a protagonist who is both homosexual and rooted in political struggles specific to Sri Lanka.[2]

Arjie is quickly established as possessing the sensitive, imaginative interiority identified with the heroines of nineteenth-century domestic novels. In the first chapter, "Pigs Can't Fly," the adult recounts his travails as a seven-year-old boy on the family's monthly "spend the days," Sundays when cousins played together with minimal supervision while the parents enjoyed a day out; he quickly maps out how the games were segregated by gender and territory. The front garden, road, and field in front of the house are claimed by the boys, whose cricket games permit them to rehearse for adult masculinity by joining the two teams' "struggle for power." Arjie, however, prefers the girls' realm, in which he leads due to the force of his imagination; his account instantly establishes him as a surrogate for the (feminized) reader, while driving away readers unable to enter this female-centered imaginary. In the favorite game, bride-bride, Arjie revels in being dressed as the bride, because cross-dressing allows him "to leave the constraints of myself and ascend into another, more beautiful self" (4). Transcending his sex, individual self, and ethnic identity, Arjie envisions himself as "magnified, like the goddesses of the Sinhalese and Tamil cinema, larger than life," an exemplary subject of the nation or, as he puts it, an "icon" adored by "the world" (4–5).

As the imaginative middle child, Arjie is contrasted with his competitive, coarse, unimaginative older brother, Diggy, and his sympathetic but conventional younger sister. In "Pigs," this structure is amplified by Arjie's estrangement from his father and his alignment with his mother (Amma). When Arjie's bride fetish is exposed to adult view, his father uses the stigma of homosexuality to insist that his mother renounce her intimacy with Arjie, her favorite, in a transparently Oedipal triangle: it seems that if the boy turns out "funny," it will be because his mother let him spend too much time in private with her while she arrayed herself for her nights out with Papa. This pattern gives rise, in turn, to the trope of exile from the mother.

Given Arjie's coding as both artistic and androgynous, he seems at first to resemble the heroine of a nineteenth-century novel, pretending to lament his lack of traditional femininity (or in his case, masculinity) while secretly celebrating his luminous intelligence, sensitivity, and originality.[3] Hence Arjie's novelistic, strangely familiar interiority is established in terms of a traditional conflict between an artistic temperament and a stultifying gender role. In this way *Funny Boy's* representation of Arjie is recuperated as a version of the "domestic woman" of realist fiction, whose humanist values are supposed to transcend local, race, or class politics, even as the story begins to introduce local politics specific to Sri Lanka. Since readers are free, until "Small Choices," to imagine Arjie either as gay or as sensitive, imaginative, and protofeminist, but straight, the text is maximally inclusive.

A second powerful device is the epiphany of loss and exile. This motif, which links the novel's six chapters, is introduced on page six, when the image of the narrator arrayed as a bride-goddess is followed by two visual images, the image of childhood as a picture emotionally tinted by the subsequent experiences of exile from Sri Lanka and emigration to Canada, and the image of Arjie as a ship being taken, unaware, "away from the safe harbour of childhood towards the precarious waters of adult life." The sea returns at the chapter's end, when Arjie, permanently cast out of both the girls' and the boys' games, mourns both the loss of camaraderie with his girl cousins and the loss of intimacy with his mother, the original film-star-goddess of his imagination (39, cited in epigraph above). Although the loss of the girls' realm may seem a childish matter, it signifies the loss of community and homeland as well as the original loss upon which selfhood is predicated, the loss of identification with the idealized mother who signifies love and plenitude.[4] So great is Selvadurai's rhetorical skill that he can suffuse the unwary reader with a sense of nostalgia, exile, and endless wandering, when actually Arjie has merely been kicked out of the house and run down the street to the beach. The trope of exile unifies the novel's sexual and political plots, and suggests that for Arjie the two forms of exile are indistinguishable. By using sexual alienation to signify political exile, and political exile to signify sexual alienation, this text doubles the points of entry for readers.

In "Pigs Can't Fly," Selvadurai sneaks in a third familiar device, the star-crossed love plot. When Amma bans Arjie from her dressing room, he experiences this as a form of romantic rejection (17). In this case, since the star-crossed lovers are Arjie and his mother, the reader may regret, yet accept, Amma's choice to renounce a kind of intense intimacy with Arjie that society doesn't sanction. In each of the next four chapters, a protagonist must choose between a beloved person representing an ideal, on the one hand, and a practical course of action, on the other; in all but the last case, convention prevails.

Closely related is the text's strategic sequencing of topics from less to more shocking. In the sentimental realm, the stories begin with child's play and a forbidden love between a Tamil and a Sinhalese, suggest both that a mother can love outside her marriage and that a father can love (homosocially) a friend and (heterosexually) an English working girl, and finally depict Arjie's own first homosexual affair. Having it both ways, these chapters enjoin readers to sympathize with rebellion *and* conformity. Arjie's political education is equally graduated. The anti-Tamil violence and government and police corruption are introduced first through remote, manageable events, then gradually become inescapable, until Arjie's home is destroyed and his grandparents murdered by anti-Tamil rioters, driving his family to emigrate to Canada. As the text trains readers progressively to condone cross-dressing, exogamy, adultery, a disavowed homosocial passion, and finally, an avowed homosexual passion, the subplot of racial hatred, violence, and persecution also escalates. Through the sympathetic portrayal of the family's repeated attempts to minimize risk by accepting the status quo, the text trains readers to understand their political disillusionment and their final choice to emigrate.

Only in the fifth story, "The Best School of All," is Arjie himself the central actor, when he is transferred to a new school in which the racial tensions of his country are enacted in miniature. The headmaster, nicknamed "Black Tie," seeks to defend the school's tradition as a site for bilingual instruction, including both Tamil and Sinhala speakers under the old, colonial name, the Queen Victoria Academy. His vice principal, Mr. Lokubandara, wants to rename the school after a Buddhist priest who had advocated Sinhala education as a nationalist principle, and to make the school a Buddhist, Sinhala-language school exclusive of Tamils, even those like Arjie who have been schooled in Sinhala (220). One sign of his hostility to Tamils is that Sinhalese students are permitted to roam the school in gangs and assault unguarded Tamils in the lavatory. A political appointee and cousin of a cabinet minister, the vice principal seems all too likely to gain control of the school. Black Tie's last defense will be to appeal at a public gathering to alumni, notably a powerful cabinet minister, by having one student recite nostalgic poems about the school and giving a speech based on these poems and calculated to raise support for its traditions. Arjie, chosen for the recitation, is urged to support Black Tie as a pluralist but finds it difficult to sympathize with the principal, who subjects his friend Shehan to hours of daily punishment merely for wearing long hair with clips. Black Tie's pedagogical practice of beating Arjie for recitation mistakes also backfires. Instead of instilling memorization and respect, the old man's canings inspire the boy to despise the poems, question the school's malice and hypocrisy, and devise a brilliant strategy for subverting Black Tie's cause.

In "Best School," the struggle to exclude Tamils from the school and its powerful old-boy network alludes to the country's unresolved political rifts. Since gaining independence in 1948, Sri Lanka has been led principally by two parties with differing views about pluralism. According to historian Kingsley M. de Silva, the United National Party (UNP) was associated with a vision of the country as inclusive of ethnic and religious minorities such as Tamils and Catholics, while the Sri Lankan Freedom Party (SLFP) won their turns in power by advocating a "democratic and populist form" of nationalism, popular with the majority, but ultimately divisive in its partisan preference for Buddhism and Sinhalese culture. A third significant faction, the Tamil "Tigers" (LTTE for Liberation Tigers of Tamil Eelam), separatists who have taken up terrorism in their campaign for a separate Tamil state, are portrayed in *Funny Boy* as provoking anti-Tamil hatred in public and mixed feelings in the Chelvaratnam family. In "Small Choices," Mr. Chelvaratnam cannot shield his protégé Jegan once the latter is publicly accused of being a Tiger. In that story, the ruling party illegally extends its term of office six years by stuffing the ballot boxes at gunpoint (167–207), and Tamil voters like the Chelvaratnams are intimidated by violence and the Prevention of Terrorism Act, under which suspects may be arrested and publicly accused without evidence. "Small Choices" refers to events in 1983, when "extended electioneering" consolidating the ruling party's power, as well as the death of thirteen Sinhalese soldiers at the hands of the Tamil Tigers, led to the anti-Tamil Colombo riots of 1983, portrayed in this novel's sixth chapter. Unfortunately, the government portrayed in "Small Choices" as openly stealing the election is, historically, led in that period by J. R. Jayawardene, the head of the supposedly more inclusive UNP. Thus in "Best School" Black Tie is a fictional surrogate for the UNP leaders of that period.[5]

The fifth, final literary device, the use of intertextuality to appeal to the reader's literary expertise, is central to "Best School," in which Arjie dissents from his family's and teachers' approval of the thuggish but pro-Tamil headmaster. The plot turns upon Arjie's recognition that the sentimental doggerel he is asked to memorize and recite at a crucial public assembly in support of Black Tie, is bad literature. If we think of the school as a microcosm for the nation, and Arjie's recitation as an exercise in nationalist ideology, his resistance to the poems marks him, both as a thoughtful postcolonial subject and as an instinctive literary critic. He finds the poems hard to memorize, and even harder to recite with conviction, because they describe a reality he doesn't "understand," apparently because it doesn't exist. While the second poem portrays cricket as promoting honesty, courage, and patriotism, Arjie has found that at his school, cricket consists of "trying to make it on the first-eleven team by any means," including "cheating and fawning over the cricket master"; it is "anything but honest" (226, 232–233). Arjie's complaint is that the poems represent an enforced false consciousness denying the social reality of the school, his "nation," in which the headmaster sets the tone by persecuting the most vulnerable boy, Arjie's friend Shehan. The text invites readers to share Arjie's interpretive labor as readers by providing, in lieu of a formal critique, a brief citation of part of the poem for his readers' own inspection (226). Here, as with its allusions to *The King and I* and the *Little Women* novels, *Funny Boy* binds its readers to Arjie with the implication that aesthetic taste is mingled with moral lucidity and a passion for justice.

What does Arjie's literary taste have to do with his exemplary subjectivity? For one thing, it strengthens his affinity with the ideal heroine of the nineteenth-century classic realist novel, whom Nancy Armstrong calls the "domestic woman," a subject deemed exemplary because, being defined by mental and moral qualities rather than wealth and status, she could function to interpellate readers across class lines into sharing or approving of her mental and moral qualities.[6] Not only does Arjie share the specifically literary side of this lineage, in which many heroines are articulate, literary, or theatrical; he also favors Anglo-American fictions along with Sri Lankan films. Arjie directs and performs in amateur plays ("Bride-bride" and *The King and I)*, convalesces with illicit Alcott novels, and keeps a journal; when he rips up the offending poems in "Best School," Arjie's friend Shehan suggests that he's a drama queen (238). By inviting readers to identify with him as a skilled producer and consumer of cultural texts, Arjie's literary artistry and critical instinct anchor this story in the tradition of the domestic novel.

It therefore seems natural that Arjie's aesthetic taste is difficult to separate from his moral judgment. In this case, Arjie's intuitive aesthetic judgment of the poems complements his lucid moral judgment—they are *lying*. Instinctively sensing the importance of this lying, Arjie resists internalizing it: he finds the poems hard to memorize, and once memorized, intolerable to recite. Thus, *Funny Boy* follows classic realist tradition by inviting the reader to identify with the narrator's moral discernment and by using aesthetic discernment to signal moral clarity.

Arjie's rejection of the poems' false nostalgia contrasts with the nostalgic passages that cap most chapters, and conveys at last his actual ambivalence toward the domestic world he seems to miss. On one hand, the novel exposes the stifling gender roles of Arjie's class; on the other, it elegizes the very world it excoriates. When Arjie finally questions the false nostalgia of the poem called "The Best School of All," he sees instead how the powerful have defined the school as a site of belonging and nostalgia by silencing and erasing those deemed unfit for membership. Selvadurai makes these insights explicit in a scene when Arjie is tempted to take a rosy view of the school, literally, at sunset. Having had his first sexual experience with Shehan, Arjie has been tempted to deny the affair and reclaim his old places, as a sexual innocent in his loving, homophobic family, and as a rehabilitated student at the school. But when he realizes that Shehan, who has no family and feels abandoned by Arjie, is being driven toward suicide by Black Tie's abuse, this knowledge alters his view of the school. Though it literally appears innocuous in Arjie's eyes, bathed in the pink haze of sunset, Arjie is moved by the "foolish lines" from the poem to see Black Tie's persecution of boys like Shehan as arbitrary, homophobic, and evocative of other kinds of injustice he has witnessed during the novel. Bitterly rejecting Black Tie's overblown punishments for innocent conduct such as blinking, licking lips, or wearing long hair, "a code that was unfair," he asks how "loving Shehan" could be bad, and why "some people" get to be the arbiters of correctness and justice at the cost of others (273–4). Although Black Tie's persecution of Shehan at first seemed arbitrary, this passage clarifies that his unfair code discriminates against homosexual conduct. Shehan, who has a reputation for having sex with the head prefect, who had concealed his long hair with hair clips, and who is described by Arjie as refined and fastidious about his appearance, is in the process of being "forced to become a man," just as Arjie's father determined Arjie himself would be (210). Seeing that nostalgia can be invoked by poetry to promote an objectionable ideology, in this case one that supports the inclusion of Tamils at the cost of excluding homosexuals, Arjie resolves to use the poems for his own purposes. He then gives the performance of his young life when he pretends to be a dull student unable to recite the hated school poems, thereby sabotaging Black Tie's intended "campaign speech" for political support.

In switching to journal format for the final chapter ("Epilogue: Riot Journal"), in which anti-Tamil violence becomes so broad and inescapable that the Chelvaratnams are reduced to nocturnal flight and permanent emigration, *Funny Boy* seems to convey a shift in its assumptions about individual agency. Whereas each prior chapter was constructed around a character's attempt to claim agency by maintaining a place in society while challenging its rules, this chapter depicts the riots as beyond individual control. The primary epiphany in the chapter is perhaps Mr. Chelvaratnam's recognition, after his house is burned and his parents are murdered in the street, that no amount of diligence, conformity, and submissiveness can secure minimal protection, much less the rights of citizens, for him and his family. In contrast to Arjie's litanies of loss, poor Mr. Chelvaratnam's life-changing recognition, which has already dawned on Arjie, his mother, and the reader, receives a paltry page of dramatization in the "July 28" entry (303–4). The form of agency he chooses, to leave, is made to seem the logical response to the state's genocidal encouragement of violence against Tamils and their property. While this is a powerful, reasonable end to Arjie's education in racial politics, it also blocks the novel from imagining alternatives to the gender discrimination and heteronormativity that have been exposed so skillfully for the first five chapters.[7] In the national crisis, Arjie renounces homosexual and feminist dissent and rejoins the family for the purpose of survival; with neither street nor home secure, neither he nor the novel can imagine how any bond or intimacy can endure outside the strictures of traditional family plots. Nor does the novel suggest that those plots, and the middle-class world they represent, will exist in Colombo once Arjie and his sympathetic readers have departed.

Connecting the Plots of *Anil's Ghost*

In *Anil's Ghost,* the three principal characters view the family neither as a refuge nor as an end but as a temporary holding site for their deeply solitary lives. The novel is set loosely in 1992, in a world in which civil disturbances, terrorism, and violence are so deeply entrenched that the locals harbor no illusions of safety or justice.[8] The novel abounds in failed romantic, conjugal, and parental relations; while such failures could be read as symptomatic of the collapse of the nation or the public sphere, one must also consider that, threaded in with the civil rights investigation and the isolation faced by the protagonist, the novel explores the possibility of an alternative community arising from flexible, provisional links among single, childless individuals. While problematic, such a community offers the possibility of greater freedom for men and women, and the development of lasting bonds between subjects not defined by heteronormative structures like marriage. Formally, the collapse of ideals of social order is conveyed by *Anil's* refusal to play out traditional plots that turn around *bildung* (marriage, star-crossed love, or apprenticeship), historical conflict and resolution, or justice through the exposure of truth (as in a detective novel). By favoring instead the illumination of isolated moments of connection, professional satisfaction, and service, the text forces the reader to give up a linear sense of narrative and the idea of historical progress it implies, and instead to exist moment by moment. In place of a literary plot of individual *bildung*, reform of mass or official institutions, or individual justice, *Anil* uses the tropes of the pietà, artistic creation, and individual transformation to signal that acts of compassionate witnessing can renew shattered spirits, inspire commitments to change, and lead to new relationships between individuals and their communities. Yet the utopian gesture of using art to signify personal and social healing leaves open a narrative gap that challenges Western readers to consider their own responses to the story of Anil's act of witnessing. The novel offers both a readerly (classic) and a writerly (unwritten) ending: in the first, the collective completion of two Buddha statues signifies the possibility of continuation and renewal in the public, but not the political, sphere; in the second, the novel challenges readers to frame a suitable response as witness to the events of the novel.

The plot is driven by the return of Anil Tessura, a Sri Lankan woman educated in the West as a forensic anthropologist, for a seven-week civil rights investigation, for which she is paired with a local archaeologist named Sarath Diyasena. Given the premise, we might expect either a detective novel or a historical novel.[9] While the classic Conan Doyle genre presumes the fundamental justice of the existing social order as well as the social benefits of fact-finding, the historical novel as defined by Georg Lukacs also requires a novel to depict history as driven by identifiable agents and victims of oppression. This novel begins with an investigation of human rights violations and ends with a political assassination, yet signals early on that it will not focus on defining the historical causes of the war; Sarath's initial briefing of Anil is characteristic of the novel's disinterest in political analysis. He says the terror, which climaxed in 1988 and 1989 but still produces weekly victims, can be traced to no single source, but is the work of "three camps of enemies—one in the north, two in the south," including the government itself. However, as no one wants to alienate foreign powers, the war remains unofficial and secret. Every side uses "weapons, propaganda, fear, sophisticated posters, censorship," every side kills and hides evidence, and every side is responsible for the vanished bodies and bodies burned beyond recognition (17–18). (Later, Sarath says that the most lawless period was "like being in a room with three suitors, all of whom had blood on their hands" [154].) To explain to Anil that the current environment requires all to surrender their notions of justice, accountability, progress, and agency, Sarath tells her that narrative itself has been rendered impossible: "There's no hope of affixing blame. And no one can tell you who the victims are" (18). Hence, Ondaatje's characteristic mode of modernist, non-linear narration may be read, not only as an aesthetic choice but also one that challenges the progressive assumptions of the realist novel.[10]

In "Writing and the Question of History," Lisa Lowe argues that a definitive "link between historical narratives of the U.S. nation and novelistic narratives of the individual is mediated by adherence to a realist aesthetic, a fetishized concept of development, and narration of a single unified subject," suggesting that in certain cases, Asian American texts *refusing* the realist aesthetic do so in order to contest its assumptions that "development" is something Westerners may bring to others, and that elite subjects may represent all citizens.[11] Lowe's argument may illuminate the ideological implications of some of Ondaatje's aesthetic choices. He pairs Anil, an expatriate in a Western profession (forensic anthropology in the service of civil rights) and Sarath, a local resident willfully burying himself in the study of his country's ancient past, and has them argue throughout the book about the local viability of the human rights paradigm framing their investigation. Sarath's objections capture both the danger and the colonial implications of international human rights work, which in his view seeks to impose Western standards around the world, regardless of local conditions. Sarath's unspoken objections early in the investigation challenge Anil's assumptions and intended narrative, contrasting them with the purity of the ancient rock images that he studies professionally. Although he knows that for her the journey to the truth is central, he likens the truth to "a flame against a sleeping lake of petrol" that will most likely lead to "new vengeance and slaughter." Yet, the narrator asserts, Sarath as a trained archaeologist still holds a high regard for truth: "That is, he would have given his life for the truth if the truth were of any use" (156–7). In Sarath's view, the human rights narrative Anil means to write is suspect, not only because the truth is too complex to be captured in a legal report, but also because Anil herself, like a Western journalist, will not face the local consequences of her work. Sarath sees only the past as safe enough to illuminate.

Anil's Ghost also challenges realist conventions by having two differently positioned Sri Lankans conduct the investigation; such a choice contrasts with the convention, found in some Western texts, of identifying historical agency with a "single unified subject," a white Westerner bringing civilization to a developing nation, a convention pointedly criticized in the novel (285–6, quoted in the epigraph to this essay). In addition to pairing non-linear narration with the investigation's wayward progress, the novel arguably supplants the traditional narrative action of the investigation with a sequence of scattered images. In these ways, I suggest, the stretching of the bounds of the realist aesthetic in this novel is linked to its questioning of Western historiography.

In addition, *Anil's Ghost* eschews marriage plots and their obverse, which I've called star-crossed love plots, above. In *Funny Boy* and novels like it, the ideals of romantic love and domestic bliss are rendered unattainable by social schisms, convention, and individual problems, but the centrality of heterosexual love and marriage to society, and to the web of institutions described as public culture by Lauren Berlant and Michael Warner, is left intact.[12] *Anil's Ghost,* by contrast, depicts a universe in which marriage and romantic plots are largely irrelevant. Elsewhere I've argued that the bildungsroman traces the individual's socialization as a citizen for the nation, and that in domestic novels, marriage often signifies that those characters have become exemplary subjects.[13] In a book like Selvadurai's, the repeated failures of marriage plots suggest the hostility of marriage and family to the homosocial subject; in other Asian American texts, the failure or absence of the marriage plot may be read as signifying the subject's failure to attain citizenship for reasons related to culture or racialization, such as the host society's racist exclusion or the immigrant's refusal to assimilate. In Ondaatje's text, the avoidance of romantic novel plots works two ways. In the case of the widower Ananda, whose wife has disappeared in a spree of unsolved abductions and murders, her disappearance exemplifies the war's fragmentation of the usual kinship ties that structure society. At the same time, it frees Ananda to bond with Anil and Sarath along different lines. Hence, *Anil's* avoidance of traditional domestic novel plots frees it to pose fresh questions about subjectivity and socialization in the public sphere.

Anil's resistance to courtship, marriage, and feminization is key to her campaign to enter the public sphere in the neutral or masculine capacity of a doctor. In contrast to Arjie, who rejects conventional masculinity, Anil claims masculine privilege by rejecting the trappings of feminine gender roles. She refuses, in quick succession, definition as her family's daughter, as a wife, and as a mistress. Having disrupted her family by claiming her brother's name and left Sri Lanka to train in the unfeminine field of forensic anthropology, Anil quickly sheds her early marriage in London to a Sri Lankan man she perceives as possessive and controlling, then flees her married Canadian lover when he shows signs of attachment. Orphaned, alienated from her brother, and released from the scrutiny of Sri Lankan family life, she chooses instead camaraderie with professional peers, expressed in nights spent bowling or watching Westerns.

The intensity of Anil's rebellion may be clarified by recalling *Funny Boy's* portrayal of the strict regulation of middle-class women's desire and physical mobility. Even in the late 1970s, it was scandalous for a Tamil woman to accept a ride from a Sinhalese man. Ondaatje likewise suggests that the cost of liberty, already high for men, is higher for women. In Anil's campaign for her brother's name, the gratuitous detail that Anil concludes her bargain by granting her brother a sexual favor suggests that Anil must be ruthless toward herself in order to claim the male privilege that is her brother's birthright. The text does not insist that gender roles are as oppressive to all Sri Lankan women as Anil seems to think. In Anil's case, however, the novel envisions her defeminization as a prerequisite for her to access the professional public society in which she thrives, a society where she may function as an equal among men, so long as she remains free of personal entanglements.

Just as Anil is a fugitive from romance plots, Sarath fails to complete a conventional narrative of professional development (*bildung*). Although *Anil* devotes much space to his teacher Palipana, the great archaeologist is portrayed as isolated by his knowledge, producing similarly isolated students rather than a community capable of embracing young scholars. Instead, Sarath works seemingly alone, unable to find a use for his calling, until he meets Anil.

The Art of Grieving

In place of traditional plots of *bildung* or of justice, Ondaatje depicts four isolated individuals who are bound together by moments of suffering and compassion. He uses the imagery of art and artifacts to highlight the slow development of bonds between Anil, Sarath, Gamini, and Ananda, bonds that transcend death to offer the novel's only hope for the creation of a new community. Though the human rights investigation founders, the novel suggests that Anil's presence has lasting, positive effects in Sri Lanka, while leaving open the ultimate response Anil, the Westernized expert, will make to what she has seen, felt, and suffered. The sign of this bond is the *pietà*.

The term "pietà," meaning pity, conventionally refers to artistic depictions of Mary, and sometimes others, contemplating the broken body of Jesus. Such works may invite viewers to contemplate Mary's sorrow, her compassion for Christ's suffering, or the magnitude of Christ's sacrifice and compassion. *Anil's Ghost* invokes the pietà, the Buddha, and the sacred eye-painting ceremony *netra mangala* to focus attention on the process of contemplating suffering deeply, even spiritually, in a variety of contexts divorced from Christian and Buddhist theology. In the end, it suggests that the heartfelt engagements with suffering and injustice marked by pietesque tableaux are the only possible seeds for survival, community, or social justice.

The book introduces Anil as participating in a forensic dig in Guatemala, where the families of the missing rise early to attend the scientists searching for unmarked remains. Anil is introduced as the witness of a woman's grief, a woman found sitting in a devotional posture, contemplating the bodies of her husband and brother in a newly opened grave. While Anil lacks words to describe the woman's face, she "still remembers" "the grief of love in that shoulder" (5). The wish to alleviate such suffering would seem to explain Anil's choice to return to Sri Lanka, yet she begins the book as an isolated Western professional, willfully cut off from family and other sentimental ties.

As the novel progresses, Anil's loss of the detachment she cultivates, both as a expatriate and as a professional, is dramatized by moments of pietà, in which the act of witnessing suffering opens the witness to compassion. Anil's first act of mercy is to recognize something amiss with a seemingly sleeping or drunk man lying on the road, to turn her driver back, to rescue the man, whose hands have been nailed to the ground "crucifying him to the tarmac" from dying of shock, and to administer, then arrange for, the medical care he needs to live (111). To read her rescue of Gunesena from the tarmac as a pietà is not to impose a specifically Christian meaning but to illustrate Anil's motto that "one life can speak for many lives": Gunesena appears both as an individual with a name and as the personification of a greater community from which, ultimately, Anil and Sarath choose not to separate themselves. The superficial intimacy that begins with her bathing Gunesena's hands and saving his life will culminate, at the novel's end, with his standing watch over her on her last night in Sri Lanka and driving her to the airport, returning in kind the gift of life she has granted him (283–5); yet the two remain remote and unknown to each other.

A deeper exchange takes place between Anil and Ananda Udugama, a local artist who had formerly excelled in the sacred ritual of *netra mangala,* in which a Buddha sculpture is completed and symbolically brought to life by the painting of the eyes (98–9). As part of their quest to give a name to "Sailor," the unidentified murder victim whose skeleton they have found,

Anil and Sarath have given Ananda, now an alcoholic mine worker, the task of reconstructing Sailor's face from his skull. Unknown to them, this task demands that Ananda confront the loss of his own wife, Sirissa, abducted and probably murdered three years earlier; he does so by imbuing Sailor's imagined features with a startling serenity, the serenity he remembers and desires for his wife. Upon learning of Sirissa's disappearance, Anil weeps for him, for Sailor, and for others. Unable to speak English, Ananda observes her weeping and comforts her with his touch, formal yet tender (183–8). Hours later, having saved Ananda from a suicide attempt and taken him with Sarath's help to a hospital emergency room, she feels "citizened by their friendship" (200). Both Ananda's suffering and his compassion for Anil open her emotionally and restore to her a sense of membership in an imagined community she had forsaken, that of Sri Lankans seeking justice.

The image of a pietà is also at the heart of Sarath's work and character. Recall that Sarath, who cherishes truth as an archaeologist, "would have" given his life for it "if the truth were of any use" (157). Like Anil, he carries within him the seed of personal transformation, the pietà he privately knows he "would give his life for, [the image of] the rock carving from another century of the woman bending over her child." Recalling "the flickering light," "the line of the mother's back bowed in affection or grief," and the "muffled scream in her posture" (156), he uses the carved pietà as a focus for his meditations on the suffering of his country, about which he feels helpless. This sketch of his inner life foreshadows the novel's surprise ending, in which Sarath chooses to help Anil complete the investigation and to save her life, risking his own. He seems moved to do so by the spectacle of Anil, surrounded by unseen enemies at the hospital, being forced to make her case in public without the crucial evidence of the skeleton. He notes her calmness, clarity, and renewed identification with her homeland:

> Sarath in the back row, unseen by her, listened to her quiet explanations. . . .
> It was a lawyer's argument and, more important, a citizen's evidence; she
> was no longer just a foreign authority. Then her heard her say, "I think you
> murdered hundreds of us." *Hundreds of us.* Sarath thought . . . Fifteen years
> away and she is finally *us* (272–3).

When Sarath steps forward as Anil's co-investigator, he tries to protect himself by pretending to be hostile, but he already knows, as he reflects, that he "would not be forgiven" for supporting her public indictment of the government (279).

What is the "use" of the sacrifice that Sarath makes in response to Anil's testimony? His brother Gamini, a doctor, must contemplate this question in the morgue, where he finds Sarath's murdered body. Mentally Gamini prepares to examine the body, to understand his brother's death and life, by explicitly broadening the Christian term of "pietà" to include scenes of conjugal love, in life and in Hindu mythology, before casting his own contemplation as "a pietà between brothers" (288), spiritual though not particularly religious. The wording suggests that Sarath's physical body serves as the object of a meditation in which Gamini will begin a "permanent conversation" with Sarath, so that his brother will be more present to him in death than he was in life (282). For some readers, Sarath's speared chest and broken hands will resonate with Christ's injuries, while others may recall the broken forearm of Sailor, the victim finally identified as Ruwan Kumara (64–5, 269). In any case, Gamini's act of remembrance, and his tacit promise to keep Sarath's spirit alive in memory, resonates with Anil's contemplation of the Guatemalan mourner and Sarath's memory of the rock sculpture as triangulated tableaux in which the contemplation of suffering is both an aesthetically powerful experience and one that moves the witness to act politically. Such tableaux are also reminiscent of the sunset scene in "Best School," in which Arjie is moved to act by the visual beauty of the landscape combined with his recognition of multiple levels of injustice and suffering. But whereas Arjie's individual insights are narratively subsumed by the riots and their consequences, Anil's quest for justice and her increasing compassion for individuals are portrayed as having power to change the lives of Gunesena, Sarath, Gamini, and Ananda—and perhaps herself.

If the pietà marks acts of psychological self-collection and reconnection to others, the literal fragmentation of self and society are linked with a more cartoonish work of art, the cardboard cutout of the fictional President Katugala, who is killed by a suicide bomber at a parade for "National Heroes Day (293)."[14] The President himself is described by the omniscient narrator in terms inviting readers to view him with compassion (291). However, he is also seen solely as a target by the assassin, the human weapon whose "own eyes and frame are the cross-hairs," just before he uses his own body to blow the President and fifty bystanders into pieces, like so many Humpty Dumpties, and to send a hundred more into the emergency rooms. This anti-pietà, and the resulting fragmentation of community and public space, is linked with the collapse of official narratives (as the public hears of the assassination via cell phone and rumor) and of hope for a rational outcome to the investigation (295).

This assassination contrasts with the novel's closing sequence, "Distance," in which Ananda's rehabilitation is implied by his successful direction of a different kind of public art. When a 120-foot-high Buddha statue in a rural area beset by political murders is exploded by would-be looters, Ananda is called to reconstruct the Buddha. Drawing upon the local community for labor, Ananda slowly reconstructs the blasted Buddha as he once reconstructed Sailor's head, in an action that symbolically reverses the explosion of the President and the destruction of another village, the one where he once lived with his wife (172–5). As this reconstruction goes on, and a new Buddha is built nearby, Ananda himself reconstructs the face of the blasted statue, deliberately leaving the traces of its damage but adding what he added to Sailor's face in memory of Sirissa—composure. When one day at dawn he finally paints the eyes of the new Buddha in a formal *netra mangala* ceremony, assisted by his nephew, he deliberately wears Sarath's shirt for the ceremony, thinking of Sarath's ghost as a legacy he shares with Anil (305). The novel ends with Ananda completing this reconstructed Buddha, which he sees no longer as a god, but imbued with human loss and sorrow (307), as is indicated by "the pure sad glance Ananda had found," whether in the image or in himself is unclear.

In the book's final images, the fields that had been used to hide murdered bodies are transformed into a beautiful landscape, in which even Ananda's sorrow for Sirissa is softened by the concerned touch of his nephew, "[t]his sweet touch from the world" (207). This is the pietà reimagined once more: in place of the living mourning the dead, the two Buddhas will gaze at each other, and watch over the fields where the work of the artisans has discouraged the murderers from bringing any more bodies, with Ananda's pure, sad, human glance, while the living man and his nephew continue together. Thus Gamini brings to the hospital, and Ananda to the field, a subtle change and renewal in response to Anil's impassioned testimony, Sarath's sacrifice. The renewal of their hearts and their commitments, as marked by moments of communication associated with the viewing of suffering or of art, is a different kind of agency than we might associate with the forms of classic realism, yet it is real and has powerful social effects. In addition, this novel goes beyond Selvadurai's in imagining how four unrelated individuals can form a provisional counterpublic, a private bond with effects in the public sphere. Of course, as an alternative to heteronormativity this impromptu fellowship is limited; it is momentary, contingent upon the principals' celibate, childless, single status, and is practically dispelled by Anil's exile and Sarath's death.[15]

Finally, what about Anil herself? What the novel does to Anil would break the heart of any ordinary character. By the time she arrives in Sri Lanka she has lost or renounced almost everything but her profession. Yet in the course of the novel, her heart is opened to the sufferings of her fellow Sri Lankans; she completes her investigation against great odds, with a determination that inspires Sarath, at the last moment, to support her. In retaliation for her bold indictment, the text implies that she is raped before she is released from the hospital (282); thus she is simultaneously disciplined, as a woman, for presuming to claim masculine prerogatives and made to share, as a citizen, the anguish of the war victims she has first championed in the abstract, then come to care for as individuals. The moment when she understands the depth of Sarath's commitment to her cause may also be the moment when she realizes she may never see him or speak with him again. In place of narrating her safe passage out of Sri Lanka, the text has her recall Gamini's disapproving remarks about Western fiction (285–6; epigraph above), as if she were reproaching herself for the departure she must make in the morning. As a result, the novel leaves us with the open question of her response to the permanent wound she has received and the memory of Sarath, Gamini, Ananda, and her homeland ("Anil's Ghost") that she carries back to North America. Thus Anil occupies a double position in the pietà: as a Westernized intellectual witnessing others' suffering, she is a double for the reader, whose compassion and engagement the text solicits; as the Sri Lankan who comes to identify herself and finally to suffer as a citizen, she is the object of contemplation for North American readers. As her final response to the story is unwritten, readers must imagine for themselves how she chooses to continue her journey, and conjecture from this what response the novel demands of them.

What is the relationship between the aesthetic and heteronormativity in these texts? In *Funny Boy* the trope of nostalgic loss and of longing for beauty is closely linked with the longing for "home" and its traditional ideological structures. In *Anil's Ghost,* the art-based trope of the *pietà* is linked with the organic emergence of an alternative social world. More fundamentally, heteronormativity is embedded in the classic realist plots and devices favored in *Funny Boy* and in *Anil's Ghost.* The choice made by Selvadurai, to use a traditional literary form to question traditional social arrangements, has a traditional effect; the choice made by Ondaatje, to build a novel's structure organically, is most conducive to imagining an alternative counterpublic within the novel and leaving open the response of the reader interpellated by the novel's double end. Finally, if the classic realist novel is as deeply imbued with heteronormative ideology as this essay suggests, what are the implications for the devotion of Asian Americanists to classic realist texts, and their relative neglect of other genres? What is lost by defining this literary tradition so strongly in familial or heteronormative terms? What can be gained by articulating the assumptions embedded in some of the genres I suggest are staples of the classic realist tradition? What counterpublics may have been imagined in literature or fashioned in life?

7

Poignant Pleasures

*Feminist Ethics as Aesthetics in Jhumpa Lahiri
and Anita Rao Badami*

GITA RAJAN

I N THE LAST FEW YEARS, some South Asians writers in the United
States have moved away from recounting thinly veiled, sociopolitical accounts of immigrant experiences to fashion aesthetically rich narratives
that create a different kind frisson and reading pleasure. This difference, evident in select contemporary South Asian fiction in North America, is based
upon an aesthetic of affect, i.e., evoking levels of poignant pleasure through
conventional literary tropes and formal devices, as for example, through a
child's narrative perspective, which blends together innocence with a sense of
helplessness in order to generate pathos. In contrast, the narrative fulcrum in
the works of Bharati Mukherjee, Sara Suleri, and Ved Mehta, for example—
works that spanned the period from the 1970s to the late 1980s—was situated in the complex identity politics of diasporic, marginalized subjects on
the cultural landscapes of Western, majority populations. In other words,
these authors relied upon the reader's ability to blend together the American
immigrant-dream metaphor with relics of images of the Raj days from which
South Asians fled real or imagined oppressions, and decode plots that either
reiterated the model minority success story or opted for the victim rhetoric
of racial marginalization. Mukherjee's *Jasmine* or Bapsi Sidhwa's *American
Brat* come to mind as representing these two modalities, which incorporated
clichéd norms from traditional narratives in an attempt to assimilate their
characters into a multicultural America as the nation of newer immigrants.[1]

Mukherjee, Sidhwa, and others crafted novels that evoked sympathy for their characters by focusing upon sociocultural inequities and injustices, with the objective of conveying a political message that was amplified in an environment of uncomfortable race relations in the nation. Such fiction serves as an example of a kind of realism, similar to that of nineteenth-century European writers whose ideology lay just under the surface of their literature, however, that is not our focus now.

By comparison, the recent works of Asian American authors such as Chitra Divakaruni, Jhumpa Lahiri, Mohsin Hamid, and Kirin Desai, for example portray subjects and situations that become memorable by invoking other kinds of aesthetic responses, something akin to brief or fleeting but pleasurable instances of shared cultural reminiscences or poignant memories of loss as they grapple with new realities. An important difference visible in the new set of South Asian American authors writing at the turn of this century, is a shift in focus that brings into play a distinctive affect through ethics. The formal devices they use create a space between readers and texts to locate one's aesthetic responses in the dynamic gap, where one encounters crises in the narratives and formulates a reaction that is based upon assessing the risk factor in not acting ethically. While the fiction of earlier writers foregrounded historical and political injustices, this new kind of fiction creates a frisson of awareness about ethical questions. Such an ethical component seems to be the simultaneous result of a younger generation of writers entering the arena (who perceive themselves as rooted within the nation space and not as diasporic or exilic actors) and a contemporary trend in fiction that responds to our globalized milieu[2] of an explosive, uncontrolled capitalism, and all its cultural accoutrements. This difference, , as practiced by writers at the turn of the 20th century , more than simply marking a generational attitude, is also discernable in the morality-ethics divide. At the risk of generalizing,[3] moral codes articulated in a public sphere rely on external, institutional mandates of good and evil, reflect upon the actor, and usually result in or from institutional initiatives (like church or state-based morés of charity). In contrast, ethical conventions are grounded in internal, intuitive notions of right and wrong, and reflect upon the actor's individual actions in the community as enacted by shouldering civic responsibilities. In other words, in our globalized, multiethnic, multicultural environment, ethics is based upon mediated and negotiated actions of one's accountability to others in society and through civic notions of *doing the right thing*, while morality suggests a set of fixed principles or actions that apply to monocultures. In praxis, the contingency of aesthetic evaluation when measured as actions in the public sphere require a moving away from the universality of standards of conduct to locality or positionality of the subject in society and in the text.[4] This form of fiction which incorporates a strand of ethics as a device to deliver pleasure is an interesting experiment in the realist tradition, and is the focus of this essay.

Speaking of ethics and this newly fashioned aesthetic in South Asian American literature in the same breath puts the problematic relationship between these two categories in a different light.[5] While older debates about aesthetics and ethics ranged from the autonomous and transcendent nature of art to the abstract and universal responsibilities of art in society, contemporary scholars broaden the scope of these arguments by incorporating the specificity of cultural productions via grounded subject positions of gender and race. Such comprehensive or inclusive theorizing not only avoids the blind spot of European (and Enlightenment) models that barred non-Western points of view from entering the debate, but also sidesteps the inherent crisis produced by the postcolonial moment that resisted a hierarchized aesthetic based upon devaluing non-Western cultural productions. Almost running parallel with this recent change in the shaping of literatures, which reflects a move from the postcolonial phase to something loosely called globalization, there is a concomitant inclination of scholars to redeploy Emmanuel Levinas's theories of the Other for debating aesthetics and ethics. The passage often quoted for this purposes is Levinas's comment, "I am defined as a subjectivity, as a singular person, as an 'I' precisely because I am exposed to the other. It is my inescapable and incontrovertible answerability to the other that makes me an individual 'I' to the extent that I agree to depose or dethrone myself—to abdicate my position of centrality—in favor of the vulnerable other."[6] Dorota Glowacka and Stephen Boos modify this view in their Introduction to *Between Ethics And Aesthetics: Crossing the Boundaries* to write, "for Levinas, Western representational paradigms are the project of an egological, imperial subject, while aesthetics, traditionally understood as producing a likeness of the Other, colludes in the appropriation of Otherness by the same. Levinas himself has never attempted to redefine aesthetics within the parameters of the Other, yet his critique has precipitated various searches for the possibility of an 'other' aesthetics, capable of accommodating radical alterity without reducing it to the measure of the same."[7]

While granting the appeal and perhaps even appropriateness of positioning Levinas as the main figure in reanimating the question of ethics inside aesthetics, some feminist scholars have taken Levinas to task for ignoring the woman question. Vicki Bell, for example, systematically challenges Levinas' statement that "indeed politics obliges one to engage in the non-ethical, so that the ethical cannot be understood as a basis of feminist politics,"[8] by responding that "ethics figures neither as a source of politics nor as a political weapon but as a check on freedom, an inspiration that prompts a continual questioning of one's own positionality, including the conditions of possibility of one's ethical sensibilities."[9] Sadly, Bell's assessment of Levinas remains bounded inside feminist critiques instead of being engaged in the wider arena of discourses on ethics. From an aesthetic angle, Marjorie Stone in a recent essay, "Between Ethics and Anguish," critiques Levinas's glaring omission or subjugation of female/feminine/gendered subjectivities vis-à-vis the Other.[10] Beyond the simplistic tendency of placing woman in the Other category, Stone's argument shows how the deeply personal moment in female subjectivity is part of an ethical crisis; yet another point of view that has not figured much in scholarly discussions of Levinas thus far. While I allude to Bell's position in rereading Levinas through a feminist lens to widen the circle of critical engagements of narrative discourses, in this essay, I will use Stone's logic to examine two South Asian texts.[11] Stone's "question [of] the relative neglect of the aesthetic in the developing work in feminist ethics and call for a more concerted analysis of the relations between feminist ethics and feminist aesthetics, between the 'real' and the representational"[12] resonates with my own scrutiny of unutterable trauma and the call to ethics in specific works of Jhumpa Lahiri and Anita Rau Badami. Consequently, I borrow some ideas from Stone's framework to explore a feminist granting of subjectivity and to read the ethical realism at work in Anita Rau Badami's *A Hero's Walk* (2001) and Jhumpa Lahiri's "Mr. Pirzada Comes to Dine" from her collection, *The Interpreter of Maladies* (1999).[13] In each of the works the protagonist is a young girl who impels readers to witness the anguish of making the right choice.

The Logic of Associations: Validating Comparisons

It is necessary to explain why I thread together Badami's novel *A Hero's Walk* with Lahiri's short story, "Mr. Pirzada Comes to Dine." To grasp the ethical import of new trends in literatures, Badami's novel about a young Asian Canadian girl's journey to India needs to be placed alongside Lahiri's short story about the experiences of a young Asian American girl in New England, and read as analogous texts. The point of comparison begins with the narrative perspective of a young girl in each case, who feels the West is her abode, and who is genuinely mystified by the idea of home that the other characters have. The reader's aesthetic responses to the two works are guided by the confident but naïve vision that the young girls have of themselves in society. Both authors deploy their own brand of ethical realism to assert their protagonists' childlike but firm sense of belonging. Upon reflection, this shows that Badami and Lahiri have crafted an identity for their heroes inside majority cultures without engaging in identity politics of minority race relations as the earlier set of authors from 1970s–80s had done. This is a crucial factor in understanding the shift from a morality undergirded by ideological motives to one that invokes an ethical response, i.e., these narratives do not solicit moral responses based upon rewriting history to correct a past injustice or racial, colonial oppressions. Instead, they create spaces through formal devices that allow readers to enter the narrative and glimpse a viable course of actions in terms of accountability to others. In fact, Lahiri and Badami deliberately use the childlike perspectives to show gaps between the actions of the older people in the works and what the readers perceive as the ethical choice in moments of crisis. Finally, reading the two works with and against each other challenges our orientation of centers and peripheries and changes our understanding of the cartography of global flows in an age of mobile cosmopolitanism—whether it is the United States or Canada—the condition of globality makes us reevaluate our paradigms of travel, migration, community and belonging, and the concomitant obligation to treat with courtesy and respect those whom we encounter. That is to say, it is not the deterritorialization of subjects that comes with *dislocation* that is fascinating in this comparison, but rather it is the unmooring of our notion of *national literatures* that comes with globalization, and our ways of reading new literatures.

But, there is also a critical difference. Lahiri's child protagonist intimates her ethical stance by glimpsing the world through television news to understand (albeit in a limited sense), the horrors of war, i.e., there is an aesthetic distance to her distress that is dramatized in Lahiri's use of the reportage genre. Badami's child protagonist hesitantly propels those around her to act ethically when she is viscerally imbricated in the unutterable trauma of loss through instances of interior monologue, i.e., the weight of non-ethical choices is more immediate as the consequences are borne by the young narrator. By looking through the prism of mirrored and distorted similarities of American and Canadian experiences of citizens of Asian origins, I posit an aesthetics that embodies the potential to articulate an ethics of/in local-global interactions. As a point of interest, there are examples of other Asian American narratives that have used child narrators,[14] such as Lan Cao's Mai Ngyen in *Monkey Bridge*, Christina Chiu's Eric Tsui in *Troublemaker and Other Stories*, and Lois Ann Yamanaka's Ivah in *Blue's Hanging*.[15] But the difference in Lahiri's and Badami's works are recognizable through their historical connections to the United States and Canada, respectively. The

Vietnamese, Chinese, and Japanese-Hawaiian authors reflect their colonial relationship to the United States and consequently touch upon oppression and marginalization, and even though seen through a child's eyes, these issues are structured along majority/minority and class/race/sexuality lines, and are confined to national boundaries. In contrast, Lahiri and Badami work from a global level, but also paradoxically from within same race familial bonds. Lahiri's protagonist Lilia, the Indian American, is unable to see the Bangladeshi, Mr. Pirzada, through the lens of geographic proximity as a neighbor or another South Asian. Similarly, Badami's Nandana, the Indian Canadian is incapable of identifying with her own maternal grandparents within the essentialized domestic space of "India." That is to say, Lahiri and Badami inflect the details of time and space—the coordinates of realism—to shade the estrangement and the process of reengagement of the two girls within their own circles of class and culture so as to enable ethical choices, even as their actions require a global context, so that social justice is articulated in vocabularies of responsibility to community and accountability to one's fellow human beings.

Badami's *A Hero's Walk*

> Do certain experiences of human anguish become so intense that a threshold is crossed when it is no longer a matter of pleasure or beauty or their absence because the very possibility of artistic expression and aesthetic response is annihilated? The substitution of anguish for aesthetics . . . is meant to shadow forth this possibility, as well as to pose the question of how such anguish affects the first (and some might say) the primary term in the coupling of ethics and aesthetics, a binary that may take the form of a dialectical opposition as well as a continuum or space of mediation? Does it become unethical even to attempt to represent what seems unspeakable? And, does such unspeakable anguish also limit our ability to make ethical judgments in the realm of the 'real' as opposed to the representational?[16]

Anita Rau Badami's story focuses upon the travails of her protagonist, seven-year-old, biracial Nandana, whose parents die in a car crash in Vancouver, to explore how she narrowly escapes becoming a ward of the state because her maternal grandfather in India is discovered to be her legal guardian. Contrary to so many diaspora stories, Badami focuses upon the dislocation and traumatic experiences of a self-proclaimed "Canadian" child in India, so that the significance of home and family are not simply reversed but radically altered. Further, the most difficult aspects of nostalgia and loss are uttered in clear, childlike tones with a beguiling banality, making understatement the artistic or aesthetic device to shed light on the girl's unspeakable trauma. The abject horror of this child's plight and the utter cruelty to which she is subjected allows readers to see the gaps in ethical action and the lapses in responsible behavior of the adults in the novel. Thus, at a formal level, Badami uses the representational power of art and the pathos of the real and deploys interior monologue as a device to create a verisimilitude to keep within the tradition of realism. This strategy further enhances the dramatic irony of Nandana's situation. It is this masterful combination of aesthetics and ethics that systematically evokes poignant pleasure in the narrative.

The novel begins with Nandana not knowing that her parents have been killed, and her inability to understand why the older people in the story will not allow her to go home, "her father had often said it was only a hop, a skip, and a jump away. She knew her address—her parents had made her repeat it nearly every day—250 Melfa Lane, Vancouver, BC, Canada, North America, The World. Her father had always added the last two, and it had made her mother laugh and say, 'Don't confuse the child, Alan'" (16). Because she doesn't know, she tries to go back *spatially to the time* when "home" was accessible and constantly attempts to escape the people who want to protect her from the trauma. A few pages later this impulse is repeated, when she runs away from Kiran's place: "She was nervous about being alone on the road, but she knew it was only a hop, a skip, and a jump away" (28). Even when she is physically transported to India to her grandparents' house, she beleives "home" was just a "hop, a skip, and a jump away" (164). The father's hyperbolic humor in positioning home as always being a "hop, skip, and jump" and located in the "world" gives Nandana a concrete sense of belonging, which in turn, creates a narrative disjuncture for the reader to glimpse the aesthetic *representational* factor of belonging that is balanced against the ethical *real* fact of not being in the right place. That is to say, the gap structured on a humorous ploy adults use teasingly, but one that Nandana believes to be legitimate, allows readers to enter the narrative and recognize the pathos of her situation and wonder what actions the adults in her life will take to correct it. This gap is heightened when Nandana, who does not fully comprehend the fact that her parents have been killed, attempts to contact her parents as spoken in interior monologue:

> Earlier today, she had tried calling home when Aunty Kiran had gone for her bath. She got the answering machine. "Mummy, Daddy, please come and take me home," she said to the machine. Then she added, in case they

had forgotten where she was sleeping over, "I am at Anjali's house. It's the white one with the maple tree, behind Safeway"

. . . .

Nobody called her back or came to get her. She was beginning to think that Aunty Kiran had decided to keep her here for ever and ever. Hadn't she often said as much to her mother? "Maya, your daughter's such a cutie pie, I think I shall keep her." And her mother would laugh, "Ah, not so cute all the time, believe me. She can be a little pest." Then, she would stroke Nandana's cheek and say, "I wouldn't give her away for a zillion dollars." She wondered if her mother had changed her mind. (18)

Recognizable signposts of diaspora narratives—the differences in cultures, in national geographies, and social and psychic environments, and the longing for home as both imagined and real—operate at an aesthetic remove, or a radical angle in Badami's novel. For Nandana, home is the private space of family, of memories, of laughter and happiness with her mother and father, and she feels consistently destabilized, be it by Kiran, who lives on the next street "behind Safeway" or her grandmother, who lives across the seas in India. Badami aestheticizes the incomprehensibility of the situation for a child by layering Nandana's grief with bewilderment, thus nudging us toward empathy by intensifying our sense of pathos:

On her last visit Nandana had crawled into her mother's closet. The clothes had smelled sweet: the white silky blouse that she wore when she had a meeting; special black pants and the regular brown ones; the sleeveless yellow cotton shirt that her father had said made her mother look like a sun drop. She sat silent as a mouse inside the closet, hoping that Aunty Kiran would leave without her. She spotted a spider creeping across the floor, towards the door and the light outside. Stupid spider, she thought and crushed it under her shoe. Dead, she told it. You are dead. Then she waited for Aunty Kiran to call her name. (117)

Here nostalgia, memory, life experiences, and trauma are all packed into Nandana's very being. It is the child's severe sense of confusion, misplaced rage, and a quiet desperation that readers glimpse. Her senseless brutality in killing the spider hints at her partial awareness of death as an intrusive fact in her life, but she is not able to deal with all the accompanying emotions. Badami begins by slowly constructing Nandana's helplessness and gradually escalates it to hysterical proportions through interior monologue, "I want to go home . . . homehomehome" (90) signaling the rising panic in the child's body as she loses control of her world, imagining "her father would be wondering where Nandana had gone. For *sure*" (90, original italics). The authorial emphasis on *sure* ironically anchors Nandana in a safe place and simultaneously reveals the threat to that safety when it is taken away. Her hopelessness becomes real when Kiran takes her back to her house to collect some things for another overnight stay, "she ran inside eagerly. She thought that the house had a lonesome smell" (91), which indicates to the reader that Nandana herself is beginning to sense "home" as a place of loss.

But, Badami does not indulge in the stereotyping of minority subjects as victims by allowing the narrative to be a litany of loss-filled events; instead, she introduces an ethical sensor, and rescues Nandana through the actions of her grandmother. It is now worthwhile to explore the potential for feminist ethics (and feminist aesthetics) in Badami's novel. In an attempt to explain the practical meaning of feminist ethics, I borrow the arguments that Robin Fiore and Hilde Linderman Nelson make in *Recognition, Responsibility, and Rights* (2000), where they write, "Responsibility, as feminists deploy the concept, is not exhausted by traditional philosophical issues of freewill and the possibility of moral judgments, of holding people accountable. For feminists, it involves human practices of responsiveness to particular contexts, of being accountable, that is taking as well as assigning responsibility."[17] The grandmother takes center stage in the child's shattered world, the person who embraces Nandana by enmeshing her in the familiarity of household routine, so that the child begins to build a sense of normalcy through the very monotony of performing habitual tasks. The grandmother serves as a stark contrast to the grandfather, who refused to speak to his daughter when she married a Canadian. And Nandana tells the reader through interior monologue that he is the "stranger," the "Old Man" who made "her mother cry," while she remembers her grandmother as the "kind Mamma lady" (154). In feminist vocabulary, the grandmother works through an *ethic of care* allowing Badami to experiment with new structures of power, where the grandmother emerges as the ethical actor in contrast to her daughter, Maya. Living in Vancouver and inhabiting the modern West, Nandana's mother Maya, for all her enlightened outlook, is only able to put in place patriarchal and juridical structures for safeguarding Nandana by *naming* her father in her will. He "saw this trusteeship as an attempt by Maya to force herself back into his life. But he signed the documents nevertheless" (86). Though resentful, he does accept this patriarchal authority.

The father, the "Old Man" resents the fact that he had to lose face when Maya broke her promise to marry an Indian man, saying "he would never avoid doing his duty, even though Maya had no compunctions about ignoring hers" (116). The power of this sentiment lies in the fact that the "Old Man" remains aloof from Nandana in Vancouver (inept at handling grief, perhaps), and stoically fulfills his duty but fails in his ethical obligation to give solace to his granddaughter. It is the grandmother, interestingly, from a small town in South India, who from within traditional, matrilineal, familial networks "pointed out, it was his duty" (116), and welcomed the distraught child into their midst. It is she who metaphorically takes Nandana's hand and walks the "hero's walk." The grandmother explains the meaning of "a hero's walk" to her dance students, urging them to "walk with dignity. Walk with courage, and humility. Lift your head high" (136). Badami's message, one could posit, is articulated in a feminist aesthetic so as to give voice both to the granddaughter and grandmother; one silenced by grief and the other by tradition, to portray a life that can be lived ethically. As Misha Strauss says, "in trying to understand one's own role in a particular situation or deliberating over a course of actions, members of a person's community can help a person reflect upon who she is and who she wants to be. Members of one's community do important emotional work . . . that both contributes to the construction of one's self understanding and provides opportunities for transformation of one's self-understanding. . . . It names the management of others' emotions—soothes tempers, boosting confidence, fueling pride, preventing frictions and mending egos."[18] In the end, Nandana and her grandmother form family and community bonds that sustain them together, as they walk the "the hero's walk."

Lahiri's "When Mr. Pirzada Came to Dine"

"When Mr. Pirzada Came to Dine" spotlights ethical issues in large-scale global contexts about wars and violence, and addresses the potential of a complex connectivity between global citizens and local subjects. Lahiri choreographs the reader's memories and embedded images of war to dramatize the difference between acting out of an abstract sense of moral convention and acting with pragmatic, ethical responsibility. The former requires little personal involvement or sacrifice, while the latter is based upon actual, transformative action, however small those gestures might be. Lilia is the young narrator who carries this message. The story is about Mr. Pirzada, a figure in crisis from war-torn Bangladesh, who benefits from the benevolence of strangers in a small, college town in New England, and who ultimately belies popular (xenophobic) expectations by going back home. Pirzada's situation, i.e., quasi refugee status, calls attention to a particular kind of discourse that is in circulation in different spaces of public culture in the United States about people's responsibility in a transnational arena in moments of global crisis. Lahiri's aesthetic device is the formalistic deployment of the reportage genre even as it negotiates the fiction-documentary divide. The duo—Lilia and Pirzada—enable discussions about the reader's preconceptions of unstable, third world countries where violence erupts as a result of national and ethnic conflicts (reiterated, for example, by media reports of Bosnia or Croatia, and more recently, of Afghanistan, or Iraq, Israel, and Palestine). The premise of such discourses is that these nations are not capable of managing their affairs, and thus need the developed West to intervene. The scope and nature of this intervention is precisely what shows the difference between ethics and morality in a global arena. By excavating memories from random spaces of public culture and United States's responses to war and disempowerment in distant countries, the story hints at the reader's own potential to act ethically by using the child as exemplum.

A comment Zygmunt Bauman made in *Liquid Modernity* (2000) is useful in understanding the sentimental responses to crises that are rooted in popular culture.[19] He notes how the United States has come to nurture *a culture of giving* over the last half a century:

It was exactly that "emancipation"—from want, "low standards of life", paucity of needs, doing what the community has done rather than "being able" to do whatever one may still wish in the future—that loomed vaguely in Harry Truman's 1947 declaration of war on "underdevelopment."... Most obviously, "development" develops the dependency of men and women on things and events they can neither produce, control, see, nor understand. Other humans' deeds send long waves which, when they reach our doorstep, look strikingly like floods and other natural disasters; like them they come from nowhere, unannounced, and like them, they make a mockery of foresight, cunning, and prudence.[20]

The reportage genre is Lahiri's formal device to wrench Mr. Pirzada's national identity from Pakistan and assigns him a Bangladeshi citizenship. By using news reports and TV coverage Lahiri knits the story together and explains the intricacies of a civil war between East and West Pakistan that created Bangladesh. In choosing this reportage mode, which lends itself to her brand of realism, she catalogues the violence of war with concise, historical, and geographical precision. Lilia, the child protagonist, begins the story with: "In the autumn of 1971 a man used to come to our house, bearing confections in his pocket and hopes of ascertaining the life and death of his family" (23), and ends by saying, "Mr. Pirzada flew back to his three-story home in Dacca, to discover what was left of it," while she and her family "went to Philadelphia to spend Christmas with friends of my parents" (41).

Lilia's guileless voice makes readers vigilant about Pirzada's precarious powerlessness and her family's unselfish response and commonsense understanding of generosity. However, the child's vision is telescoped by the author's ironical gaze that points to the inevitable limit of liberal generosity. Lilia's casual documentation of her family's willingness to help a stranger motors the story, and shows how Pirzada accepts their benevolence (comes to dinner) and its limit (returns to Dacca). It also reveals how Lilia's parents have assimilated into a form of public culture in the United States and, as members of the general public, have unconsciously internalized Truman's dictum of "emancipation" from "want" (Bauman). But once that obligation is fulfilled, the interruption is glossed over and their lives go on, as seen in their Christmas jaunt. In contrast, Pirzada is permanently marked by their kindness, as Lilia reveals in the end saying he "thanked us for our hospitality [upon returning to Dacca], adding that although he now understood the meaning of the words 'thank you' they still were not adequate to express his gratitude" (42).

By not making Pirzada a permanent liability, Lahiri reveals the other face of liberal generosity, i.e., the moral obligation and the necessarily temporary nature of transnational aid in today's tense geopolitical reality. Lilia's comment of Pirzada's "gratitude" points to public sentiments about social obligations, which in turn, enables readers to access sedimented memories about expected responses to human suffering while ensconced in the safety of their own homes. Lilia helps excavate such submerged memories by relaying the events as a composite report of the horrors of war overlaid upon the normalcy of everyday life:

> That year Pakistan was engaged in civil war. In March, Dacca had been invaded, torched, and shelled by the Pakistani army. Teachers were dragged onto streets and shot, women dragged into barracks and raped. By the end of the summer, three hundred thousand people were said to have died. In Dacca Mr. Pirzada had a three-story home, a lectureship in botany at the university, a wife of twenty years, and seven daughters between the ages of six and sixteen whose names all began with the letter A. (23)

By juxtaposing scenes of rape and genocide in the violent splitting of Pakistan with the placidity of hearth and home, and the familiarity of a modern university life with the strangeness of other's cultural practices,

Lahiri allows readers to go back to the hazy *topoi* of news reports they, too, might have witnessed over the years. The scene brings back memories of other wars fought elsewhere, gradually creating a fundamental similarity about peoples' lives in war-torn zones. By skillfully using the reportage form, Lahiri couples distance and immediacy, war and peace, and a chaotic sameness out there with the stable sanctuary in here so as to suture together the representational aspect of aesthetics with the real issues of ethics. The next scene emphasizes this fact, when Lilia recounts, "That night, like every other night, we did not eat at the dining table, because it did not provide an unobstructed view of the television set. Instead we huddled around the coffee table, without conversing, our plates perched on the edges of our knees. From the kitchen my mother brought forth the succession of dishes: lentils with fried onions, green beans with coconut, fish cooked with raisins in a yogurt sauce" (30). Lahiri may be speaking of a war that birthed Bangladesh in 1971 while eating exotic Indian food, but today, the scene could very well trigger images of atrocities in other war-torn parts of the globe, as we too watch the evening news and eat dinner. These images of war, haphazardly stored and evoked from public memory sites become Lahiri's pretext for asking questions about one's ethical conduct in global contexts.

The latent sense of distance, safety (and privilege) that readers have stored in the vast and irregular spaces of public culture in the United States often gets mediated through communal acts of generosity. Giving money to feed the hungry and tending to refugees are familiar responses to war, which allows readers to engage their moral obligation, albeit impersonally. Lahiri's story suggests that the impulse behind such impersonal, institutionalized gestures of goodwill needs to be examined, and Lilia serves as her heuristic device. Lahiri manipulates public memory to probe this question by appealing to two sets of readers. On the first level there is the general reader, who merely recalls war scenes and formulates obligatory responses of generosity, and on the second level there is the more astute reader, who recognizes the subtle message about flaws in liberal humanism (and its corollary, liberal guilt). Lilia aligns herself with the first set of readers by saying "my father and Mr. Pirzada deplored the policies of a general named Yahyah Khan. They discussed intrigues I did not know, a catastrophe I could not comprehend. 'See, children your age, what they do to survive,' my father said as he served me another piece of fish" (31). Obligation here arises simply out of one's sense of safety in the face of the other's danger. Images of distant wars mapped outside the borders of the United States underscore one's security while also requiring one to engage in appropriate action. Lahiri adroitly builds upon such an unclear or unsure sentiment of moral obligation by having

Lilia admit that her understanding of war came from learning about the American Revolution in school, a war that had both rational purpose and moral underpinnings.

Interestingly, Lilia's comment about her mother is meant to appeal to the second set of readers who know, and now are reminded again of fault lines in liberal generosity. The mother says, "'We live here now, she was born here.' She [mother] seemed genuinely proud of the fact, as if it were a reflection of my character. In her estimation, I knew, I was assured of a safe life, an easy life, a fine education, every opportunity" (26). The mother fits the outmoded, melting pot paradigm of immigrants, and reveals dichoto-mous moral impulses of gratitude and guilt based upon gifts received and sacrifices made in her life in the United States. She manifests such confused motives by cooking elaborate meals for Pirzada's daily dinner visits. Guilt, an unpredictable emotion, makes the cost of liberal humanism high indeed. Readers catch a brief glimpse of the fraying edges of her conflicting emo-tions when Lilia recalls that during the actual days of the war between East and West Pakistan, "my mother refused to serve anything other than boiled eggs with rice for dinner" (40). The mother's scaled-down dinner preparation points to this "procedural" sense of obligation. And, by switching to a quasi omniscient, news-anchor voice, the narrative gestures toward the fact that, in reality, liberal humanism is founded on the *unspeakable* immunity of first worldism. Her generosity is based upon parochial nationalism rather than a real willingness to help, and is seen in Lilia's remark that is informed by a nascent understanding of local-global connectivity:

What they heard that evening . . . was that India and Pakistan were drawing closer and closer to war. Troops from both sides lined the border, and Dacca was insisting nothing short of independence. The war was to be waged on East Pakistani soil. The United States was siding with West Pakistan, the Soviet Union with India and what was soon to be Bangladesh. (40)

The matter-of-fact reporting of the bloody exchange glosses over the fact that super powers tend to divide parts of the globe with self-serving political and economic motives, while using euphemisms to formulate policies. Lilia's factual tone gives the reader an opportunity to reflect upon *ethical responsi-bilities* to Pirzada, given that the United States is ideologically at odds with a Soviet-backed Bangladesh. Lahiri tries now to point to the sequel nature of international accountability, i.e., figuring out which nations the United States needs to help, and for how long its citizens feel responsible for those in war-ravaged nations. This implication of liberal generosity is underscored,

particularly as the media seems invested in routinely and graphically proliferating reports of overwhelming global chaos aided by its unrelenting coverage
of sensationalized violence.

That is to say, when images and information about war and ethnic cleansing in Croatia, for example, get sequentially superimposed upon images
from Afghanistan, it becomes increasingly difficult to imagine the world
out there, and to prioritize which nation and for how long disempowered
people merit generosity. Political alliances, which add to the confusion of
one's willingness to help, further problematize such a blurring of nations
and peoples in need, especially in a world gone mad with violence. Using Lilia as the narrator and the reportage genre as her vehicle, Lahiri's
story draws attention to the media's technique of creating a repository of
indiscriminately blurred images in the public sphere, such that differences
between moral obligation and ethical responsibility become distorted. Lahiri
uses the form, i.e., the reportage genre, to challenge the *meaning of truth*, and
alerts readers to their own roles as global citizens. Lilia's parents feel they owe
Pirzada some charity and kindness, but Lilia connects with him at a visceral
level in a not-yet-articulated effort of ethical, global community building.[21]
Bauman expresses this sense of obligation in another way when he writes,
"that to live is to live *with others* (other human beings; other beings *like
us*)—is obvious to the point of banality. What is less obvious and not at all
banal, is the fact that what we call 'the others' we live with . . . is what we
know of them. Each of us 'construes' his or her own assortment of 'others'
out of the sedimented, selected and processed memory of past encounters,
communications, exchanges, joint ventures, and battles."[22] When horren-
dous images of war-torn places promote immediate but uncritical responses
from people, how does one decipher the nature, meaning, and significance
of ethical responsibility? If one agrees that the media obliterates national,
ethnic, and religious barriers in order to sensationalize information and grab
viewer attention (playing the ratings game), where does one turn for getting
and assessing the *truth of the events in order to enact social justice?*

The ethical fulcrum of Lahiri's story rests on awakening readers to their
own actions in this messy world. She points to the difference between
an older generation of liberal humanists like Lilia's parents who feel morally
obliged to be kind, and a younger generation of Lilias who are still working
out a complex, ethical connectivity between peoples of this globe. Lahiri
marks Lilia's place in a new generation of global citizens, citizens forging
connections through genuine, radical kinship bonds. The story ushers in a
cautious note of optimism through Lilia, a child who is not yet socialized or
internalized that ideology of liberal generosity. When she hears Pirzada and
his family are finally safe, Lilia recalls:

To celebrate the good news my mother prepared a special dinner that evening, and when we sat down to eat at the coffee table, we toasted our water glasses, but I did not feel like celebrating. Though I had not seen him for months, it was only then that I felt Mr. Pirzada's absence. It was only then, raising my water glass in his name, that I knew what it was to miss someone who was so many miles and hours away, just as he had missed his wife and daughters for so many months. (42)

As a child who has not yet internalized the codes of adult gestures of civility, she embodies Lahiri's powerful note about the interdependency of human lives in a disproportionately globalized society. Lilia's sorrow, nay her empathy, is her bond of solidarity with Pirzada, one that reaches across transnational spaces.

Throughout the story, Lilia sees Pirzada as a friend, for example, by accepting his little gifts of candy, initiating him in the foreign act of carving a Halloween pumpkin, and praying each night that his "family was safe and sound" (32). But her parents see him merely as an object to be used as repayment for their good fortune in the United States, and thus feel a need to feed him curries. Lilia's sentiments and actions hint at the possibility of a nascent understanding of ethical, reciprocal community building. In today's world, alliances are temporary, fickle, and often politically motivated and/or market driven, hence ethical action cannot be based upon absolute commitments but upon small and consistent efforts of valuing and nurturing connections, even fleeting ones, between people. Lilia symbolizes such a connectivity that will make asking for and giving help not a matter of generosity, but one of solidarity. In this story, the Bangladesh war is a ploy for readers to reflect on the volatility in developing nations, the willingness of developed nations to help maintain peace, albeit a fragile peace, and the necessary actions each one of us takes as global citizens in this negotiation. Lilia tries, but doesn't fully succeed in revealing the full potential of global citizens to forge an equitable society that can affirm individual freedom and communal existence on a slippery balance between self-interest and responsible group interest.[23] Lahiri takes up the challenge of articulating an *ethical discourse* when claiming she is *telling us a story*.

Conclusion

A child's voice, whether spoken in interior monologue as in Badami's case or articulated lucidly as in Lahiri's work, becomes a mode of experimentation on numerous registers. As a vehicle for deploying a version of feminist ethics, both authors move away from rigid, universalized moral codes, and suggest instead intimate gestures of friendship and solidarity that help build community. As seen, these bonds are not hierarchized via relations, but enabled through empathetic moments of doing the right thing. At a formal level, as expressions of feminist aesthetics, both authors use a child's voice to bring to the fore a contemporary issue of the ethics of care, taken up by feminists such as Alison Jaggar, Seyela Benhabib, and Marion M. Young in a larger debate that spans the spectrum of the rights and responsibilities of global citizens. Both authors attempt to awaken readers to their own responses and actions when faced with dilemmas that are becoming more and more part of our lived, globalized reality.[24]

Part III

Intertexts: Asian American Writing and Literary Movements

8

"A Loose Horse"

Asian American Poetry and the Aesthetics
of the Ideogram

JOSEPHINE NOCK-HEE PARK

ASIAN AMERICAN POETS have a singular plight: they write within the constraints of an American poetry indelibly marked by Orientalism. American poetry was reborn in a modernist revolution spearheaded by Ezra Pound's Imagist movement. Pound took seriously what had been a fad—adding an Oriental flourish to poetry in the early twentieth century—and made it a centerpiece of his argument for a new American poetry. In search of a remedy for what he considered the excesses of the recent past, Pound turned to the East in order to purify modern poetry. To insist on objective values is a hallmark of modernist poetry, and Pound looked to the formal properties of the Chinese character, with its clean strokes, as a visible model for clarifying American poetry. In his monumental study of Pound, Hugh Kenner asks, "is the surest way to a fructive western idea the misunderstanding of an eastern one?"[1] Pound's American revolution in poetry was an exercise routed through an Orient understood as an aesthetic ideal. As modernism's poet-pedagogue, Pound has taught us how to read and fashioned the tenets of what we consider good poetry today, and the residue of his particular fascination with the Orient has endured in American poetry. Traces of an Asiatic influence linger today in

"After the Three Characters" and "A Symphonic Poem: Unfinished" used by permission of Ho Hon Leung.

the dominant mode of American poetry: all short, piercing lines and sudden turns.[2]

Asian American poets writing in the wake of the modernist revolution forcefully turned away from the Poundian legacy, and it is only in the eighties that American modernist influence returns to the scene of Asian American poetry. The Asian American poet-pedagogues of the sixties and seventies wanted to instruct their audience in a new literary terrain, and they were especially careful to keep their poetry untainted by an Orientalist inheritance. This essay reconsiders Pound's Imagism in terms of his interests in the Orient, focusing on the influence of the American Orientalist Ernest Fenollosa on Pound's work. From establishing these origins, my analysis examines one contemporary poet's attempt to tackle the vexed question of the Poundian inheritance head-on. In two lyric poems collected in Walter Lew's 1995 collection *Premonitions: The Kaya Anthology of New Asian North American Poetry*, Ho Hon Leung addresses the fascination with Chinese writing that fueled Pound's Imagist revolution, ultimately interrogating the position of the Asian American poet as he faces this legacy.[3]

Images of the Ideogram

Pound's serendipitous discovery of Chinese poetry provided the impetus for his poetic instigations. In 1913, Pound was bequeathed the papers of the American Orientalist scholar, Ernest Fenollosa, and these manuscripts were a gold mine for Pound: through them he translated Japanese Noh plays, found the fodder for his volume *Cathay*, a handful of translations of Tang Dynasty poetry, and discovered evidence for the core formulation of his poetics of Imagism. In his landmark manifesto "A Few Don'ts," Pound defined the Image as "an intellectual and emotional complex in an instant of time."[4] The power of the Image is such that it literally provides a lens for the emotion and intellect that Pound identifies as constitutive of poetry; the successful Imagist poem brings together minutely observed particulars to create a powerful, visible complex of intellect and emotion. Pound insisted on both an intellectual and emotional response simultaneously, in the flash of his "instant of time." It is the single moment of the Image that frees the poem from being a lesser imitation of the world; in its instant of time the poem achieves a thingliness of its own, one that incites a formal complex of intellect and emotion superior to experiencing the world in the absence of art. The Image is the word as we dream it would work; it is what Pound, in a discussion of his most famous Imagist poem, "In a Station of the Metro," calls "the word beyond formulated language."[5]

In 1918, Pound edited and published Fenollosa's treatise on the unique properties of Chinese writing and its possibilities for English, *The chinese written character as a medium for poetry*. The essay begins with a parenthetical editor's note, in which Pound tells us, "We have here not a bare philological discussion, but a study of the fundamentals of all aesthetics."[6] According to Fenollosa, the Chinese language is a vital, instructive tool because it makes apparent the process of thought. Fenollosa demonstrates this by claiming that the sentence marks the cognitive pathway of the thought process, in the correct order. Further, because Chinese and English are both uninflected languages, they rely on word order to relay the expression in the sentence; and this shared grammatical affinity leads him to poetry because, as Fenollosa writes, "All that poetic form requires is a regular and flexible sequence, as plastic as thought itself" (7). Because Chinese characters enact thought processes, then, examining the Chinese sentence can lead us to poetry in English.

The Chinese sentences that Fenollosa shows us are carefully chosen to reveal sketches of natural processes; he chooses these sets of ideograms because they demonstrate process and movement. Fenollosa's most famous exemplary sentence appears early in the essay: "Man sees horse." Fenollosa discusses what he sees in these "visible hieroglyphics":

> First stands the man on two legs. Second, his eye moves through space: a bold figure represented by running legs under an eye, a modified picture of an eye, a modified picture of running legs, but unforgettable once you have seen it. Third stands the horse on his four legs.
>
> The thought-picture is not only called up by these signs as well as by words, but far more vividly and concretely. Legs belong to all three characters: they are *alive*. (8–9, original emphasis)

Fenollosa goes on to elaborate the experience of reading such images: "In reading Chinese we do not seem to be juggling mental counters, but to be watching *things* work out their own fate" (9, original emphasis). These three characters have a vitality that almost escapes the page; each ideogram can "work out its own fate." This life attributed to the word is especially entrancing to modernist ideals of objectivity, a fantasy of an impersonal poetry that can vividly present its objects to the reader, in which the poet's job is not to infuse the components of his art with life but to find a formal means of expressing life itself on the page. Pound discovers in Fenollosa the culmination of a thesis he insisted upon years before seeing this essay: namely, that language is not separate from life. As Fenollosa writes, Chinese "retains the primitive sap"—unlike English, in which etymologies can no longer be heard and the word is "cut and dried like a walking stick" (24). According to Fenollosa, the ideogram is a uniquely true instance of language, and, crucially, its visible etymology can assist in reviving a long-deadened English.

The essay ends with another now-famous sentence: "Sun rises in the East." Fenollosa explains the characters to us:

The sun, the shining, on one side, on the other the sign of the east, which is the sun entangled in the branches of a tree. And in the middle sign, the verb "rise," we have further homology; the sun is above the horizon, but beyond that the single upright line is like the growing trunk-line of the tree sign. This is but a beginning, but it points a way to the method, and to the method of intelligent reading. (33)

With this line at the close of this study, Fenollosa claims that he has created "a beginning" that "points a way to the method." He has taught us how to read intelligently by showing us the delicate images embedded within the sign. This Chinese sentence provides us with an image of the importance of Eastern influence, which, like the rising sun, can illuminate the West. Fenollosa ended with an opening, and Pound takes up these ideas, incorporating the ideogram into his Imagist movement, in which "Luminous Details," like the strokes that compose the Chinese sign, come together to produce an Image. Fenollosa's meditations on precise seeing and the poetic nature of the ideogram take root in Pound's poetics, and in his extension and application of Fenollosa's work, accurate poetry, like the ideogram, can demonstrate a one-to-one correspondence between the thing and the marks put together to designate it on the page.

The Chinese character is unique in its visibility. Fenollosa takes this commonplace observation—already rather tired in his era—and renews it by arguing for its applicability to the West. The fact of the difference of Chinese is the least of Fenollosa's interests; instead, he wants to enliven English with the beauty he locates in the Chinese language and argues that crucial similarities between East and West make this rapprochement possible. Fenollosa's early transpacific vision dims the rest of the globe to show us the special connections between America and the Far East. He uses his philological claims in order to demonstrate a shared essence between East and West: according to Fenollosa, our thoughts progress in exactly the same way on either side of the Pacific, and Chinese characters have the unique ability of revealing to us the inherently active properties of English that have been obscured by centuries of ill use.

In *Of Grammatology*, Jacques Derrida heralds the potent combination of Fenollosa and Pound as a significant historical moment in his philosophy of writing. Derrida calls their poetic discoveries "the first break in the most entrenched Western tradition"; according to Derrida, their "irreducibly graphic poetics" "caused to vacillate the transcendental authority and dominant category of the episteme: being."[7] Along with Nietzsche and Mallarmé, Derrida cites Pound's and Fenollosa's Orientalist revolution as a significant force in ushering in a new discourse, one in which attention to the word itself becomes a crucial component of philosophical inquiry.

The full import of Fenollosa's and Pound's combined faith in language is demonstrated in Fenollosa's conviction that he had discovered a means of understanding the process of thought through the lens of the Far East. Pound's extension of Fenollosa's endeavors helped him formulate an idea of poetry that could capture the entirety of a moment by following the visible dictates of the Chinese character. They are responsible for a crucial moment of dislocation in Western writing, in which a newfound aesthetic faith is discovered in the Chinese sign. They shared a belief in the ideogram's ability to present the thing itself, unmediated by the troubling arbitrariness of Western writing. Clearly, Fenollosa and Pound never speculated on the nature of language as arbitrary sign; their work proceeds from the opposite assumption.[8] Ultimately, this belief in the commensurability between the thing and its presentation in language finds an echo in the spirit which brings East and West together simply by setting an aesthetic moment of accord.

Pound picks up where Fenollosa left off, including Fenollosa's closing image of the rising sun in his 1934 textbook for teaching poetry, *ABC of Reading*. Pound tells us that "anyone can see how the ideogram for man or tree or sunrise developed," and he shows them to us as proof.[9] Pound's version, however, moves down the page, showing us the ideogram for "man," "tree," "sun," and, finally, "east." His translation of the last character brings together the previous ideograms: "sun tangled in the tree's branches, as at sunrise, meaning now the East."[10] Pound, then, dispenses with the sentence that had been so crucial to Fenollosa's argument. In fact, Pound's recapitulation is missing the verb altogether and instead shows us an Imagistic scene, in which the first three characters seem to come together to produce the last. In fragmenting and rewriting Fenollosa's sentence, Pound includes "man," the agent previously left out in the final Chinese sentence of Fenollosa's essay;

despite his insistence on the obviousness of the visions themselves, Pound is famously unwilling to let things work out their own fate.

The importance of the Far East to Pound's poetry simply cannot be overstated: his fascination with the ideogram shaped his lyric revolution in the 1910s, and his later obsession with Confucianism was a centerpiece of both his epic, *The Cantos*, and much of his lamentable and disturbing polemical writing from the 1930s on. Both ends of his poetic legacy—the lyric and epic poles—are deeply informed by his idiosyncratic interest in the Far East, and his infamous will led to the bitter end of his epic and his career. Pound's aesthetic values go well beyond poetry; they infect his politics and economics because, just as life and art cannot be segregated from each other, he cannot imagine keeping them separate. In training redemptive values onto art, Pound was singularly captive to his aesthetic beliefs, fashioned early on with the help of Ernest Fenollosa's American Orientalism. In the arc of Pound's career, the trappings of Fenollosa's aesthetic fundamentals so crucial in the beginning sparked a belief system that, at its nadir, resulted in Pound's actual imprisonment at Pisa.

The Image and the Asian American Poet

Ideally, the Image can function in the manner of the ideogram. On the following page in the *ABC of Reading*, Pound writes, "Fenollosa was telling how and why a language written in this way [i.e., in Chinese characters] SIMPLY HAD TO STAY POETIC."[11] The ideogram is always and automatically a poem. This hallucinatory belief in Chinese writing fueled Pound's poetic revolution, and the poets who follow him contend with this legacy. Until fairly recently, Asian American poets have chosen, understandably, to turn away from this inheritance altogether. The dangers of imitating an imitation of the Oriental style is a trap the activist poets of the sixties and seventies chose to avoid. Writing in the late sixties and seventies, during the activist era of Asian American poetry and the time of an ethnic nationalism that borrowed its terms from Black Power, these poets forcefully turned away from this modernist legacy.[12]

Indeed, the deliberate cordoning off of modernism by activist Asian American poets at the critical moment of pan-ethnic formation may be a reason behind the very different experiments in this poetry, which have resulted in an exuberant poetic voice that has escaped the academy and is presently only rarely studied within it. It is certainly the case that the lyric has a marginalized existence in literary study as a whole; lyric is seen as either irrelevant because it cannot accommodate history in its "instant of time" or, in a more positive light, as a minor subversive jab at these larger interests, but one that does not acquire a full presence on its own.[13] Yet Asian American poets have a particularly difficult relationship to the mainstream American lyric, still suffused with the minimalism learned from Pound's example. The influence of Pound's Orientalist turn simply can't be overstated; poetry workshops today adhere to the dictates of Pound's Imagist manifesto "A Few Don'ts," paring down rhetoric and sharpening the poetic line in order to show us sudden collisions of intellect and emotion. In response, Lawson Inada flees from the thought of what he terms "a quaint collection of cricket haikus," turning instead to jazz rhythms in order to express an Asian American consciousness.[14]

The American lyric that bears its Poundian inheritance has come to be seen as a kind of prison house for activist Asian American poets, but later Asian American poetry has returned to these confines in order to address its complicated position in American literature. George Uba discusses this gradual turn to modernism in the wake of the activist poets, and he notes that post-activist Asian American poets have returned to this legacy, albeit gingerly and with crucial differences.[15] I contend that it is the Orientalism at the heart of the modernist revolution in the poetic line that freights this inheritance with a difficult weight that many poets still choose to avoid.

Two short poems by Ho Hon Leung in Walter Lew's *Premonitions* directly address Pound's legacy. "After the 'Three Characters'" takes its title from Fenollosa's paradigmatic three-character sentence, "Man sees horse," and elaborates the position of a very different poetic persona who registers these Orientalist revelations long after the appearance of Imagism. Leung writes a page that looks as though it could have been taken out of *The Cantos*, and the opening lines of "After the 'Three Characters'" launches us into Poundian quirks of spacing on the page and abbreviation:

After I read yr poem
I felt depressed

Perhaps this opening apostrophe is an address to Pound himself: we can imagine the Asian American poet facing one of Pound's translations from the Chinese, taken from Fenollosa's crib notes. This is the simple and honest response of the Chinese American poet reading these fantasies of Chinese language: "I felt depressed."

This opening has the markers of Pound, but its tone is altogether different. Leung's poem formally invokes Pound's epic in order to address the lyric inheritance; hence, he brings together the two poles of Pound's legacy. Pound wrote both the shortest lyric ("In a Station of the Metro") and longest epic (*The Cantos*) of high modernism—both of which were inflected with very different understandings of the Orient—but it is Leung's innovation to use Pound's epic style to interrogate his lyric revolution. Pound discarded the Imagist lyric in his own work because of its inability to account for the duration and fantasy of history that obsessed him in *The Cantos*. Leung, however, uses the epic form of *The Cantos* to address Pound's interest in Fenollosa's work on the Chinese sign, and in using the form that superceded Imagism to address it, Leung brings together both ends of the Poundian legacy to critique the Orientalist vision that undergirds the Image. Leung writes in an epic mode in order to address the lyric innovation of the Image, thus avoiding the dangers of producing another Poundian lyric in critiquing the Image; he makes these two extremes collide and writes out of the resulting fissure.

"After the 'Three Characters'" describes an experience of going through a tunnel and emerging on the other side:

> After I went thru the tunnel
> & saw the unity no more
> I cried loudly.
>> I had confronted
>> the chaotic world.

After this early description of movement into "the chaotic world," however, nearly half of the poem remains in the past tense, in the world before the tunnel. This world is characterized by light, a light the speaker misses terribly on the other side:

> W/out light I cldnt
> see images thru wch
> I sought forms

The light before the tunnel serves to illuminate images; in poetic terms, this is the world of Pound's Image, and it is figured in the past tense. Thus, the speaker describes learning the lesson of Imagism, that a method can be learned through this light, and Leung has given us a shorthand for Pound's Imagist revolution.

The poem goes on to detail the poet's study of the image:

As I learned more,
I REALized the images/
(REALity)
wch went thru the symbols
as light thru a prism
were being crystallized &
    formalized:
        the sun rises
        behind a tree
        wch is the "EAST.")

The poet learns that the images are themselves reality, and, more important, that if reality is imagined as light, notably the light of this pre-tunnel existence, it is a reality "crystallized & / formalized." By virtue of this process of filtering the light through the prism just as reality is pushed through the symbol, the real may be presented in the poem. Leung shows us Pound's fantasy of presenting the real in poetry, refined through a formalizing light.

Leung reminds us of Pound's famous deconstruction of the ideogram for "east." Pound, we recall, described the finished character as "sun tangled in the tree's branches, as at sunrise, meaning now the East." In reciting this moment, Leung points to the fact of the sun as a light shining through the tree: we imagine not just the layering of different ideograms on top of each other as in Pound's example; we see what has become of the initial light. Leung traces the shapes made by the light, a light that will be lost once we pass into the tunnel and out to the post-Imagist world: the light of the sun scattered and ordered through the branches of the tree has been formalized and crystallized into an Image. Leung's version is a further abbreviation of Pound's reference to Fenollosa; he doesn't bother showing us the ideograms that Fenollosa and Pound reasoned were components of the character for east, and the light itself—which I read as an unwavering faith in the ideogram—emerges as the primary force behind the Image. In fact, as Leung's poem progresses, he shows us the evolution of the Chinese word for "east," from its supposed primitive origins to its present appearance in simplified Chinese.[16] Leung's etymology stands as a corrective to the fanciful etymologies that Fenollosa saw in the Chinese sign, and his presentation of the evolution of the Chinese character proceeds apace with the poem's elaboration of the changing fate of Pound's Image as it took hold in American poetry.

Leung presents the next step in thinking through the Image:

> Later, characters traveled
> beyond themselves
> & became the subject matter
> of a work of art.
>
> A deep emotion about
> a flying bird.
>
> The imagination of
> an ideal bird wch
> stands as still as itself—the ideal language—

In what happens after this "later" we see the conflation of the reality of the image and its automatic status as art. Leung's mention of "deep emotion" recalls the "intellectual and emotional complex" of Imagism, and the equation of ideal bird and ideal language leads us to the fantasy of an ideal poetic language that Fenollosa and Pound found encapsulated in Chinese writing. This identity between ideal bird and ideal language catapults the figure into movement.

The notion of the "characters traveled / beyond themselves" reminds us of the "third character," the ideogram for horse that Ernest Fenollosa delighted in seeing galloping off the page. This horse appears in the next section of Leung's poem:

> I see a horse
> run across
> a bar of
> my prison.

The liberation of this horse stands in stark contrast to the poet's prison. The horse has surpassed the poet; it has become a work of art despite itself; the poet has been left behind. Although the poet's imagination drives this written character beyond itself, through the force of his belief in the living properties of the image, the poet is left without it, locked in the prison of his own fantasy. Leung shows us the dangers of both Fenollosa's things working out their own fate and Pound's belief in his aesthetic method; one frees the horse, and the other imprisons the poet.

The horse appears on the prison bars, and by this time we have returned to the present tense and the "chaotic world" after the tunnel. The horse, which had been born in the light of the previous world, now runs free outside of it. As Leung writes:

> The horse evolves
> as I evolve
>
> But I can see it
> no more.
>
> A car runs
> across my eyes
> (It reminds of the old
> RED WHEELBARROW)

The horse outruns the poet, turning into something a world away from Fenollosan fantasy—a car. The appearance of William Carlos Williams' red wheelbarrow is a bit surprising here; I can imagine it in the other world of modernism's light. Yet perhaps even by the time that Williams applied Imagist innovation to his art in *Spring and All* in 1923, in which he published his now-famous image of the red wheelbarrow, the horse had already evolved away; Williams took Imagism's fascination with the Orient and evacuated his image of Oriental content, creating instead an image suited to a nativist vision of America. It may be that the horse had escaped already for Williams, just ten years after Pound's Imagist manifesto.

At this point the poet turns and sees the "character: RETURN." This return to the world of light, of balance, of image, however, is impossible: "But the horse wants / to race & / wants to be a superhorse / competing in the computer world." The leap from horse to car to computer is sealed in a parenthetical remark:

> {One told me, "the world is of computers, of numbers
> 101010 . . . to simplify our language is good for development . . .
> easier to be learned by the machine-brain . . . "}

In the chaotic world, this is the chilling endpoint of the Image: the ideal language imagined through the ideogram finds a truly ideal machine language. We see that what emerges when "characters traveled / beyond themselves" is an image that no longer needs the artist—and what falls away from the poem is emotion itself. The original complex of intellect and emotion falls apart in the waning of modernism's light in the chaotic world beyond the tunnel. The poem closes:

> We can't return, but
> where can/will we go?
>
> a loose horse

The unleashed fantasy of the ideogram can't be retrieved, and Asian American poets in particular must negotiate a field with the dangers of "a loose horse."

A New Image

The formal fantasies of Imagism have imprisoned the poet and left us with a character that flees art. Leung's second poem in the anthology, however, provides a surprising kind of answer to the final question of "After the 'Three Characters.'" "A Symphonic Poem: 'Unfinished'" is a surprisingly direct love poem. It opens in what seems like the desolation of the end of the previous poem:

> Walking on a
> bare mountain
> in the Western night.
>
> Nothing is left,
> except an unstable
> image with a pair of
> blinking EYES.

What seems like another dangerous terrain, a specifically Western terrain, with another treacherous and movable image, becomes something rather different in the course of this poem. These "EYES," we will discover, are in fact two first-person "I"s, two people walking next to each other on the "bare mountain."

The question of the lyric "I" is a complicated one for Asian American poets: the activists unleashed their voices, following the lead of the American

romantic resurgence in the fifties, in which the poetic "I" could commune
with the world in order to express its howl against it.[17] The Poundian first
person vacillates from almost no "I" at all—R. P. Blackmur indicts Pound
for his masks, the different consciousnesses his poetry adopts in the service
of producing a purified art[18]—to the *ego scriptor cantilenae*, the irascible
artist whose astonishing will created an epic with ambitions beyond poetry.
Leung's poem shows us two "I"s, thereby avoiding privileging both the "I" of
Pound's epic and that of activist poetry; this lyric "I" is, ultimately, a part of
the poem and the particular kind of image it creates. It is Leung's innovation
to embed his "I" into a surprising and lovely new kind of image beyond the
limits of Imagism.

Leung's image is unstable because it is composed of two moving people,
not because it is ready to bolt away. The beauty of this image proves to us that
images can still be art and yet not become dangerous, but only if the image
includes the poet himself, thus barring its escape from him. In exchange for
the dangers of the Image in the previous poem, however, this image remains
unsteady and tenuous:

> Both of us are
> > in the West &
> > feel bound
> > > in cells.

This is still the world of the prison bars, but the poet finds a moment
that "belongs to us":

> At 5:59.59
> you're willing
> to look at this I.

It is literally a vanishing moment, and this precise time-telling reminds
us of Imagism's "instant of time": we remember that that was how long an
image lasted. For Pound, the instant of time freed his image and lent it a
vital actuality; Leung knows that the image cannot transcend the cell, but
this momentary glance can offer a human connection. And "this I" is a part
of the poem who can be admired by the other "I" the poem has introduced to
us, on the bare Western mountain. Further, the ephemeral quality of these
two "I"s suggests the provisional nature of identity prevalent in minority
literature's theories of subject formation. This fragile and momentary
positioning has been carefully elaborated by Stuart Hall, in his argument

that cultural identity is "Not an essence but a *positioning*."[19] Perhaps the legacy of the modernist lyric can be uniquely useful for minority poets; in a post-activist era, the lyric can present more provisional formulations attentive to a constant destabilization of identity.

"A Symphonic Poem: 'Unfinished'" includes a few lines of Beethoven's opus 27, and the image, like the piano sonata, is a time-bound art; the unsteady image is more beautiful for its transitoriness. This poem demonstrates the negotiation of the poet in this world populated with loose horses, and in these two poems we see two sides of the legacy of Imagism: both the oversimplification and mechanization of the formula and the great beauty it can still produce if captured at the right moment. In particular, Leung suggests the possibilities of a human connection through the difficult art he's unflinchingly chosen to examine. These poems contend with the question of how to function in an artistic world without modernist light yet unable to free itself from its influence, and the lyrical innovation Leung lights upon uses the facts of his modernist inheritance in order to express both the difficulties and gains of facing this darkened world.

Ho Hon Leung's poems grapple with a difficult inheritance. The split second of his living image obeys Pound's Imagist dictates, but it is Leung's innovation to incorporate the poet himself and make his position visible through a newly imagined image. Leung never imagines that the poet can run free like the loose horse; it is simply never a possibility for his speaker and, in particular, for Asian American poets caught in the wake of this difficult legacy. Yet to examine aesthetic innovation shows us another way of considering the role of the Asian American poet; Leung shows us the flash of an image comprised of two "I"s on the bare mountain of the West, and the poet in this instance can see himself within the landscape of the poem. Through this renewal of the image, he finds a way of expressing his position within an aesthetics learned from the Orient.

9

"A New Rule for
the Imagination"

Rewriting Modernism in Bone

DONATELLA IZZO

> *"Call me Ishmael." See? You pictured a white guy, didn't
> you? . . .*
> *A new rule for the imagination: the common man has
> Chinese looks. From now on, whenever you read about those
> people with no surnames, color them with black skin or yellow
> skin.*
> —MAXINE HONG KINGSTON, TRIPMASTER MONKEY

EVER SINCE MY FIRST reading of Fae Myenne Ng's *Bone* when it was published in 1993, I was struck by its stylistic and compositional subtlety. Despite the deceptive simplicity of its prose, *Bone*—written over a ten-year span—is very far from documentary realism or autobiographical straightforwardness. Quite the reverse, the peculiarity of this novel seems to me to lie in its full, deliberate, and even openly displayed engagement with the structural, stylistic, and thematic features typical of some of the more canonical novels of mainstream American modernism, such as *The Great Gatsby*, *The Sound and the Fury*, or *Absalom, Absalom!*: a preoccupation with time as a philosophical, historical, and existential category and experimentation with temporal disruption in narrative discourse; an epistemological interest in subjectivity and perception, mirrored in a variety of treatments of narrative perspective and voice; a reliance on metaphor rather than metonymy as a favorite connective trope operating to create a coherent, spatialized texture for the novel; a metatextual self-awareness and self-reflexiveness.[1] One reviewer of *Bone* explicitly mentioned Fitzgerald's *The Great Gatsby*, and indeed there are several resemblances between the two texts, in terms of both their overall structure and the rich texture of their prose, which plays on the recurrence and variation of images and keywords revolving around the themes of memory, hope, and the promise and nightmare of America.[2]

My reading of *Bone*, however, does not aim at demonstrating the intertextual influence of Fitzgerald's novel on Ng's; while I believe that several echoes do exist between the two novels, my point is different. By highlighting the relevance of modernist compositional techniques to *Bone*, I will be taking it as a case study for the relation of the Asian American novel to modernist aesthetics—not just the aesthetics of modernist literature, but the ideology of the aesthetic as a separate sphere that modernist literature problematically elaborated, New Criticism refined into critical dogma, and today's literary theory frequently seems to have internalized even while reacting against it. What I hope to show is that engaging the aesthetic standards of modernism—as Asian American texts can and frequently do—does not automatically entail subscribing to an ideology of the aesthetic; that the kind of close reading traditionally applied to canonical modernist literary works can in fact enhance our perception of the aesthetic direction of Asian American texts; and that as the formal is never disjointed from the ideological, so does the aesthetic fully subsume the political—not in the sense of aesthetic transcendence, but quite the reverse, in the sense that an *aesthetic* engagement with the mainstream canon is simultaneously and inevitably a full engagement with the ideological, political, and racial issues underlying the canon's formation. Reading *Bone* as a self-aware rewriting of modernism, then, does not aim at claiming for it the canonical authority or aesthetic rarefaction of modernist texts, but at raising questions about the cultural significance of the novel's positioning vis-à-vis both the mainstream and the ethnic canon within an overdetermined literary space. What I will contend is, finally, that the relation of Asian American literary works to the dominant canon should not be represented as one-way—that is, as inevitably one of either aesthetic assimilation or political resistance to the gravitational tug of an inherently more powerful dominant literary model. Indeed, confronting the canon can be an empowering move, enabling the ethnic author to shape it in his or her turn. As suggested by the "new rule for the imagination" tactically proposed by Wittman Ah-Sing in *Tripmaster Monkey*, learning to visualize the narrator of the American epic *par excellence* as black or yellow-skinned can be a way to "conjure up and inscribe our faces on the blank pages and screens of America's hegemonic culture."[3]

One Mile Forward and Eight Miles Back: Compositional Structure and the Quest for Origins

> We were a family of three girls. By Chinese standards, that wasn't lucky. In Chinatown, everyone knew our story. Outsiders jerked their chins, looked at us, shook their heads. We heard things.
>
> "A failed family. That Dulcie Fu. And you know which one: bald Leon. Nothing but daughters."[4]

The "hermeneutic code," as Roland Barthes termed it, takes center stage from the very inception of *Bone*: "everyone knew our story"—there is a story to be learnt, as yet undisclosed to the reader, whose task it will be to reconstruct and interpret it.[5] It takes about ten pages for the narrating voice and eldest sister Leila to mention Ona's suicide, the focal point of the narrative's attempt to probe and reconstruct the chain of occurrences, the "story" or "stories" (a constantly recurring word) leading to that event. "Why" is constantly echoing in the novel (not just with reference to Ona's death): interweaving questions and answers are played out on different planes and in different registers, producing the persistent interrogative mode that haunts the narrative.

The hermeneutic quest produces a retrospective orientation through the backward movement of the narrator's memory. The fourteen chapters move gradually backward from the present, first to the immediate antecedents of the opening scene (Leila's return to Chinatown and her search for Leon Leong and Mah to announce her New York marriage to Mason Louie), then to the mourning, conflict, and anguish following Ona's death, then to the news of Ona's suicide, and beyond that, to the events that might have caused it, and to the earliest memories of the three sisters' childhood. This overall shift from the present to the past, however, is effected in a far from mechanical fashion: each chapter interlaces different chronological layers, offering short anticipations of episodes that will be extensively presented later and inserting memories of earlier incidents. The last chapter brings us back to the recent past, only to proceed to the remotest chronological fragments of both Leila's and her family's story (Mah's first marriage to Leila's father and their immigration to the United States), and then opens out toward the future, in the final scene of Leila leaving Chinatown to live with Mason—a future, however, that was already past at the beginning of the novel.

This structural pattern, arranging the *récit* in an order that reverses the diegetic unfolding of events, bears some further attention. While recalling the retrospective structure that is one of the more familiar patterns of the modernist novel, the treatment of narrative time in *Bone* has implications that both contradict and complicate the modernist emphasis on temporal disruption. The latter has mostly been read in connection with the attempt to subsume existence into aesthetic transcendence and time into spatial form, evading the "nightmare of history" into the timeless perfection of art or the atemporal flow of inner subjectivity, both capable of giving order and significance to the otherwise meaningless fragmentation of life. As for the hermeneutic task of reconstructing and interpreting the past that *Bone* shares with a tradition ranging from *Heart of Darkness* to *Absalom, Absalom!*, this has been customarily related to the primacy of the cognitive sphere in the modernist novel from James onward, and to its prevalently epistemological orientation, foregrounding and questioning the relation of the individual subject to perception and knowledge.

The backward quest in *Bone*, however, partakes neither of traditional historicism nor of the teleological detection pattern that William V. Spanos associates with modernism as the epitome of Western onto-theology. It discovers no final explanation, unearths no inexorable logic or necessary concatenation, produces no transcendental panoptical vantage point from which events may be reviewed and revised in their inherent order and meaning—rather, it offers a multiplication of intertwined, contradictory subjective explanations: Mah's reading of Ona's suicide in terms of guilt—her own for her "bad choices" (51) and her affair with Tommie Hom, the owner of the sweatshop, and Leila's for the "bad example" she set her younger sister by leaving home to go and live with Mason; Leon's twofold explanation, both in terms of traditional Chinese culture (the "bad luck" brought by his failure to ship his adoptive father's bones back to China) and of America's failure to fulfill its promises; Leila's conflicted and contradictory effort to interpret Ona's suicide as an act of free will by reiterating the notion of "choice," simultaneously emphasizing the opposite notion of Ona's yielding to the inescapability of family pressures, outer prevarication, or fate.

More important, the analeptic narrative structure of *Bone*, while contradicting its more customary associations in mainstream modernist aesthetics, takes on specific connotations in terms of the Asian American literary tradition. The primacy of a retrospective cognitive quest and its simultaneous failure both tend to sabotage the stereotypes traditionally associated with Asian American literature as primarily centering on a quest for origins and/or identity. Indeed, the very notion of origins is undermined here. In spite of its interrogative, retrospective thrust, the narrative does not achieve its Quest. No point of origin, no final cause is found: "narrative reversal works to criticize the overdevelopment of temporal contextualization as a source of meaning" and *"causality* as a means of investigation is disorganized."[6] The quest for origins is simultaneously evoked and denied in episode after episode: the search for Leon's "true" documents, resulting in the discovery of a document that is nothing but the attestation of a fictitious, although legally valid identity; the search for Grandpa Leong's tomb, eventually leading to a ritual gesture of faith rather than knowledge ("Bow to the family headstone, it's all the same, the right gesture will find your grandfather" [78]); and finally, Leila's own quest for her origins, in hopes of gaining acknowledgment and getting explanations from the father who abandoned her as a child, and who in the end will only send his greetings. All causes, all origins are confused and irrecoverable: there are no overarching entities, no transcendent horizons (be they individual, familial, or national) capable of providing experience with a final sense or significance, but only successive layers of events, memories, and interpretations.

If narrative fragmentation and retrospection do not eventually allow for either a univocal causal reconstruction of the past or an epiphanic moment of transcendence of time into higher understanding, no more successful is the quest for identity: family, community, and nation equally fail to offer any linear path or unambiguous landmark. China is virtually absent from the scene, and unlike many other successful Chinese American novels, *Bone* features it as neither mythical and legendary nor fantastic and baroque, yielding to neither Orientalistic nor nostalgic fantasy. America is less a mythical promise than a lusterless daily actuality. Community is experienced as both supportive (its help in coping with mourning over Ona's death) and oppressive (its social control and omnipresent gossip).[7] Family genealogies, in turn, are mixed, broken, and uncertain: Leon is not Grandpa Leong's son but just his paper son; Leila is not Leon's daughter but the daughter of Mah's first husband; there is even a hint that Ona's father may not be Leon but Tommie Hom.

Identity in *Bone*, then, is less the heritage of blood or nation than the daily negotiation of one's place in a shared network of emotions and events. The narrator's identity, in particular, seems to emerge only as a response to and elaboration of the events concerning the suicide sister, the family, and the family's position in a societal network. Indeed, as we read on the very first page of the novel, "it's time that makes a family, not just blood" (3)—a statement that underscores the performative, anti-essentialistic construal of identity throughout the novel. While foregrounding an accumulative notion of time that counters the modernist evasion of temporality through spatialization, this reliance on time as productive of unpredictable patterns of identity simultaneously subverts both the traditional Chinese emphasis on blood and family connections and the American myth of the Chinese as a "model minority" drawing sustenance and support through hardships from its reliance on close family ties and traditional patriarchal structures. Indeed, rather than the (re)construction of a viable identity through the appropriation of an assimilatory pattern or the recollection of an ethnic patrimony, *Bone* seems to feature a scrupulous deconstruction of both. A metaphor of separation and consequently of the underlying theme of the novel,[8] Ona's suicide can also be read as a metaphor for the deconstruction of a monological (Ona = one?) model for identity, her literal fragmentation figuring the explosion and erasure of the colored body, that is, of an identity submitted to the authority of ethnic tradition, while also functioning as an emblem of the threat of self-destruction inherent in too radical an attempt at escape.

Individual identity, thus, is finally presented as one's place in a narrative network:

> We're lucky, not like the bondmaids growing up in service, or the newborn daughters whose mouths were stuffed with ashes. The beardless, softshouldered eunuchs, the courtesans with the three-inch feet and the frightened child brides—they're all stories to us. Nina, Ona, and I, we're the lucky generation. Mah and Leon forced themselves to live through the humiliation in this country so that we could have it better. We know so little of the old country. We repeat the names of grandfathers and uncles, but they have always been strangers to us. Family exists only because somebody has a story, and knowing the story connects us to a history. To us, the deformed man is oddly compelling, the forgotten man is a good story, and a beautiful woman suffers (35–6).

Stories and history are thus presented as closely connected: only through stories can history be experienced and acknowledged, whether by the younger generation of Chinese Americans or by the mainstream reader of the novel itself. Rather than serving to evade or devalue history in modernist fashion, the fragmentation of narrative continuity in *Bone* seems to obey the opposite project of recovering a history disrupted by immigration and investigating its relevance to the self. While the horizon the novel outlines is fully historical, however, its notion of history is a neo-historicist rather than a historicist one, in that the truth value of narratives is ultimately unattainable. The impossibility to sort out "the real" and "the fake" is thus reconceptualized not as mystification, as Frank Chin would have it, nor as postmodernist interrogation of the ontology of narrative, but as the distinguishing trait of a whole generation, born and raised in America, as well as a condition main-stream readers inevitably share.[9]

The modernist interrogation on the subject's epistemological predica-ment thus takes on a specific ethnic twist. History exists in *Bone* and, as Jameson would put it, "it hurts." Although it is conveyed and experienced through narrative, history—the novel makes it clear—cannot be reduced to mere textuality. Rather, it is the lasting weight of the former generation's material oppression, economic struggle, and individual sacrifice extending into the next generation's awareness and guilt: "What wasn't simple was my guilt about having a better life than Mah" (12). The past reaches out into the present, as Leila realizes when visiting the recently immigrated families of her pupils:

Being inside their cramped apartments depresses me. I'm reminded that we've lived like that, too. The sewing machine next to the television, the rice bowls stacked on the table, the rolled-up blankets pushed to one side of the sofa. Cardboard boxes everywhere, rearranged and used as stools or tables or homework desks. The money talk at dinnertime, the list of things they don't know or can't figure out. Cluttered rooms. Bare lives. Every day I'm reminded nothing's changed about making a life or raising kids. Everything is hard (17).

The depressing similarity between the lives of the former immigrants and of the new ones points to the inexorable continuity of immigration as an enduring economic structure rather than mere personal experience. Con-tradicting the hidden teleology inherent in the whole tradition of immigrant autobiographies, which portray the individual's economic progress and suc-cessful assimilation, *Bone* unveils the serial, repetitive quality of the immi-grant experience when regarded in terms of ethnic community, that is, of the continuing circulation and exploitation of the workforce on the labor mar-ket. Thus, the denial of linearity inherent in the fragmentation of narrative temporality acquires the added implication of a denial of the self-enclosed teleology of the one-way assimilationist narrative.

Memory, then, far from being a question of subjective psychological expe-rience, is the necessary link connecting the present to the past, the fictional to the historical, the individual to the collective dimension of experience: "Remembering the past gives power to the present. Memories do add up" (89). Unlike the prevalently epistemological orientation of modernist ret-rospection, the backward movement of narrative in *Bone* has an eminently political import: it stages the narrator's, and sets the stage for the reader's confrontation with a past that is not presented as irrecoverable on philosophical or psychological grounds—as an insoluble hermeneutical problem or a lost and not fully comprehended experience—but rather as the lasting object of an unremitting negotiation. Only by moving backward can one hope to move forward, as the recurring image of the ship moving through the ocean suggests: "Ships are massive, but the ocean has simple superiority. Leon described the power: One mile forward and eight miles back" (145). In spite of the powerful pressure of the ocean, signaling the massive resistance offered by material conditions and the weight of the past, the ship never ceases to exert pressure in her turn. Retrospection, then, is the paradoxical sign of an unrelenting will to move forward: "And all our promises, like all our hopes, move us through life with the power of an ocean liner pushing through the sea" (193).

Paper is Blood: The Texture of Language

Bone is, in its structural complexity, a demanding novel for the reader, who is required to be at once intellectually alert and emotionally empathetic, as well as capable of practicing the arts of memory on her own. The novel's linguistic texture is just as demanding: its prose, while deceptively simple, is very closely knitted and intense. Syntactically there is a prevalence of simple, short, and direct sentences; the register is mostly denotative. However, this apparent dryness is the result not of poverty, but rather of utmost condensation. The formal restraint lends each sentence an extreme intensity, and the bone-like essentiality of the prose makes each word stand out in relief, endowed with a precise and powerful significance. Simultaneously, though, the novel weaves these simple words into a closely knit texture of recurrences. Keywords acquire strong symbolic overtones by being repeatedly employed on different planes and with different implications; they are not congealed once and for all into a univocal meaning or symbolic equivalence, but travel through the text, interact with each other, and multiply their resonances, in ways that are not unlike some of Henry James's uses of imagery in his later phase. Needless to say, both styles of diction fully belong in the mainstream tradition of modernist experimentation: again, it is as if Ng were simultaneously drawing inspiration from Hemingway's terse conciseness and from Fitzgerald's reliance on a rich metaphorical fabric.

Metaphor, as several critics have shown, is one of the devices whereby modernism creates a spatialized perception of the novel. By creating a linguistic system of coherence independent of the progression of the plot, metaphor contrasts linearity, that is, temporality, and enhances instead a perception of the work of art as simultaneous, foregrounding its self-referential, linguistic quality and its evocative capacity to transcend contingency by association. Ng's use of metaphor, however, is different: while certainly providing the text with depth, coherence, and linguistic self-awareness in ways that are fully within the mainstream of modernist diction, the recurrent images in *Bone* systematically point to the material conditions of immigrant life and, simultaneously, to the novel's way of negotiating its textual relation to these conditions.

Virtually each word in *Bone* creates an isotopy, and virtually each isotopy connects terms endowed with a strong symbolic, universalizing import to the concrete realities of Chinese American experience. While each of these lexical clusters would reward separate consideration, I will now concentrate on those strands of the imagery that to my mind more directly connect the formal texture of the novel with its ways of negotiating the Chinese American experience.[10] Foremost among these is food. Associated with the mother figure, food articulates a number of material, psychological, and cultural implications, intertwining in a complex way sweetness and bitterness, love and death, ritual and guilt, never yielding to those exoticizing ethno-gastronomic descriptions that Frank Chin has stigmatized as "food pornography."[11] In the immigrant's subsistence economy, food stands first and foremost for survival and/or for economic failure (as witness the unsold merchandise getting stale on the shelves of Mah and Leon's grocery in Chapter Twelve). In connection with food, Mah appears capable of dispensing in turn love (the family celebrations, the banquets for Leon's return) and death (the skinned frog, the birds and fish raised in the house to eat). Chinese food is both healing ("bringing the right foods was as delicate as saying the right words" [105]) and oppressive, tied as it is with tradition (the wedding banquet Leila refuses) and family obligations: "How can I tell her my tastes have changed, like everything else?" (48). It has nothing to do with pleasure or gastronomic exoticism, and everything to do with exploitation and social subalternity:

> When I suggested Chinatown, Nina said it was too depressing. "The food's good," she said, "but the life's hard down there. I always feel like I should rush through a rice plate and then rush home to sew culottes or assemble radio parts or something."
>   I agreed. At Chinatown places, you can only talk about the bare issues. . . . "I don't want to eat guilt," Nina said (26).

Feelings and family relationships in turn have a taste and fragrance: the bitter taste of ginseng, constantly connected to Mah and to China, as well as to the humiliation of an immigrant's life—"only a bowl of bitterness to show for his life as a coolie" (148)—and Leila's heritage of shame and suffering due to her abandonment by her father (whose name, Fu, sounds like "bitter" in their original dialect). Guilt, however, is also related to a secret core of sweetness:

> Fault. In English or in Cantonese, that was the word we were all afraid of. I held it like a seed in my mouth. As kids, the three of us loved to suck on dried plums. Long after the sour and salty fruit dissolved, the seed stayed sweet, the true secret. Now I was afraid my secret guilt would start to grow sweet, and I would never want to spit it out (106).

And the association seed-secret is again played out with reference to Ona, "holding the seeds of herself secret from us" (112). Secrecy, in turn, is presented as another ambivalent cultural trait, connecting the collective fear of the first, newly immigrated generation with the wish for privacy of the new, Americanized one: "They were always saying, Don't tell this and don't tell that. . . . We graduated from keeping their secrets to keeping our own" (112).

Thus the manifold implications of food, by way of the immigrant condition and the older generation's defensive emphasis on secrecy, connect to Ona's secret and to the hermeneutic quest and interrogative thrust of the novel. Equally linked to food is the core image exhibited from the very title of the novel, recurring from first to last page, and played out in a variety of meanings and associations. The author has stressed its assonance with the Chinese term for "good" and its implications of resistance and endurance, which she associates with the older generation's virtues;[12] she has also pointed out that the Chinese character for "bone," resembling an abstract human figure, was for her a source of inspiration, the image wrapping together the pain pervading the novel and the separation that is its main theme, of which Ona's suicide is a metaphor.[13] A recurrent use of the word centers on Grandpa Leong's bones and consequently looks backward to China as the "old world": the old-timers' wish to retrace their journey after death and Leon's superstition that his failure to grant his paper father's wish has brought them bad luck, all seem to point to a continuity of belief between the present and the past. Again, however, continuity is denied and the past, fragmented and scattered, is literally irrecoverable, as the graves have been disinterred and the bones regrouped and reburied. Witnessing to the novel's problematic position vis-à-vis Chinese tradition, bones are also related to the traditional beliefs that connect the individual to ancestors and to heavenly powers,[14] thus making Ona's jump from the thirteenth floor of a building not just a terribly self-destructive gesture, but also a gesture that wilfully destroys her connection with the past, and particularly with the father and with the whole Confucian tradition.[15]

One of the most evocative uses of the bone image is again related to the mother-food nexus, Leila's memory of her mother sucking the bones of pigeons after giving her daughters the meaty parts: "'Bones are sweeter than you know'" (30). Apart from the usual associations with the mother figure (her love and self-sacrifice but also her formidable power of dealing death within the family) and with the ambiguity of sweetness—whose plea-sures arise from meatlessness, that is, from economy and dearth, but are also claimed as value: "'Clean bones . . . No waste'" (31)—this use of the metaphor is worth noting for its metatextual reverberations. The same bone-like essentiality—everything functional, no waste—applies of course to the novel itself, whose very title is meant to underscore the self-referential impli-cation of the image. Bones stand for architectural precision and essentiality of design: toward the end of the novel, they are connected to the mother's craft as a seamstress—"Mah knew all the seams of a dress the way a doctor knows bones" (178)—a craft in turn related to the storytelling accompanying the sewing-ladies' work and to the author's own: as Ng herself has declared, "learning to sew helped me learn to write."[16]

The last lexical cluster that I propose to examine shares the same poly-semic metatextual radiation. "Paper" is a word recurring in a dazzling variety of meanings: from the more ordinary ones—the pink butcher paper, the newspapers, the pupils' papers, the construction paper for an art class—, through the paper money ritually burnt at Chinese traditional funerals and the papers required by the cemetery administration to start the search for Grandpa Leong's tomb, to the police papers associated to Ona's death, an-other paper ritual impersonally regulating death in the American world. Prominent among them all, of course, are the heterogeneous but equally meaningful papers carefully kept in Leon's suitcase, bearing witness to a lifetime of attempts and failures: the documents that made him a paper son, the letters recording his adoptive country's lifelong rejection, the pho-tos and aerograms collected during his travels, the family memorabilia, the receipts and IOUs, the paper clippings: "From *The Chinese Times*: a pic-ture of Confucius, a Japanese soldier with his bayonet aimed at a Chinese woman, ration lines in Canton, gold lines in Shanghai. From *Life* magazine: Hitler, Charlie Chaplin, the atom bomb" (59). Ranging from literal, legally valid but false identification papers, to fragmentary scraps evidencing the constructed, tentative, and heterogeneous process of identity formation across two cultures, Leon's papers—as Thomas Kim argues, drawing on Butler, Fuss, and Foucault—bear witness to Ng's anti-essentialistic critique of subject-formation.[17] Leon's wish to keep his papers is presented as the result of both his traditional Chinese respect for everything written and his wish to appropriate the new country: old and new, memory and hope, backward and forward movement, again are one and the same: "These letters marked his time and they marked his endurance. Leon was a paper son. And this paper son saved every single scrap of paper. I remember his telling me about a tradition of honoring paper, how the oldtimers believed all writing was sacred" (58). While performing their deconstructive task, though, the papers simultaneously display an extraordinary connective power both at the stylistic and at the conceptual level. A single word links traditional China and contemporary America, personal and world history, death and daily life, the ancestors' traditions, the immigrants' suffering, and the children's Westernized lifestyle, truth and lies, memory and its different versions:

> The letters were stacked by year and rubberbanded into decades. I only had to open the first few to know the story: "We Don't Want You." . . .
>
> Leon had made up stories for us; so that we could laugh, so that we could understand the rejections. . . . Now, seeing the written reasons in a formal letter, the stories came back, without the humor, without hope. On paper Leon was not the hero.
>
> Maybe Leon should have destroyed these papers. They held a truth about a Leon I wasn't sure I wanted to know (58).

It is of course another paper product, the novel itself, that weaves together all meanings and versions of the word into a single complex texture, extending the paper son's respect for memory into the typically modern, secular, Western genre that is the novel. The older generation's stories are explicitly claimed by the narrator as her own at the end of Chapter Five: "For a paper son, paper is blood. . . . I'm the stepdaughter of a paper son and I've inherited this whole suitcase of lies. All of it is mine. All I have are those memories, and I want to remember them all" (61).

By claiming her inheritance of this "suitcase of lies," the narrator is using metaphor in a way that is both self-awarely metatextual and extremely political—a way that, as I have tried to show, is typical of the use of imagery in Ng's novel. The lies are, of course, the defensive lies enabling Leon to circumvent immigration laws, but also America, "this lie of a country" (103); they are the patrimony of stories, both personal and traditional, whose truth value cannot be either recovered or ascertained; and they are the "fake," that is, fictional stories that the choice of the novel as a form produces. While endowing the novel with a degree of coherence, self-referentiality, and self-awareness in every way comparable to those of the more celebrated modernist masterpieces, Ng's metaphors do not construe the work of art as a separate transcendent world. Quite the reverse, they emphasize the ways in which *Bone* is *both* a work of art, an aesthetic product capable of self-referentially drawing attention to its style, rules of composition, and aesthetic assumptions, *and* a political work intent on confronting, rather than sublimating, the harsh actualities of its subject in an ever-renewed performance of memory and storytelling.

Backdaire: Conquering New Spaces

As the willing inheritor of a heterogeneous, cross-cultural suitcase of narrative, Leila is primarily defined by her relation to her inheritance, not just as a past to be recovered and understood but also as a present to be negotiated and performed. As the narrating voice, she is further committed to sharing what knowledge she gains in the process with us as readers, acting as the mediator of the experience she is in the process of discovering, interpreting, and organizing. In that, her function is no different from the statutory function of the typical autodiegetic narrator of early twentieth-century fiction. What does make a difference, however, is that in this case the narrator's mediation is not just cognitive, but linguistic and cultural, and that her function as mediator between the diegetic world and the reader is mirrored by her function *within* the diegetic world, pointing to potential and actual communicative problems that reverberate from the narrative world to the relation it entertains with its readers.

Indeed, Leila's role is that of an institutional mediator throughout: a "go-between" (53) for her mother and Leon; a telephone intermediary with her sister in New York; a dutiful daughter shuttling "back and forth between Mah and Mason" (50) to reconcile her family duty with her wish for independence; and finally, a linguistic and cultural translator, not just for her parents but also, officially, between immigrant Chinese parents and their children's school: "my job is about being the bridge between the classroom teacher and the parents . . . opening up a line of communication" (16). From the very beginning, two separate worlds interact within and through Leila: "My middle sister, Ona, jumped off the M floor of the Nam. The police said she was on downers. But I didn't translate that for Mah or tell her everything else I heard, because by then I was all worn-out from dealing with death in two languages" (14–15). The linguistic and cultural split between the two worlds is reproduced in the binary spatial arrangement of the novel, entirely organized around opposites: America and China, San Francisco and New York, Chinatown and Mission (where Leila moves with Mason), Salmon Alley (Mah's house) and the San Fran Hotel (where Leon takes shelter).

Not surprisingly, then, Leila's job is described as "being the bridge" (16). Bridges—a literal presence in San Francisco, but also a metaphor for transit and communication—are mentioned everywhere in the novel, and never unproblematically. The dual arrangement of space offers no easy positioning, nor is mediation a comfortable stance. An essential medium, the bridge is also, however, a problematic and unstable place to be: "Rush hour, and we were stuck in the middle of it: the late-afternoon glare, the heat, the thick gasoline smell of idling motors, the tension of everyone wanting to be anywhere else but on that bridge" (113)—incidentally, "stuck in the middle" (139) is also the expression used to describe Ona's position, leading her to suicide. Characters look for escape along less limited routes: Leon sailing the ocean; Nina traveling as a flight attendant; Ona inexorably "flying through the air" (106) in her fatal jump; Leila "flying" or "sailing" riding fast along the freeway (42).[18]

Still, while recognizing the uncomfortableness of transitionality and the limits of translatability— "I have a whole different vocabulary of feeling in English than in Chinese, and not everything can be translated" (18)—the novel articulates a patient, obstinate work of transition and translation. The whole narrative in *Bone* is a sort of literary and linguistic bridge, an act of "translation" echoing the well-known closing sentence of *The Woman Warrior*. But one should not take it for granted—as most white readers may be inclined to do—that this bridge is a one-way structure, a Chinese-English translation of which mainstream readers are the obvious addressees. A narrative act is always an act of interpellation that simultaneously positions both its narrator and its narratees with respect to the diegetic and, implicitly, to the outer world; we should ask, therefore, where is the narrating voice speaking from, and where does her narrative act position us as readers?

Riding in a car with Mah and Leon immediately after announcing Ona's death, Leila briefly looks at Chinatown from the outside:

From the low seats of the Camaro, I looked out at the streets and saw the spidery writing on the store signs, the dressed-up street lamps with their pagoda tops, the oddly matched colors: red with green, green with aqua blue, yellow with pink.

Looking out, I thought, So this is what Chinatown looks like from inside those dark Greyhound buses; this slow view, these strange color combinations, these narrow streets, this is what tourists come to see. I felt a small lightening up inside, because I knew, no matter what people saw, no matter how close they looked, our inside story is something entirely different. I knew the dangers of closing up, but I didn't care. Right then, I didn't want people looking in at us. I wanted to slide down deeper into myself; I wanted to hide from everything (144–5).

A complex *mise en abyme* of point of view, this passage closely echoes similar moments of doubled vision in *The Great Gatsby*; instead of the modernistic subjectivism of point of view, though, it foregrounds its ethnic and cultural positionality. The "small lightening up inside" operates as an epiphany relating to the cultural function of the narrative act and of its reception. Simultaneously positioned *within* and *without* Chinatown, in endless transition between both, Leila as narrator defines herself as neither a "native informant" nor an assimilated "honorary white"; moreover, in a dizzy act of identification and disidentification with different spaces that produce different, ethnically marked reading protocols, she projects herself as reader, and projects her readership as sharply polarized between an "inside" and an "outside," adumbrating the possibility that the two readerships ultimately read two different texts.

What such a passage tells us is that, if this novel is a bridge, it is no bridge into Chinatown for complacent literary tourists to cross. Like the unuttered pain of loss and separation, the "inside story" of an ethnic community can neither be perceived by a fleeting glance from the outside nor be displayed from the inside—nor, indeed, as the unanswered question on Ona's death shows, is it so univocal and self-transparent as to be entirely contained, subsumed, and represented in each of its component "stories." Even though "the dangers of closing up" are explicitly denounced as a temporary, regressive temptation, the silence, secrets, and unuttered answers echoing throughout the novel are possibly the sign of a programmatic limit—a psychological, epistemological, linguistic, and cultural limit to translatability. After all, as Leila states at one point, "not everything can be translated" (18). To my mind, this is not the limit of the ineffable, but rather of restraint—a reserve pertaining as much to Leila's in-between position as to the novel's way of relating, linguistically and culturally, both to the Chinese American community and to the mainstream canon and readership.

Throughout the novel, there is a constant emphasis on the ambivalent involvement of language both in emotional and in power relations. This is made clear in the Social Security episode in Chapter Five, where Leila bitterly realizes that Leon's bursting out into curse "like a string of firecrackers popping" (56) only replays the cursing he had himself undergone by his shipmates. While Leon's linguistic violence can hardly be seen as a mutual relation, and recalls rather Stephen Greenblatt's reading of Caliban's "learning to curse,"[19] the overall power relation between the two languages is depicted as reciprocal, neither ethnically polarized nor axiologically oriented toward assimilation. English, it is true, is the language conveying the political and administrative authority of U.S. institutions, but Leila is herself part of that system, and English gives her authority vis-à-vis the latest immigrants; conversely, though, Chinese is the language of interpersonal relations, and her inferior knowledge of it sets her at a disadvantage whenever she has to personally confront either immigrant families or her mother: "What could I say? Using Chinese was my undoing. She had a world of words that were beyond me" (22).

In other words, if bilingualism inevitably underlies the project of translation, it just as inevitably undermines it, articulating separateness even while building communicative bridges. While written in English, *Bone* is tuned, as the author herself has declared, to the sound and cadence of Cantonese; its language is interspersed with homophonies and puns between Chinese and English that can only be perceived by bilingual readers.[20] The same applies to biculturalism. The assumed encyclopedia of the audience and the author's chosen affiliation are signaled by an underlying texture of references to the Chinese American literary tradition—from Edith Eaton/Sui Sin Far, after whom Leila's school is named, to the episodes and expressions evoking other classics like Chu's *Eat a Bowl of Tea* and Kingston's *The Woman Warrior*. Simultaneously, though, the novel's way of engaging the expectations of its readers is a critical one. In spite of its partly autobiographical content, *Bone* presents itself from its very cover as "a novel," a genre definition that should not be underestimated in view of the polemical debates that have accompanied the question of autobiography and fiction in Chinese American literature. Rather than aiming at authenticity or a documentary effect, the book offers on the copyright page the ritual disclaimer "*Bone* is a work of fiction. Names, characters, places, and incidents either are the products of the author's imagination or are used fictitiously. Any resemblance to events or persons, living or dead, is entirely coincidental." The full fictional quality claimed for the text officially seals its recourse to the stylistic and compositional resources consecrated by the modernist "art of fiction." The insistent recalling of the most celebrated loci of the early twentieth-century American canon—such as, as will be seen, the closing paragraph of *The Great*

Gatsby—should not be taken as a perfunctory literary homage, or else as an act of complaisance or capitulation to the mainstream reader's literary tastes. Rather, I think it should be taken as a conscious challenge.

In order to better illustrate the terms of this challenge, let me now take up one character I have not hitherto analyzed, Leila's fiancé and then husband, Mason. A skilled mechanic, a *homo faber*, who unlike Leon "finishes whatever he starts" (19), Mason does not live in Chinatown; he is represented as neither traditionalist nor forgetful, neither macho nor subaltern, neither aggressively militant nor a doomed loser—possibly an ideological role model for Chinese American manhood, Ng's response to the polemical debate on gender representation in Chinese American literature.[21] In the last chapter, while preparing to leave the house in Salmon Alley and Chinatown, Leila briefly comments on Mason's attitude to the space that surrounds him:

> Mason is a little strange about having been born and raised in Chinatown; sometimes he's proud and sometimes he's not. Most of my other boyfriends didn't feel comfortable outside of Chinatown; they didn't even much like doing things outside the family. Mason likes to ski and he goes to Tahoe as much as he can. He doesn't care if he's the only Chinese guy on the expert runs; he knows he's good enough (183).

This young Chinese American who, aware of his personal worth, skis on the expert runs all alone seems to demand a metatextual reading: he is a proud manifesto, a self-aware invitation to try one's worth on the heights. If, as the author says, this is a novel about separation, the bridges it builds lead out of Chinatown, not in an invitation to reject it, but rather to conquer new spaces—geographical, cultural, and literary.

Conquering new spaces is what Ng does in her novel, where the adoption of a modernist aesthetics of rarefaction, selection, and control serves not to sublimate and transcend, but rather to unearth and investigate the archives of Chinese immigration, with all its material harshness and severe psychological, emotional, and intellectual traces. Negotiating a complex set of identifications and disidentifications with the spatial, symbolic, historical, and aesthetic terms of *both* dominant American culture *and* the cultural nationalism and essentialism of first-generation Chinese American literature, *Bone* simultaneously engages both. On one hand, by rewriting the Chinese American immigrant experience in terms of mainstream canonical literature, she defines the Chinese American cultural identity, as well as her own identity as a writer, in anti-essentialistic fashion, as an open-ended and layered process of affirmation, denial, and contestation. On the other hand, by rewriting the canonical literature of the United States in terms of Chinese American experience, by adopting its aesthetic standards, and by sounding out in a different ethnic context the controlling metaphors and evocative images that the mainstream has celebrated as its own heritage, she contests the alleged universality of the dominant canon and unveils the racial character of the "American dream."

The structural, linguistic, and metaphorical achievement of this process is the novel's ending, where Leila leaves Chinatown and her guilty feelings toward her mother behind and moves with Mason to a third space, neither Chinese nor white ("'No Chinese there, you know,' she said. 'There are some,' I said" [191]), neither ghetto nor assimilation:

> All my things fit into the back of Mason's cousin's Volvo. The last thing I saw as Mason backed out of the alley was the old blue sign, #2—4—6 UPDAIRE. No one has ever corrected it; someone repaints it every year. Like the oldtimer's photos, Leon's papers, and Grandpa Leong's lost bones, it reminded me to look back, to remember.
>
> I was reassured. I knew what I held in my heart would guide me. So I wasn't worried when I turned that corner, leaving the old blue sign, Salmon Alley, Mah and Leon—everything—backdaire.

This strongly symbolic finale explicitly echoes Fitzgerald's celebrated "so we beat on, boats against the current, borne back ceaselessly into the past" but simultaneously inverts its direction. Being chronologically prior to the opening of the novel, the closing sentence contradicts its teleological suggestion, while also positing itself as a final achievement—a beginning that is also an ending, an ending that is also a beginning. In a telling, final graphic synthesis of the process at work throughout the novel, Mason's car is *backing out* of the alley—moving forward in reverse, with Leila looking at her past in front of her while riding in the opposite direction. Hope, the future, the forward movement incorporate memory, the past, the backward movement. Lending an added twist to Leila's final look back, this future-oriented version of the modernist narrator's retrospective quest conflates two different and contradictory linguistic and cultural systems. Whereas the Western imagination figures the past as what is behind us, in the Chinese language a single ideogram, *hou*, conveys the two meanings of "back, rear, behind" and of "afterwards, later, in the future" (as well as "offspring, progeny").[22] "Backdaire," then, is the future to come. Rather than sounding the note of translation as a relentless shuttle between two distinct and distant linguistic and cultural realities, the last word in the novel offers itself as a moment of hybridization, where Chinese and English mark each other inextricably not out of linguistic incompetence or inadequacy, but as the result of deliberate choice—an empowering new language that opens the way to the conquering of new spaces, literary or otherwise, where the past is made one with the future.[23] In just such overlappings of culturally determined opposites, new rules for the imagination can begin to emerge.

Part IV

Rewriting Form, Reading for
New Expression

10

Performing Dialogic
Subjectivities

*The Aesthetic Project of Autobiographical
Collaboration in* Days and Nights in Calcutta

ROCÍO G. DAVIS

SUBVERTING TRADITIONAL AUTOBIOGRAPHICAL structure to deploy originative formal and aesthetic concerns—a correlate to revised perceptions on subjectivity, identity, and ethnicity—is a prevalent strategy in contemporary Asian American life writing. The increasingly dialogic nature of life writing reflects a multi-voiced cultural situation that allows the subject to control the tensions between personal and communal dialogues within texts that signify discursively. Issues of self-representation—with its attendant concerns with identity politics, the rewriting of history, and the attempt to validate personal and social experience—become central to the autobiographical strategies employed by many Asian American writers as they perform individual and relational processes of self-awareness. Maxine Hong Kingston's *The Woman Warrior* and Michael Ondaatje's *Running in the Family,* for example, articulate physical and psychological disruption through postmodern collagic texts. Similarly, Sara Suleri's *Meatless Days* and Garrett Hongo's *Volcano: A Memoir of Hawai`i* use the short-story cycle to enact their accounts of personal and locational affiliation.[1] In this essay, I read Clark Blaise and Bharati Mukherjee's collaborative autobiography, *Days and Nights in Calcutta,* as a formal subversion of genre that occasions a renewed aesthetic.[2] Via a doubled journal that offers contradictory/complementary perspectives on the experience of a year in India, Blaise and Mukherjee enact a regenerated formal and aesthetic experience based on a dialogue between two independent texts, suggesting an alternative model for self-inscription.

Collaborative autobiographies challenge the fundamental paradigm of the unified self of traditional autobiography, as well as the concept of monologic representation. Indeed, the renewed formal and aesthetic experience of these autobiographical texts stems precisely from the tension created by a dialogue. Collaborative writing, defined succinctly as a text composed by more than one person—as-told-to, ghostwritten, and coproduced or collectively produced texts—is the clearest textual manifestation of this phenomenon.[3] Asian American collaborative life writing exercises illustrate how this strategy was, on occasion, fundamental to the writing and/or publication of the text. Jeanne Wakatsuki Houston's story of Japanese American internment, *Farewell to Manzanar*, was written with her husband, James.[4] The role of the editor was crucial to the publication of Mary Paik Lee's *Quiet Odyssey: A Pioneer Korean Woman in America*, as it was Sucheng Chan's enthusiasm for Lee's story that led her to revise, complete, and publish it.[5] Autobiographic collaboration also features ostensibly equal participation of both subjects, such as that evidenced in Blaise and Mukherjee's texts, or enacted by May-lee Chai and Winberg Chai in *The Girl from Purple Mountain*, a dialogue between a father and daughter about his mother, where familial, historical, and diasporic concerns are woven into the story of three generations of a Chinese American family.[6] The interaction between the participants in this autobiographic act reconfigures the traditional idea of a monologic narrative as it interrogates the relationship between lives and narrative construction, stressing the discursive potential behind generic choice.

Collaborative texts that enact a dialogue between two voices—two positions—radically alter not only the idea of individual self-representation but also that of autobiographical form and process. To authorize a dialogue, rather than the traditional monologue, as the central discursive strategy in life writing texts suggests a multilayered project with formal and cultural resonances. One of the constitutive thematic/textual markers of this renewed autobiographical exercise involves an emphasis on the intersection of biography and autobiography, locating the narrating subject most often in a community—family or ethnic group.[7] The relational configuration of autobiography controls the shape of the text, leading to originative formal choices. By reading Blaise's and Mukherjee's *Days and Nights in Calcutta,* I address the project of collaborative autobiography as a performative act that renegotiates critical concepts of the self-in-autobiography and proposes a new literary form of negotiating the transcultural position of Asian American writers.[8] Deploying an innovative formal operation, *Days and Nights in*

Calcutta advocates a renewed aesthetic mode of performing the narrative processes of subjectivity: the text *enacts* the relation as it/that it *narrates*. Moreover, this form of collaboration is increasingly being reinterpreted, as Sidonie Smith and Julia Watson suggest, "as arenas and occasions of a dialogical process shared among two or more voices."[9] As Susanna Egan notes:

> Parallels between life and text become even closer when both subjects are involved in the preparation of the text. Narration then takes the form of dialogue; it becomes interactive, and (auto)biographical identification becomes reciprocal, adaptive, corrective, affirmative, as is also common in life among people who are close to each other.... These autobiographies, in other words, do not reflect life so much as they reflect (upon) their own processes of making meaning out of life.[10]

Days and Nights in Calcutta illustrates the writers' negotiation of immigration and ethnic affiliation, as these inform their relationship and their writerly processes. Blaise and Mukherjee combine their journals to emphasize the intersection of ethnic, social, familial, and personal positions precisely because each of them, as individuals, occupy differing locations in the structure. Questions of position, power, and agency are assessed through dialogue. As separate but significantly linked individuals with different perspectives on the manner in which racial and ethnic identity functions in their societies, the dialogic structure of the text dramatizes the processes that lead Blaise and Mukherjee to rethink their positions. These autobiographical documents factor their innovative formal process through simultaneous operations of conflict and dialogue, and by providing a sense of both performance and mutual spectatorship. To have one's opinions, perspectives, and stories complemented or challenged by an (ostensibly) equally authoritative voice *within the text itself* stresses the dialogic element, making the relationship, rather than the individuals, the center of the text. Blaise's and Mukherjee's chronicles—written independently but structured in the published text to perform the dialogue—gives the reader a renewed life-reading experience that promotes the potential of narrative structuring in transcultural contexts. Importantly, it also requires us to reexamine autobiography, as Albert Stone suggests, as *"occasion, script, performance, process* rather than simply as form or literary genre."[11] Collaborative autobiography illustrates the points that Stone notes in superlative ways, and this paradigm allows us to discern the nuances of Blaise and Mukherjee's formal and aesthetic project. By privileging the relational and the dialogic, the text acquires elevated discursive potential. Moreover, the dialogue textually enacts the complicated transcultural positioning that the writers have to engage in their lives. This collaborative autobiographical act becomes, simultaneously: an *occasion* for dialogue, the negotiation of the *script* of that dialogue, the *performance* of subjectivity, and a discursive *process*. The analysis of *Days and Nights in Calcutta* will proceed according to the approach Stone proposes and that I negotiate paradigmatically in the context of both formal renovation and transcultural position. This approach organically deploys the literary, critical, and cultural concerns of the texts as they intersect with personal and social issues in the context of self-representation.

In the first place, the *occasion* is, as Egan notes, the "real presence" of the speakers, confirmed "by the responsiveness of each to the other and by the fact that their dialogue is comprehensible only in terms of the involvement of both"[12] and authorized by the autobiographical pact. *Days and Nights in Calcutta* is composed of journals that Blaise and Mukhejee kept on a year's sabbatical in India, after a series of unfortunate accidents (Blaise breaks his wrist, their house burns down, and their car is wrecked) led them to leave Canada with their two young sons. The journals are framed by a prologue by Blaise and epilogues, written for the book's publication in 1977 and reissue in 1995. The first part of the text is written by Blaise and the second by Mukherjee; similar events, themes, questions, and changing perspectives are engaged by each. Notably, the two sections do not directly refer to each other and there is no textual evidence that the two writers read each other's journals. This structure evinces how Blaise and Mukherjee posit the center of their autobiographical exercise as occurring precisely in the space between their individual positions and independent texts. The autobiographical occasion occurs in writing that creates a dialogue, opening up a third space for relational selfhood. Their contrasted positions on cultural and ethnic affiliation, family obligations, the role of the writer, and questions of diasporic belonging obliges them to reexamine the basis of their marriage. The challenge of a journal, and the tension that characterizes it, derives from the writers' lack of foreknowledge about outcomes of the plot: there is no critical reworking of events nuanced by hindsight, and the reader accompanies Blaise and Mukherjee on this doubled journey of rediscovery of India and of themselves.

India is the central focus of both diaries, and the force that compels them to reappraise their social, cultural, and personal positions. Blaise claims that "From the moment we landed, India conspired to write this journal" (10). As a white Canadian married to a Bengali Brahmin, Blaise is welcomed by his wife's relatives and given privileged access to cultural and intellectual events. But Mukherjee has to rethink Blaise's position in her life and what she gave up when she married him. In a sense, Blaise's account might be read as a travel journal, as he continually reexamines and rewrites himself in transit. He explains his position in these terms:

> I had my books, my notes, and my husband's heart to say yes to anything my wife's city offered me. Not to hold back, not to judge, not to be shocked, never to say no. I was the *jamai*, the son-in-law, collecting all his wedding gifts ten years late. Though we'd been married ten years, it has been ten years of knowing Bharati on my terms and in my language. The only big adjustment in my life (accomplished with all the groans of a youthful identity crisis) had been a thirty-mile drive over the border to Montreal, the dropping of an accidental American passport, and the reassertion of the Canadian. (96)

Barry Fruchter suggests that Blaise "at least semiconsciously recuperates the traditional narrative of the Orientalist traveler . . . he uses his senses of irony and ambiguity . . . both as markers to distinguish the writer from his complacent ethnocentric compatriots at home and as badges of pride to keep him aloof from the 'natives' abroad."[13] His eagerness to engage the multifariousness of India reality reinscribes the rhetoric of the "European Grand Tour," where traveling subjects "recorded their observations as educational journeys through successive cultures."[14] Yet, due to his conjugal connection to India, Blaise's intention is more urgent, even if as naïve. Moreover, because of his own history of cultural displacement, Blaise believes that his biracial children also need to connect with India and their family there.

Mukherjee's position is more complex: her marriage to a non-Bengali and, perhaps more important, her economic independence, alienate her from the traditional society she was raised to belong to. The return to her family home and city becomes a painful journey of tentative and frustrated reconnection. The couple's processes are contrasting: Blaise looks outward and moves forward, in a stimulating voyage of discovery as Mukherjee journeys inward and to the past. She finds herself reviewing, reworking, and rewriting the inherited texts of the configuration of the Bengali Brahmin woman she was and has become. In her 1995 epilogue, she admits that the project she had originally embarked upon, "a communal autobiography of the women of my age and my vanishing class who had stayed on in the riot-pocked hometown," was transformed in the process into the "real" story about North America (301–2). Her journal reports her difficult process of trying to reenter that world and the impossibility of belonging to what she had left behind. Her ambivalence is resolved at the end, with her decision to return to Canada, albeit temporarily.

Interestingly, the few published essays on *Days and Nights in Calcutta* read the book as unilaterally Mukherjee's autobiography. Barry Fruchter, Pramila Venkateswaran, and Anindyo Roy, for example, discuss the text primarily from the point of view of Mukherjee, relegating her husband's text to, at best, a 164-page introduction.[15] But to discuss Mukherjee's text independently of her husband's is to disregard their generic choice in their life writing exercise. To read this text as anything *but* a carefully constructed collaborative autobiography disables the discursive potential of the text, and fails to acknowledge dialogism as constitutive of the couple's formal and aesthetic strategy. Though Fruchter does acknowledge, without further discussion, that we cannot discuss Mukherjee's "contribution" to the volume without "[at] least touching on her husband's section, which in a sense sets up a pattern to be answered by hers,"[16] Venkateswaran, obsessed with locating Mukherjee in the context of Indian women believes that the text "derives its power by allowing the collective voices of Calcutta women to take over the narrative."[17] This critical perspective, though it provides fascinating insights to the situation of Indian women and does negotiate the issue of collectivity and collaboration, limits this notion only to the context of the polyphony of voices pertaining to Mukherjee's interactions with women, really only a minor section of her account. Blaise's role as "witness" to his wife's narrative is interpreted in the narrowest possible sense by Venkateswaran. This narrow reading might be explained by Mukherjee's position as a leading Asian American writer, and a political need to privilege her contribution and foreground her section.[18] Roy's essay focuses on Mukherjee's complex aesthetic project, but ignores the evidence that the formal strategy is radically collaborative. Surprisingly, none of these critical articles foreground the fundamental paradigm set up by the writers: the performance of subjectivity precisely *in the act of dialogue* through a specific formal process.

In the second place, the *script* of both dialogues centers on the question of immigration, as well as ethnic, cultural, social, and national affiliation.[19] The experience of India requires both Blaise and Mukherjee to reexamine their views of belonging in society. Blaise's strategy consists of deploying literary and/or journalistic conventions: his acute observations and critical analyses attest to a curious and well-informed intellect at work. His sincere attempts to understand and, in a sense, find a home in his wife's culture illustrate his own perspectives on ethnic affiliation. Yet, having lived all his life in mainstream (read *white*) North America, he cannot comprehend the intricate nuances of Indian cultural and societal norms. He is uncomfortable with his imposed sahib status, the fluidity of social relations, and easy connections with celebrities like Satyajit Ray—the effortless entrance into high society motivate his ambivalence.

The issue of the Indian definition of identity and the manner it is negotiated on a personal and national level fascinates Blaise. "In India, of course," he explains, "identity never has to be sought; it is the lone certainty, and one's identity determines nearly everything. The father decides the son's career as surely as he chooses his daughter's husband. It is his duty to do so, and duty in India is discharged guiltlessly" (93). The peaceful coexistence of apparent contradictions confound him: the position of family servants, the role of parents in organizing their children's lives, the sanctioned separation between classes and castes. This ambivalence, and the equilibrium between things that appeared diametrically opposed, is partially resolved as Blaise negotiates the nature of Hinduism. Astonished by "moment-by-moment inventiveness within the rigidity" (161) in the elaborate ritual of a relative's wedding, he comprehends: "Of course there was order, even precision, to the ritual, but it was the order and precision of oriental carpetry, of intricate design endlessly repeated and varied, without a clear vanishing point or center of attention" (159). As Egan notes, "emblematic of space absorbing difference and time, Hindu rituals absorb all the contradictions of this composite travelogue."[20] Blaise watches his two sons "praying" with their grandfather, young Bernie transforming the Hindu prayers into his own multilingual chatter: "*Lufthansa, Lufthansa, let down your hair*" (38), to the delight of both Canadian father and Hindu grandfather.

Mukherjee's journey of self-examination yields a painful conflict. She is angered by Westerners' (including her husband's) attitudes toward India, even as she chafes under the restrictions imposed upon her by a position she had abandoned years before. Aware that she is simultaneously envied and pitied—for similar reasons—she finds herself needing to find a place to belong, to call her *desh*, her homeland. She explores the motivations of her immigration, and what her marriage to Blaise has implied—culturally, socially, and personally. She describes herself as a "late-blooming colonial who writes in a borrowed language (English), lives permanently in an alien country (Canada), and publishes in and is read, when read at all, in another alien country, the United States. My Indianness is fragile; it has to be professed and fought for, even though I look so unmistakably Indian" (170). Because of her family history—education abroad and at an elite school run by Irish nuns— Mukherjee and her sisters had grown into another version of the traditional Bengali Brahmin woman. These multiple locations lead her to uncomfortably occupy a liminal position wherever she finds herself. Though Mukherjee makes her home in Canada, it continues to be alien to her, and, as she insists, she to it. She argues that Canada has relegated her to second-class citizenship—she cannot hope to achieve the writerly recognition her husband easily enjoys because of her status as a visible minority. "I am tired of being exotic, being complimented for qualities of voice, education, bearing, appearance, that are not extraordinary," she complains (169). Because of her painful awareness of her multiple liminality, in this time of "sliding convictions," Mukherjee renounces the attitudes of well-meaning scholars at the residence in Calcutta as patronizing or even contemptuous of India; even her husband was not "exempt from my growing disgust" (220). Her suspicions derive from her growing insecurity. As her foreign husband becomes more and more comfortable, she, the native, occupies a more precarious position.

This gap weights more deeply as Mukherjee's narrative progresses and she faces the contradictions of her current intellectual and social dispositions with what she finds in India, within her family and among friends like her. Interestingly, one of the many contradictions of India that this text illustrates is the manner in which, as Egan explains, Mukherjee's conversations with friends "expose both the rigid structures of possibility for women and the permeable nature of boundaries encountered by the talented, the beautiful, the rich, or the lucky."[21] The social formation of high-class Bengalis—outwardly elastic, open, and friendly—was "simultaneously rigid, hierarchical, and exclusive" (213). As Mukherjee reacquaints herself with old friends and finds new ones, she is repeatedly astonished by the flexibility and inconsistency of their concerns: a conversation about Mother Teresa segues easily into a discussion about hairstyles, each one just as passionate. Her eagerness to explore "the social life I had once regarded with irony" (199), marks a crucial point of ambivalence. Her reintroduction into this world requires a complex retrospection of cultural and social awareness. Mukherjee knows that ethnic affiliation in India is inextricably linked to social position, and her place will be defined by the latter as much as by the color of her skin: "In a city [Calcutta] where there are no natural outsides and insides, the phenomenon of the party, like the walls of the compound, is a strategy of self-definition" (213). This phenomenon, unknown and unimaginable in Montreal—and beyond her husband's understanding—modifies preconceptions harbored from a distance. The paradox of her own position—insider/outsider, daughter/prodigal—seen through the eyes of others, begins to significantly alter her own view. She regards the question of leaving India, and returning to it, from the prism of possibilities of reconnecting and reconfiguring a selfhood from a lost history.

This dilemma leads to the third point in the analysis: as Blaise and Mukherjee negotiate the inherited scripts of national and ethnic affiliation, they perform highly unique itineraries of subjectivity. Smith and Watson explain that "a *performative* view of life narratives theorizes autobiographical occasions as dynamic sites for the performance of identities constitutive of subjectivity. In this view, identities are not fixed or essentialized attributes of autobiographical subjects; rather they are produced and reiterated through cultural norms, and thus remain provisional and unstable."[22] Another way of understanding the performative quality of life writing centers on the "act of composition," as Eakin proposes when he posits life writing as a process of "narratively constituted identity."[23] Eakin invites us, in the analysis of these texts, to note the "performance of the collaboration . . . , the relation between the two individuals involved."[24] The roles each writer plays and how one's narrative stance and perspective nuances the other's account must be addressed. This process has implications for Asian American formal negotiations of life writing, which recurrently engages multiply positioned itineraries of subjectivity, as Blaise and Mukherjee demonstrate.

Their differing cultural histories and ethnic posturing are the subtext of Blaise and Mukherjee's performances. In Canada, an officially multicultural nation, Mukherjee's Indianness was an issue negotiated daily, particularly in her professional life. In India, this ethnic affiliation is again subject to interrogation as it intersects with social position. But both writers enact ideas of evolving selfhood in their journals, as individuals and in dialogue. This doubled journal stresses the separate individuals Blaise and Mukherjee are and how their self-revelations, linked to how differing perspectives on ethnic affiliation, torment their relationship. She now confronts the questions that Blaise often asked visiting Bengalis in Montreal: "'What have you given up? Is it worth it?' For the next year, I was to hear her answers, and it has shaken our marriage to its core," he says (104). As the couple examines their relationship through the prisms of ethnic and national affiliation and social class, their text becomes a performance of their evolving perspectives. The experience of India, viewed almost as a rebirth after their Canadian home is consumed in flames, allows them to engage in a significant act of self-invention, a re-presentation in writing. As both had renounced citizenships and made their place in other countries, their multi-locationality contributes to their processes of liminality. To perform these processes in a journal—the form that most clearly rejects finality—signifies discursively.

G. Thomas Couser asserts that collaborative autobiography is "inherently ventriloquistic", obliging us to consider the positions of power in transcultural dual-authored texts.[25] As much as a collaborative text of this nature ostensibly presents a relationship of symmetry and balance, subtle manipulations appear that might correspond to the writers' public roles. Before the writing of the *Days and Nights in Calcutta*, Blaise and Mukherjee were—to differing degrees—already recognized public figures in Canada, the United States, and India. Blaise was a renowned Canadian writer; Mukherjee was denied access to this recognition there. In India, she was the star, he the consort. Perhaps because this book was written in India and deals primarily with India, Mukherjee appears to dominate the text. Her presumably authoritative position leads her to, consciously or not, control the dialogue and performance in the act of collaboration. This point is arguable on many levels: specifically, Blaise's narrative comes first and is longer than his wife's. Yet there is a sense in the text that his account functions as a frame, or even introduction, to hers. In India, Blaise's identity as Mukherjee's husband opens doors and allows him to be accepted as an equal. The identity he performs is, in a sense, intact—he leaves India basically as the same person he was when he arrived. Indeed, the most significant transformations in the text are Mukherjee's revisions of her own ethnic and social position. Blaise returns to Montreal much skinnier (though he gleefully notes that his wife has gained thirty pounds), but essentially the same Canadian intellectual, satisfied by the productivity of his experience.[26]

Mukherjee's performance of identity is much more vexed, and remains unresolved, as her epilogue assures us. The titles of her chapters— "Emblems," "Intimations," "Calcutta"—suggest a romantic impulse to reclaim memories, to find the self she had lost or invented, and reconcile herself with the scripted performance expected of her as a middle-class educated woman of Ballygunge and Calcutta. But her trajectory has subverted that script: she defines "three disproportionate parts"—the traditional joint family, life as a single family, and her reincarnation in the West—where "[e]ach phase required a repudiation of all previous avatars; an almost total rebirth" (179). The third avatar is the most crucial: it signals, in Blaise's words, her obligation to trade in "something in the bargain—their innocence, perhaps, their *place* in some ongoing, creative flow" (75). This is precisely where Mukherjee's complex struggle for position lies: in her attempt to find her place in that "family"—nuclear, joint, and national. Interestingly, some of Blaise's observations elucidate his wife's dilemmas and hint at an important point of contention between them. His initial enthusiasm for his wife's family in Ballygunge ends in frustration. "In India all is finally family," he complains, "If we in the West suffer the nausea of disconnectedness, alienation, anomy, the Indian suffers the oppression of kinship" (92). He likens their stay in her father's house as "a *No Exit*, a closet drama of resentment and dependence among people who, like cellmates, know each other too well to hide a thing" (80). Mukherjee, because of her sense of continual dislocation, yearns for that sense of comfortable stability. She writes that she envies her acquaintances in Montreal, capable of effortlessly enacting image changes, their "confident attempts to remake themselves" (175), something she cannot conceive for herself because she knows that "excess of passion leads only to trouble. I am, I insist, well mannered, discreet, secretive and above all, pliable" (175). Yet she acknowledges her awareness of how an acute sense of irony—developed from her years of study of British novels and membership in English departments—has altered her perspective. Reinserting herself in that place and that family, Mukherjee again falls into the timeless routine of family visits, gossiping with aunts and cousins, listening to All-India Radio. In Calcutta, where they escape to, she occupies another position, that of an Indian memsahib. These separate and contiguous lives "impinged but did not collide" (239). She learns to perform the roles that place demands and expects of her, even as she watches herself, gauging her reactions carefully and analyzing her actions.

Identification with family links with connection to the city, and location in India plays a pivotal role in self-identification. Blaise and Mukherjee's descriptions of Calcutta's streets, alleys, marketplaces, hotels, and homes necessarily limn the intricate relationship of the city with its inhabitants. As Blaise notes, "Bengalis love to explain Calcutta; the identification with the city is so complete that the standard question put to an outsider—'What do you think of Calcutta?'—is a shorthand way of asking, 'What do you think of Bengalis? What do you think of me?'" (64–5). Mukherjee's observations of her husband's way of functioning in her city reflects this identification: he is stereotyped as the typical foreigner, and she observes him as though a stranger, from a distance, appropriating the perspective of her friends who do not understand her choice. More important, propelled by this "misplaced bitterness," she accuses him of forcing expatriation on her, in a desperate fight for her "sanity," understood as her increasingly fragile position (221). As her husband happily performs his role as consort—"[m]y idea of hospitality while in Calcutta would be to give the largest number of people the greatest number of opportunities to entertain me" (95)—he tries to understand her increasing insecurity. Mukherjee reads his well-meaning interest and support as critical interventions to her increasingly complex process of self-negotiation.

This aspect dramatizes the suitability of the collaborative text as a vehicle for the concerns of transcultural subjects: by privileging individual voices as they occupy diverse positions in the retelling of their own history, the genre enacts as it signifies. The discursive process, the fourth element in the analysis, is evidenced as the shifting voices illustrate the negotiation of perspectives, power relations, and the adjustments required in this dialogue.

Each voice represents a different position, and the text itself enacts the process of adjustment that Blaise and Mukherjee—Canadian and Indian, white and brown, writer and writer, husband and wife—experience in their year in India. As Mukherjee seeks redefinition by measuring herself against the world she left behind, positing this as "a time to subvert memory, to hunt down sly conciliatory impulses," Blaise's role is that of "witness" to his wife's process (221). But this concept must be interpreted in complex sense—as he watches, his presence interrogates and his conversations provide crucial counterpoints to Mukherjee's engagement with liminality. Significantly, the narrative enactment of that process requires the participation of both parties—a formal and aesthetic choice made consciously by the writers. As Egan argues, "Adjustments between the two narrators also establish each one as the critical reader of the other.... Just as this journey calls into question the cultural securities of the Western white man, requiring him to listen in new ways to his Bengali wife, so too the qualities of narrative, shifting significantly from part one to part two, function responsively, pointing up both harmony and dissonance."[27]

Ultimately, both Blaise and Mukherjee realize that the immigrant positions they have chosen make them outsiders, both in Canada and in India. Moreover, their complacent acknowledgement of the superiority of the West is undermined by the dialogues they have with many in India. After a long conversation with a groom-to-be, one of Mukherjee's cousins, Blaise perceives a concurrent thread of understanding, as he and the boy smile, "doubtless pitying the cultural constrictions of the other's society" (95). Mukherjee repeatedly asks her friends if they would rather live elsewhere, and the answers were inevitably the same: they considered themselves "the luckiest people in the world" (201). After analyzing in detail these women's lives, which continued where hers left off after she immigrated to the United States, Mukherjee increasingly comes to see things from their point of view—acknowledging, for instance, that Western critiques of the Indian system are forms of political and cultural imperialism. These renewed perspectives become weapons that defend her right to self-definition in her marriage, and, in arguments with her husband, she notes that "[t]o defend my friends was to assert my right to differ with him" (202). For Blaise, as for Mukherjee, time in India exposes their different brands of Eurocentrism and deepens their understanding of each other. In her discussion of Mukherjee's aesthetic project, Roy notes the writer's determined amalgamation in limning the possibilities of accommodating "a decidedly Hindu imagination with an Americanized sense of the craft of fiction."[28] In these assertions, Roy argues, Mukherjee negotiates the aesthetic to construct a scheme that readily locates forms of "identity" and "difference": "[t]hese forms are clearly indicative of the stabilization and commodification of a colonized culture by a postcolonial writer whose own authorial gaze corresponds to that of the Orientalizing West."[29] The ambivalences they negotiate require them to refocus their perspectives on the West and India, and the fundamental relations between the two, enacted in their marriage, a microcosm of immigrant complexity. As Egan notes, in this transaction, "center and periphery shift, providing critiques for each other."[30] This is precisely the location of the dialogic enactment of subjectivity, exhibited textually to stress the advantages of the formal mode they deploy.

Mukherjee's section ends with a conciliatory note that illustrates the middle ground arrived at after a painful journey of antithetical and contradictory cultural and social negotiations. Her fervent examination of the malady of the culturally dispossessed and socially disenfranchized becomes muted by the erosion of time. She acknowledges that her idealized—"faintly Chekhovian" (297)—image of India, which had sustained her in cold Canada, had buckled under the reality of the heat and dust. The journal—her "accidental autobiography"—traces her journey "from exile to settler and claimant," secure once more in the decision to return "home" to a city she knows herself displaced from (302). In a sense, it marks a closure to her vexed self-definition as a Bengali and an Indian, as she acknowledges the limitations of the society she had, in immigration, idealized.[31] Her conclusion in the final epilogue promotes a renewed definition of affiliation, wrought out of the processes of the palimpsestic movement: "I want to think that our story—Clark's, our sons', and mine, braided together—is a happy one. Happy because we made our fates out of the many possibilities offered us by destiny. We build our 'homeland' out of expectation, not memory" (303).

For Blaise and Mukherjee, therefore, the construction of their story—individual, interacting, and intersecting lives—enacts a fundamental aspect of their distinct processes of selfhood. This collaborative autobiography charts itineraries of subject dialogue and positionality that obliges us to reevaluate formal and aesthetic paradigms. The resulting text becomes a dynamic chronicle that charts their writers' individual processes of adaptation and renegotiation of previously accepted models, prejudices, and stances. Readers witness the formal dialogue that makes this change happen, participating in the evolution of this relationship. *Days and Nights in Calcutta* demonstrates how collaboration as a generic strategy effectively augments possibilities of inscribing the autobiographical project, attending to the relational quality of our lives. Albert Stone has suggested that, if we approach collaboration having abandoned "the belief in literature as a collection of autonomous aesthetic icons and sacred texts, . . . dual-authorship may cease being a literary problem to become rather a cultural solution."[32] The plural positions of these writers, performed though their dialogic life-writing exercise, reflects the shifting boundaries of immigrant representation and illustrates the possibilities of the autobiographical form. *Days and Nights in Calcutta* functions as a powerful tool for cultural criticism because of the discursive possibilities of the act of dialogue as the principal strategy life writing exercise that multiplies meaning. As writers explore the genre as *occasion, script, performance,* and *process,* the dialogue signifies on a literary and cultural level. In the context of Asian American life writing, collaborative texts, emblematic of the transcultural position, accommodates not only issues of ethnicity, culture, or nation but, importantly, limn the formal approaches to the narrated subject in his or her act of inscription.

11

Bicultural World Creation

Laurence Yep, Cynthia Kadohata, and Asian American Fantasy

CELESTINE WOO

FANTASY IS PERHAPS entering a golden age within our culture. Thanks to J. K. Rowling's *Harry Potter* series as well as the recent Tolkien films, fantasy books for both children and adults are proliferating at a seemingly magical rate. As society has grown more multicultural, fantasy as a genre has become increasingly pluralistic, and so the time is ripe for the delineation of Asian American fantasy. By writing within this nascent subgenre, Laurence Yep and Cynthia Kadohata begin to transform both fantasy and Asian American literature, appeal to a broader audience than each separate genre traditionally reaches, and model an imaginative space that showcases the most compelling and inspiring aspects of each.

Fantasy is inherently literary and aesthetic, for inasmuch as the aesthetic has constituted a paradigm since the classical theorists to explore beauty, pleasure, ethics, and the affective power of art, fantasy by definition is constructed from the belief that literature and imagination can conjure these qualities. By defining Asian American fantasy, I delineate how fantasy enriches Asian American literature through foregrounding the interaction between the aesthetic and sociopolitical issues that form the central exploration of this volume. I thus progress in several of the directions Sue-Im Lee outlines in her Introduction: I perform formal and generic analysis; highlight the constructedness of literary conventions; and sketch a pattern for avoiding the reduction of literary discourse to the narrowly political. Central to my approach to aesthetics is the question of what can be distinctly Asian American within fantasy.

What a well thought out, richly depicted fantasy world prompts in the reader is an interrogation of our assumptions about customs, cultural norms, ethics, and human relations. Entering into an imaginary world showcases and explores what humanness is comprised of, what transcends and exceeds the particularity of locale, chronology, culture, and circumstance. Fantasy inspires by extrapolating possibility; as science fiction provides visions of how ethics would be different with expanded technology and space exploration, so fantasy foregrounds the norms and fundamental values that constitute culture. The appeal of the non-realistic[1] inheres in the staying power of storytelling, myth, imagination, and evocation; of magical creatures, powers, peoples, and lands; of meaning unanchored by particularity of time and place. As serious readers of fantasy will agree, envisioning a fictional society attunes you to nuances of human behavior, systems of government and authority, ethical and moral values.[2] Sadly, to date, there is little scholarship or theory pertaining to fantasy, and there is still a widespread tendency to denigrate "escapism" or "escapist literature" as pure indulgence, elite and effete absurdity, devoid of social or political transformative power.

Asian American literature offers the Asian American reader a sudden recognition of his or her world, no longer elided and silenced. Yet the plethora of stories about culture shock and generational conflict usually lack the wonder of the fantastic. Conversely, fantasy worlds are frequently populated by "white" people, with societies and values replicating those of mainstream Western European cultures. Exceptions abound, but the norm remains: fantasy worlds tend to resemble pre-industrial Britain, and be written by, about, and for whites. Yep and Kadohata are the only authors, from what I can ascertain, who have written fantastical stories with identifiably Asian American elements. They achieve a transformation of fantasy by adducing ethnic consciousness, and thus augment its contemporary social applicability and mainstream respectability. Both authors inject Asian American elements into their plot, setting, and characterization, and draw upon their personal experiences as Asian Americans to do so. These Asian American aspects to their fantasies differ from, and therefore call attention to, the standard Anglocentric assumptions undergirding the typical fantasy novel.

The confluence of these two categories, Asian American literature and fantasy, enriches both: fantasy provides Asian American literature a sense of imaginative non-realism and an expanded repertoire of modes of representation. Yep and Kadohata allegorize the representation of Asian American experience through the lens of fantasy. This infusion of ethnic consciousness into fantasy broadens its inherent penchant for multicultural-ism and underscores how it has been culturally constricted and constructed.

Let me define the "whiteness" of fantasy, in order to narrate its exclusion-ary aspects and development of ethnic consciousness. In the majority of high fantasy stories, one or more of the following is true: the characters are Anglo or Western European in appearance, possessing fair skin, hair colors ranging from blond to red to brown, and eye colors such as blue, hazel, green, gray, or brown; the "default" culture resembles Anglo or Western European cul-tures; Anglo ways of thought and perception are portrayed as either universal or the default/norm—to wit, that one naturally describes physical appear-ance by noting eye and hair colors. Sometimes, contemporary readers can easily identify racialized or outright racist assumptions structuring imagined peoples: in C. S. Lewis's *The Horse and His Boy,* Narnians, who are clearly portrayed as "good," resemble Britons, whereas the dark-skinned turbaned Calormenes represent "evil," worship the wrong god, and ultimately are con-signed to "hell," except for one lone convert who repents from his misguided adulation and redirects his faith toward Aslan, the Narnian Christ-figure.[3] Lewis wrote his books in the wake of World War II, when J.R.R. Tolkien wrote *The Lord of the Rings.*[4] In Tolkien's anthropocentric Middle Earth, certain species (like the dark Orcs) are innately evil and deserve nothing better than to be killed. Lewis and Tolkien must be understood in terms of their historical and sociopolitical moment, but clearly, both of their created worlds privilege white peoples and logocentric habits.

Fantasy has grown more multiculturally aware as society has altered. Raymond Feist's Riftwar Saga, published in the 1980s, focuses on a Tolkien-like world, Midkemia, complemented by another world, Kelewan.[5] Although cross-cultural conflicts inform Feist's saga, the Britannic Midkemians remain the default culture, and the vaguely Japanese Tsurani from Kelewan, the aliens. Though Feist's worlds exhibit more cultural relativism than Lewis's and Tolkien's, nevertheless, "white" ways are the norm—as cover artists for most fantasy novels inevitably demonstrate by depicting fair-skinned peo-ple unless (one surmises) explicitly instructed to do otherwise.[6] The Asian American reader receives the mainstream message from these books that her own experience is other, foreign, and odd.

Anne McCaffrey's Pern series further establishes a pluralistic world by acknowledging the multiethnic Earth origins of the Pernese.[7] (Tellingly though, she does not do so until 1988, when American society had embraced multiculturalism; *Dragonsdawn,* the prequel I refer to, is the ninth in the series.) McCaffrey envisions a future Earth society (which spawns the space excursion to found Pern) in which cross-cultural marriages and interchange are the norm. Nonetheless, both bearers of Anglo-sounding names, "Benden" and "Boll," are the leaders of the expedition, the default point of view in much of the novel, and the ones who have places named after them in later decades. The more foreign names "Kwan Marceau" and "Mar Dook" are lost to Pernese posterity. So fantasy continues to be white-dominant.[8]

The stage is set for deeper ethnic interpolation into fantasy conventions. Yep and Kadohata permeate their worlds with a bicultural sensibility: their protagonists are intensely conscious of cultural norms and struggle to assimilate to different cultures' mores. While Yep's characters are literally Asian American, Kadohata foregrounds within an imaginary world issues germane to Asian American life, such as assimilation, cultural clash, discrimination against immigrants, and traditional versus contemporary sexuality. Their Asian American fantasies invite investigation of how imaginative literature is culturally constructed, for by decentering what goes frequently unexamined, Yep and Kadohata undermine its neutrality. For instance, by depicting a protagonist who questions her or his cultural context, Yep and Kadohata tacitly highlight other fantasy protagonists who never acknowledge their cultural formation.

In turn, Asian American fantasy salutarily broadens Asian American literature. I used to wonder whether the cultural identification I so prized in Asian American writing could coincide with the imaginative and culturally analytical power that rendered fantasy so compelling to me. Genre is ineluctably entwined with evaluation: as Sue-Im Lee states in the Introduction, an aesthetic can form a category of evaluation, and what made Asian American literature valuable to me fifteen years ago as a reader and potential writer differed from what rendered fantasy valuable. Back then, I could not envision a way to reconcile the imaginative and lyrical beauty of fantasy with the quotidian reality and personal relevance of Asian American literature. Yep and Kadohata exemplify in their fantasies what is meaningful and inspiring about both genres: cultural delineation, imaginative creation of characters and customs, and quandaries of ethics and identity.

As discrete traditions, fantasy and Asian American literature engage readers differently; their fusion enlarges the palette of what may be termed "Asian American" and what aesthetic, literary, and rhetorical tools are available to communicate to readers. Yep and Kadohata each present a model for allegorized representation of Asian Americans: distanced from the direct portrayal and realism of Asian American literature, their works offer novel ways to apprehend the nuances of Asian American experience. In so doing, these writers widen Asian American aesthetics by weaving in the lyricism, mystery, inventiveness, and transcendence of fantasy, supplementing its quotidian vividness and sociocultural critique. Fantasy as an aesthetic mode inspires wonder and connection to the realm of the infinite and supernal. Yep and Kadohata interject a bicultural sensibility into the aesthetics of world-creation, and outline how an Asian American worldview affects perception of societies and values other than the narrowly factual.

Yep muses, "I think of fantasy and writing in general as a special way of seeing. It's a way of looking at the world more intensely and more sensitively and more sharply than we normally would."[9] He adds that "reality" is social consensus, not an absolute, and hence, what happens to "people whose society's sense of reality corresponds very poorly to their experience of the world" is that "[t]hey become lovers of fantasy."[10] He expresses his shared task with the greater Asian American community in terms of fantasy: "Like Aslan, each of us must sing our own Narnia into existence."[11] Yep's world-making demonstrates to Asian American readers and writers the possibility of scripting a reality with the charms and boundlessness of the fantastic, without necessitating an absorption into the parameters of white fantasy—an absorption reiterating the cognitive dissonance between socially defined reality and Asian American lived experience.

In his introduction to the newest edition of *Sweetwater*, Yep remarks, "without *Sweetwater*, I'm not sure I would have had the courage to have begun that journey into Chinese America in the first place."[12] Yep views his reading and writing of fantasy as a crucial interlude that enabled him to explore his Asian American identity in ways unavailable to him elsewhere. This indirect exploration is what I term allegorized representation: in both Yep's and Kadohata's works, the fictitious nature of the society, characters, and situations evokes real-life analogues in provocative ways, without being delimited by them.

The setting of Yep's Dragon series[13] vaguely resembles Chinese mythology in possessing dragons and a monkey as magical beings and authority figures. Dragons of course are also common in Western fantasy, but monkeys are not. Another figure of Asian origin is the Lord of the Flowers, an immortal being with a band of flower-like riders. The world of the books is noticeably different from the usual Eurocentric world of forests, hunters, and castles. Yep also tinges his stories with elements characteristically (if not exclusively) American: the feisty underdog protagonist; the irreverence and wry humor evinced toward figures and systems of authority; the controlling idea of individuals on a personal quest, benefiting from companionship but maintaining separate aims.[14] Yep's series contains classically appealing elements of fantasy with an Asian twist, such as a dragon's magic pearl that effects transformations; a boy and girl turned into fish; Monkey's magic golden

needle, and his hairs that become hundreds of mini-Monkeys. Magical objects and transformations into animals are standard fare in fantasy; they
captivate the imagination and stimulate curiosity about the world's workings. In the slightly unexpected world Yep paints of undersea kingdoms and
caves, the archetypal American values of rugged individualism, resourceful-
ness, and humor-tinged resilience take on a fresh hue amid the trappings
and appeal of fantasy.

Correlatively, Yep's series draws on conventional aspects of Asian
American stories. The narrative of a protagonist feeling at sea and making her
way in an unfamiliar, often hostile, culture resonates with readers acquainted
with systemic discrimination, generational differences, the status of misfit
and outcast, and a yearning to belong. These familiar motifs are enlivened
when applied to outlandish characters like an exiled dragon princess and a
spiky-haired underwater orphan girl. Yep's series amasses unusual ingredi-
ents into a narrative identifiably Asian American in ethos and appeal.

Amazon.com reviews of *Dragon of the Lost Sea* testify to the book's
attractiveness on its merits as "straight" fantasy, as well as its potential to
provoke generic interrogation. Reviewers find Shimmer charming, comment
on how much they like dragons and magic, and usually label the book as
fantasy. Two of the twenty-one reviews[15] cite the Chinese aspects as part of
the story's appeal. "kandladin" writes, "I have always loved reading mythology
of all kinds and though I had dabbled a bit in chinese [sic] here and there I
didn't take a real interest in it until I read this book . . . I would recommend
this book to any fantasy fan."[16] This reviewer enjoys the book as fantasy
and as mythology, and notes that Yep has prompted his/her greater interest
in Chinese subjects. Another reviewer, "la_solinas," designated by Amazon
as a "Top 50 Reviewer," writes, "An intriguing and unique fantasy story
based on Chinese mythos . . . An excellent, classic fantasy."[17] Presumably,
the "uniqueness" consists of using Chinese mythical elements to formulate
a "classic" fantasy tale.

One unhappy reviewer unconsciously foregrounds both the problems and
the promise inherent in crafting Asian American fantasy. This anonymous
writer, identified only as "A reader," submitted two reviews on August 13,
1999, both entitled, "A little bland, especially if you're Chinese . . .". The
reviewer complains, "Thorn is like any other fantasy hero. Shimmer is not a
Chinese name. Chinese dragons have no wings, and use magic to fly. Their
pearls are in their mouth. Monkey King's master was not born old, nor was
he called the Old Boy."[18] The reviewer objects to features in Yep's fantasy
world that are not sufficiently culturally authentic, for Shimmer has wings
and a magic pearl secreted in her forehead. The second review continues

the harangue: "I didn't really like Thorn—for one thing, most human heroes would have done what he did." It is unclear why this writer produced two nearly identical reviews, but the remarks are telling: s/he is displeased with Shimmer's name and physical traits for not being sufficiently Chinese. The writer compares Yep's world with Chinese mythology and carps at the inconsistencies. S/he criticizes the delineation of Monkey and refers inaccurately to the character as "Monkey King," the traditional Chinese mythical figure. Thorn is criticized for being "like any other fantasy hero" and because "most human heroes would have done what he did"—in other words, Thorn is deficient in being too generic and not identifiably Chinese.

Whether Yep knows the authentic details of Chinese folklore, and whether the reviewer's knowledge is accurate, are not as important here as the fact of Yep's having created a world engrossing to American readers and containing recognizably Chinese aspects. These reviews underscore that Yep's readership does not yet have a concept within their literary vocabulary of Asian American fantasy, in which conventional fantasy elements coexist with foreign elements altered or adapted for American accessibility;[19] nonetheless, Yep's stories enthrall fantasy fans, and introduce a wider audience to Asian American writing.

His novel *Child of the Owl* is a mostly realistic story that utilizes myth and fantasy in ways that speak to my notion of Asian American fantasy.[20] Casey[21] is the sassy no-nonsense daughter of Barney, a lovable gambling ne'er-do-well hospitalized after having been beaten up for unpaid debts. Casey's mother is dead, so she is to live with her obnoxious rich uncle, "Phil the Pill," who has no use for Casey's audacious sense of humor or refusal to wear pink frilly dresses. Phil sends his obstreperous niece to live with her grandmother in Chinatown—a terrifying punishment, he hopes. Casey discovers, though, that she likes living with "Paw-Paw" and learning about Chinese culture.

In the midst of this award-winning[22] coming-of-age story, Yep devotes a hefty twenty-two pages to his adaptation of a Chinese folktale about owls. Although the tale does advance the plot, it seems that Yep delights in the tale for its own sake, and expects the reader to do likewise. Though fantasy and mythology differ, one subcategory of fantasy gaining greater currency is that of the retooled myth or fairy tale, and it is in this vein that I consider Yep's owl myth as "fantasy."[23] Yep remarks, "I find that a myth can act like a lens that helps bring an experience into focus."[24] He elaborates in the Afterword to *Child of the Owl*, "Chinatown is not so much a place as a state of mind—or to be more accurate, a state of heart ... But the heart is a difficult place to enter, let alone describe, unless one wears some sort of disguise ... I think in the end an owl mask is one many of us could wear."[25] Generically, Yep's use of the owl tale in a realistic story allows him to have his cake and eat it: he can revel in fantasy, and also have the fantasy explained and applied to real life, as Paw-Paw does for Casey. Like all well-crafted and satisfying fantasies, the owl story is rife with magic, mystery, and ambiguity, and devoid of a simplistic sense of right and wrong; it thus nicely complicates the plot. Yep's interpolation of the owl story performs the inverse of what he does in the Dragon series: rather than infusing Asian American features into a standard fantasy, here he inserts fantasy elements into a typical Asian American story. Structurally, the owl tale functions in a bicultural and Asian American manner, for it is a Chinese tale deployed to help Casey the American survive and establish an identity in her foreign new Chinese environment; moreover, the values affirmed in the tale include the typically American ones of independence and the pursuit of individual fulfillment apart from family, as well as characteristically Chinese values such as fierce familial loyalty and a long memory. Thus, Yep's tale both instances and instigates an allegorized representation of Asian American identity formation.

After hearing the tale, Casey responds, "[I]t was like there had always been this person inside of me that I had never been able to name or describe—a small, feathery me lost inside this body—and now I not only knew her name but I could tell part of her story" (81). Appropriately, Yep uses an ambiguous and disturbing tale to trope the process of coming to terms with bicultural identity. Casey realizes, "I didn't have to be just like a [violent, ungrateful, vengeful] Chinese owl. I could be like an American one too . . . as wise as an American owl" (214). Casey self-consciously constructs her future to be informed by a Chinese mythology to which she applies a new and distinctly American interpretation.

Other than the incorporation of the owl tale as a whole, several characteristics of fantasy within the novel indicate Yep's familiarity with and appreciation for the conventions of the genre. It is the power of story that infuses and marks fantasy, and Yep employs devices such as a protagonist's active imagining, identification with animals, and magical transformation—all of which prompt her to reflect upon the implications of her imaginative experiences on her sense of identity. Casey dreams one night of being transformed into an owl, an experience evoking T. H. White's classic fantasy *The Once and Future King*, in which the boy Arthur transforms into a series of animals and takes on their qualities.[26] Casey relates, "my fingers curled inwards toward the palms and I could not straighten [them] . . . my fingernails had grown down over and around my fingers so they were shut up in shining, smooth casings, hard and sharp as talons" (170). The vividness with which Casey's dream is rendered forms a crucial part of the appeal and mystery of the story. At the novel's conclusion, after Casey has been disillusioned by her father who has stolen the owl charm, she reproaches him, "The charm was given to us by the Owl Spirit" (202). Barney scoffs at this "superstition," but Casey proceeds to explicate the meaning of the charm and the family owl spirit, and undaunted by her father's befuddlement, maintains her new vision of human nature. Yep uses the story's fantastic aspects to deepen its impact, and to provide Casey a new paradigm with which to make sense of her life. He thus allegorizes Asian American experience by having an Asian American character construct a reading of a myth—itself transformed from Chinese to Chinese American in Yep's retelling—that becomes a rubric for bicultural identity. The rubric is allegorical in that the tale's elements—talking animals, dream visions, and so forth—are fantastical, but are applied to a re-envisioning of Asian American existence.

Fantasy draws upon a mythology: a people's foundational stories of origins, identity, cultural values, trials, and homeland. On the surface, it sounds oxymoronic to envision an ethnic American fantasy, since ethnic Americans have seemingly no mythology inherently their own. An old-fashioned identity schema might proffer the overseas, non-American culture as the necessary Other that validates or deepens one's American identity. But the truth and convenience of this paradigm is proportional to the degree to which the Asian American identifies with the foreign culture. What the emergence of Asian American fantasy achieves is the creation and substantiation of a mythology innately "hyphenated" and displaced. It bears reiterating that most ethnic American groups, such as African Americans and Latino Americans, initially hyphenated their self-designations, and eventually deleted the hyphen in order to underscore the equivalence and non-subordination of each term. I choose here the term "hyphenated" to showcase the hyphen as bridge or link, and to imply the *connection* between Asian and American identity in this genre I am calling Asian American fantasy.

Richard Mathews characterizes American fantasy as possessing a "bottom-up approach" exemplified by Mark Twain's "deflating" of "epic grandeur and heroism," and Thorne Smith's "antiheroic" ethos.[27] Yep fits neatly into this tradition by displaying an American penchant for humor, impertinence, and posture-puncturing in his writings. Moreover, Yep names Twain as influential upon him, recalling, "I was … studying Mark Twain and other period writers in graduate school, [and] I wound up giving a pioneering nostalgia to [*Sweetwater*]."[28] Yep evinces an aptitude for "deflating" grandiose traditions that serves him effectively in crafting Asian American fantasy; Shimmer the dragon, for instance, seems to whimsically evoke first-generation immigrants as she learns to relinquish her pride and rigidity in

tradition and old customs. As ethnic American literature excavates and deconstructs cultural fantasies and stereotypes,[29] likewise, Asian American
fantasy addresses the disjunction between the imaginative world that compels suspension of disbelief and the more Americanized mode that deconstructs the mechanisms of fantasizing. Yep and Kadohata effect an innovative
synthesis of the wonder of world-creation and the analogical representation of Asian American experience, thus crafting a new poetics. This new
type of fantasy allows an empowering self-consciousness of its formal and
generic choices without hampering that suspension of disbelief that gives
delight.

Cynthia Kadohata's *The Glass Mountains*, set in an imaginary world,
incorporates features possibly arising from her experiences as an Asian
American.[30] Her characters perceive the world in Asian American–inflected
ways, and wrestle with cultural issues familiar to Asian Americans such as
prejudice, cultural assimilation, and differences in sexual mores. It is interesting to note for instance the protagonist's comments on black hair. Mariska,
the narrator and protagonist, observes, "I marveled at the beautiful blackness
of his hair and eyes. Since everyone in Bakshami possessed black eyes and
hair, one learned to distinguish between the nuances of the various shades of
black. His eyes were huge, and the blackness held no other colors, no blues
or browns or reds" (13). Kadohata addresses a mainstream white audience
whom she assumes will be unaccustomed to thinking of "black" as encom-
passing a variety of hues and qualities. This small scene, insignificant to the
plot, will no doubt speak powerfully to Asian American readers (or African
American, for that matter) raised in a society that often considers black hair
to be unattractive and monotone, that distinguishes between blond shades
but has few if any equivalent terms for brown and black shades. Kadohata's
point that black hair can be attractive and nuanced, followed by her lesson
on *how* to evaluate blackness (in terms of reds, browns, and blues), constitutes a tiny but telling window onto what could be identified as Asian
American experiences or perceptions. Mariska, raised in the heart of the
land of Bakshami, has no rational reason to internally expound her views on
black hair; what is extraneous to the movement of the plot, though, gestures
significantly to the concerns propelling Kadohata's writing.

Another Asian American–inflected feature in *The Glass Mountains* is
the concept of cultural integration: in the land of Soom Kali, visitors are
strictly patrolled and only permitted to remain one night, under supervision.
If they remain longer they must integrate, which means taking on a Soom
Kali name and identity to such a degree that they willfully forget their own
culture and country of origin. When Mariska's brother, Maruk, integrates,

Mariska reflects:

> [merely] pretending to be who he was not had not made him a Soom Kali.
> His Bakshami childhood was forgotten . . . He'd pretended to be Soom Kali,
> and to protect himself and his children, strove to make the pretense real . . . I
> couldn't help respecting the way he'd invented himself . . . But in the process
> he'd become more like a Soom Kali soldier than many of the real Soom Kali
> soldiers. (298–9)

Maruk concurs, "It would not be possible for me even to remember the [ritual drumming] rhythms I once knew by heart because I am no longer what I was" (299). Mariska responds to this statement in turn by playing mourning rhythms that night for her brother, as if he had died.

Asian Americans encounter the notion of cultural integration, or lack thereof, frequently, even daily. It is not far-fetched to conjecture that Kadohata has Asian American cross-cultural issues in mind when delineating the Soom Kali culture. By limning a scenario in which assimilation is mandated to such an extent, Kadohata can both affirm the achievement inherent in the process and grieve for what is lost. By draping in exotic fantasy what to Asian American readers is overdeterminedly familiar, Kadohata prompts the reader to ponder anew the process and ramifications of cultural assimilation. She concomitantly implies, by its lack, the desirability of a cultural blending that would reap the riches of each culture without having to choose irrevocably between them.

Kadohata's novel also reflects Asian American experience structurally: the typical Asian American child is intimately acquainted with the experience of being an outsider and minority, and of having to adapt quickly with little preparation or explanation to a multitude of (sub)cultures. Analogously, Mariska spends much of the novel alone, encountering four cultures of which she knows nothing, learning to her surprise how much she enjoys her isolation, and discovering her reserves of buoyancy and fortitude. Kadohata describes each culture in terms of its underlying values as well as exterior appearances and behavior—perhaps testifying to her everyday experience of cultural observation and analysis. She especially permeates her discussion of Forman culture with an awareness of immigrant life: Mariska finds her parents in misery and semi-slavery in the land of Forma, where they are mistreated because they are "partials," or noncitizens. Kadohata writes:

> We'd inquired about a driver but had been told there were few people who
> would work for partials, especially partials who owned only a few provi-
> sions . . . Apparently a minuscule minority of partials had sufficient funds to

purchase other partials, but one look at us told all onlookers that we were not among the privileged . . . The person who told us all this chastised us for speaking only Artroran and not bothering to learn Forman. She said the "best" partials were the ones who learned the language. (246)

Kadohata evokes here the experience of many an immigrant: prejudice only partly mitigated by wealth, and the automatic presumption of the superiority of the local language, English, to whatever other language(s) the immigrant might speak. While observation of the misunderstanding and unjust treatment of immigrants is certainly not an exclusively Asian American ability, Kadohata's experiences growing up as a Sansei in the 1960s, moving around the country through Chicago, Arkansas, Georgia, Michigan, Los Angeles, and Boston, doubtlessly exposed her to situations and societies in which unsympathetic assumptions were commonplace.

Mariska's experiences with sexuality also invoke the Asian American immigrant experience. Bakshami culture views sexuality pragmatically and unromantically: young people aim to find a strong person to "mate" with so they will bear hardy children; they "copulate" when they "come into season" (250). When Mariska first experiences physical romance from her non-Bakshami lover, Moor, she is so astounded by his gentle touches and kisses that she "took a stunned step back and fell over [her] pack to the floor" (163). Moor quips, "How do you expect to breed with anyone if you act like that?" She retorts, "[M]y mother has told me how to breed. Do you think I'm a child?" He replies laughingly, "Everyone breeds . . . But I can assure you, their mothers aren't there at the time." To which she queries, "Then how do they know what to do?" He remarks, "At least I won't be wanting for amusement on this trip." Mariska, a virgin, is sensible and unimaginative about sex, whereas the suave Moor is looking forward to teaching her the joys of lovemaking, and he is warmly amused that she doesn't get the joke. In this interchange, Kadohata rehearses a typical—even stereotypical—encounter between an innocent immigrant accustomed to thinking in traditional ways and a savvy American who wittily and proactively prompts the former to reconsider his or her assumptions.

Kadohata's construction of Mariska and Moor's relationship depicts scenarios familiar to Asian Americans, yet the fantasy setting and fictive cultures prevent the interaction from being predictable or clichéd. The imaginary cultural setting provides a distance from which the Asian American reader can apprehend Kadohata's social analysis and relate it to his or her own experiences without naming certain aspects as Asian or American and thus linking it to all the other aspects of Asian American culture. The generic application of fantasy allows Kadohata to eschew the need for accuracy and the avoidance of generalities that a discussion of factual issues entails, and instead focus on the emotional dynamics at play. Here, she can explore conflicting cultural values about sexuality in a fluid discourse, unconstricted by the bounds of any actual culture, embellished and extrapolated by imagination, yet rooted in Asian American experience.

Kadohata's framing device of a journeying protagonist allows her to foreground the process of cross-cultural exploration and interplay that seems closer to the purpose of the novel than the actual plot. Bakshami culture is ancient, traditional, technologically backward and unsophisticated, content to exist with a deliberate avoidance of the advances and complexities of surrounding societies. As such, Mariska's venture away from Bakshami represents the situation of many Asian immigrants: coming from a simpler, more traditional society into America, they find themselves facing rampant sexuality, bewildering technology, mind-boggling diversity in goods and services, and influences from other cultures. The story concludes with open-ended issues and indications of impending cultural change; Kadohata seems less intent upon wrapping up the narrative coherently than extending and elaborating upon her motif of cross-cultural exploration. Mariska encounters several different cultures—the Soom Kali, Artrorans, Formans, and Hathatu-me—according to no compelling plot-driven logic, but seemingly for the joy on Kadohata's part of inventing and pondering cultural differences. In particular, there is no necessity for introducing the Hathatu-me man whom Mariska meets near the story's close, since he is not a developed character (he is not even given a name), and their interaction does not advance the plot except arguably to cement Mariska's determination to fight for her land. Rather, the delight in this episode inheres in the adumbration of yet another culture: we learn that the Hathatu-me are optimistic, quiet, resigned, rather Zen Buddhist–like; they do not believe in humans owning each other, and this philosophy extends to their unwillingness to fight to protect themselves. Kadohata's novel exhibits Asian American affinities: she infuses her story with concerns about cultural identity and adaptation ranging from minor details about perception of physical appearance to broad societal norms such as definitions of nationalism. Her use of fantasy as a mode to explore facets of different cultures illustrates concretely one ingredient of the wonder inherent within the genre.

Yep's work shares Kadohata's sympathy for the figure of the outsider and the survivor; he avers in his forthcoming essay, "[F]or what sort of child do I write? I speak to the children similar to the children I knew when I was young—the outcasts and the survivors."[31] Whether writing fantasy or realism,

Yep creates spunky marginalized protagonists easy to empathize with, and thus contributes viably to the ongoing negotiations by Asian American writers of the vicissitudes of bicultural selfhood. His use of Chinatown as a mapping of the Chinese American heart, ordinarily secreted and hidden, eschews the Orientalizing tendencies of Amy Tan and Maxine Hong Kingston that script Asian Americans as ultimately more Asian than American. Yep also avoids Frank Chin's essentializing of Chinatown: by injecting magic and fantasy into a real-life setting, and by inscribing imagination as a necessary component to the protagonist's forging of a self-conception, Yep destabilizes the extent to which Asian American identity must be located in an actual Chinatown, because in his tales, Chinatown is fantastical and metaphorical.

Yep and Kadohata establish a provocative blending of two genres, infusing imaginative wonder into Asian American literature, and sociocultural implication into fantasy.[32] Both genres possess these capacities without need of the other, but their fusion within Asian American fantasy loosens the tendency of Asian American literature to be irrevocably anchored in historical time. History is crucial to Asian American consciousness, but nevertheless, such works as Yep's and Kadohata's hint at what there is within the Asian American experience that can transcend and aestheticize chronology. Conversely, Asian American fantasy anchors fantasy more solidly within history and lived experience, and thus conveys how empowering and transformative an attention to imagination can and ought to be.

12

Dismantling the Realist Character in Velina Hasu Houston's *Tea* and David Henry Hwang's *FOB*

KIMBERLY M. JEW

SCHOLARS INTERESTED IN STUDYING formal aesthetics in Asian American theater have been challenged by a canon dominated by realist dramaturgy. In fact as a representational model rooted in the close correspondence to observable, physical life, realism has become a signature feature of the past thirty years of Asian American playwriting. Audiences of Asian American dramas have therefore been witness to a life-like mise en scene, one filled with psychologically complex characters carefully drawn so as to embody not only specific social and environmental conditions, but the motions and gestures of everyday life as well. This embrace of realist aesthetics by Asian American playwrights has been inspired by a political imperative to control the manner by which their dramatic storylines and characters are perceived and interpreted. In other words, realism's promise of "truth in the material fact" has appealed to writers seeking to portray a persuasive vision of a "real" Asian America.

But what can be said of those rare theatrical visions of an "unreal" Asian America? How can experimental aesthetics influence a dramatic tradition grounded in the materialist objectivity of realism? To begin to answer these questions, I will first explore the theoretical function realism has served for Asian American playwrights. Second, I will focus on the relatively unexplored possibilities of non-realistic aesthetics in Asian American playwriting, particularly in the area of character construction and development. Towards this end, Velina Hasu Houston's *Tea* and David Henry Hwang's *FOB* will be examined for their use of expressionist and surrealist techniques, innovative dramatic effects that address the particular challenges in representing Asian American identities onstage.

In his study *Contradictory Characters: An Interpretation of the Modern Theatre*, Albert Bermel clarifies the standard rubric for assessing modern realist characters. Equating realistically drawn dramatic figures to living human beings, Bermel argues that realist characters derive their power through the enactment of the contradictory forces of human life. Through their self-destructive and irrational acts, realist characters reflect the "inner-selves" of the audience members, initiating an empathetic mirror relationship between viewers and characters.[1] Inherent in this aesthetic paradigm is the belief that the characters play a special role in dissolving the audience's self-conscious separation from the theatrical event. Though Bermel does not directly specify this function in his study, he alludes to it in his description of the impermeable spatial relationship between realist characters and their audiences: "From our padded seats we watch them in their padded cells between a curtain line and a backdrop as they behave unreasonably. Like human beings."[2]

As evidenced by Bermel's references to the auditorium seats, curtain line, and backdrop, spectators are acutely aware of the theatrical artifice of the characters onstage. That audience members may also experience safe aesthetic distance from the characters, as well as from the theatrical event itself, is reinforced by the imagery of the stage as an inescapable, or perhaps impenetrable, prison cell. Nevertheless, according to this aesthetic framework, the characters' persuasive realism counterbalances, and momentarily transcends, the audience's disbelief. The realist characters' effective dual expression of *reality* (the direct correspondence to observable life) and *realness* (the apparent possession of viable human consciousnesses) elicits the spectatorial empathy and identification necessary for realism to function successfully.

This character-centered realist paradigm has significant implications for Asian American playwrights. From the early works of Wakako Yamauchi and Momoko Iko to later dramas by playwrights such as Philip Kan Gotanda, audiences have been presented with living, true-to-life depictions of Asian American people, dramatic figures whose realism often dominates over the stories they tell. Indeed, the question of a character's authenticity—is he or she real?—has long been held as a standard for excellence in Asian American playwriting.[3]

While the dominance of realist aesthetics may be viewed as a sign of disempowerment,[4] it may also be interpreted as a deliberate effort to control the perception of Asian Americans onstage. To counter the history of representational distortion faced by the community, many critics have urged writers to turn to the reifying and subtly manipulative techniques of the realist apparatus.[5] Hoping to resculpt a truer vision of Asian American life, writers have built upon realism's positivist assumptions, developing a materially grounded discourse on Asian American life. As Josephine Lee notes: "Asian American realism would thus operate by using the stage to reform 'reality,' to counter how Asian Americans are often seen, and to teach audiences how to see 'real' Asian Americans."[6] In other words, to counter historical misperceptions of Asian Americans, playwrights have utilized realistically drawn characters to inspire empathetic identification among audience members.[7] As audience members momentarily overcome the artifice of the theatrical event, they may also temporarily cross the distance from cultural stereotype to human engagement.

Given the strategic importance of the realist character in Asian American playwriting, what can be learned from those rare instances when Asian American characters are constructed outside the boundaries of realist dramaturgy? Without question, innovative Asian American playwrights have more readily experimented with non-realistic narrative structure than with character, a trend seen in the works of Elizabeth Wong, Diana Son, and Chay Yew. Each of these playwrights has produced dramas that confound the typical features of the realistic dramatic narrative: a singularity of space, a linear continuity of time and action, the presence of the climactic structure, and the inability to acknowledge the outside world of the playwright or audience. From a theoretical viewpoint, these writers have begun to dismantle Peter Szondi's definition of the "Drama," challenging the viability of a traditional, hegemonic form that is self-centered and self-sustaining, dependent on the moment-to-moment, interpersonal interactions of the characters.[8] According to Szondi's vision of the history of modern drama, the "Drama" comes under heated attack during the 20th century as playwrights seek to integrate social thematics into their works, a movement that results in a myriad of dramatic forms and styles. As will be discussed in this essay, the theory that formal aesthetics can be shaped, if not inspired, by social thematics has significant implications for Asian American theatre.

Like the previously mentioned playwrights, Houston and Hwang experiment with non-realist narrative structure. In the two plays under review, however, they also explore non-realistic character development, allowing their dramatic figures to serve as the motivating forces behind the structural innovation. The aesthetic effects of experimental character construction are limitless in scope, ranging from symbolism's reduction of character agency, action, and dialogue, to epic theater's focus on the character's performative social and economic aspects. Characters emerging through expressionist and surrealist techniques, as seen in *Tea* and *FOB*, may evidence high degrees of abstraction and destabilization. While the magnified, subjective perspective of the expressionist protagonist shapes the dramatic events onstage, the surrealist character may act strangely and irrationally, confounding reality with chaotic shifts of identity and fantastic actions.

In contrast to realism's tendency toward materialism and its manipulation of truthful appearances, what these highly diverse, non-realistic aesthetics have in common is "the potential to interrupt the illusion of reality and directly interrogate spectatorial privilege."[9] Hence non-realistic aesthetics can potentially offer more consciously theatrical strategies to reformulate the processes through which Asian American personas are dramatized. Velina Hasu Houston's *Tea* and David Henry Hwang's *FOB* effectively dismantle the realist character paradigm in favor of more theatricalized representations of Asian American identity. Through these bold explorations, Bermel's padded seats may become decidedly less comfortable.

Tea, which premiered in 1987, constitutes the final segment of a dramatic trilogy in which Houston chronicles her mother's life as a Japanese army wife living in Kansas.[10] At the beginning of the play, four living women (Teruko, Atsuko, Setsuko, and Chiz) have gathered at the home of Himiko, one of their estranged community members who had recently committed suicide. They meet at Himiko's home to clean and organize her house and to perform a cleansing tea ceremony that will placate her restless spirit. The women are introduced to the audience through a poetic choral ode, one of the many non-realistic episodes in which the characters break away from the realistically-drawn present-moment action (i.e., the "real-life" tea ceremony in Himiko's living room) and speak artfully as a group:

Teruko: We Japanese women drink a lot of it.
Atsuko: Become it.
Setsuko: Swallow the tempest.
Chiz: And nobody knows.
Atsuko: The storm inside. (164)

To evoke this hidden "storm inside," and to allow it to materialize on the stage, Houston passes beyond realist preoccupations with surface appearances and physical reality, and explores the imaginative *interior* spaces of her characters. In order to understand the lives of these marginalized, foreign-born women living in Midwest America, she argues that one must look beyond the outward details of their public appearance. Within their private relationships, thoughts, memories, and even deaths, five unique and vital subjectivities are expressed in full force. This approach to character construction may be necessitated in part by the cultural background of the characters, as Teruko says pointedly, "It is the Japanese way to carry everything inside" (172). More important, Houston's application of an experimental strategy of dramatic representation that values interiority strengthens her greater project of dispelling negative stereotypes and humanizing her often overlooked Japanese American characters.

Houston's desire to explore spaces of interiority is first signaled by the given circumstances of the play. Himiko's tea ceremony, a culturally specific event, solicits a momentary exclusivity among the living women, who seldom meet in this fashion due to divergent lifestyles and personal tensions. In this private moment of common culture, gender, and social experience, the women are given the rare opportunity to pass beyond their reticence and reach new understandings of each other as kindred spirits. Indeed, the major action of the work, which develops through both the realistic living room scenes and non-realistic episodes of choral odes, flashbacks and fantasies, lies in the bonding process that occurs among the women as they share their private memories and feelings.[11]

The absence of the exterior world of their husbands, children, and other community members further enhances Houston's focus on interiority by offering a structuralist prism through which the women are defined in relationship to one another. Such a closed system allows for the emergence of their differences, relevancies, and oppositions from one another, highlighting their typically submerged individual personalities. Moreover, the women are also shown to be different *within* themselves, complicating the initial impressions of their stereotyped and simplified personas.[12]

Undoubtedly, the greatest resource for Houston's non-realist exploration of interior spaces lies in the construction of Himiko's ghost, a constant stage presence who is unseen and unheard by the other living characters. Using the imaginative potential of theater, Houston materializes Himiko's disembodied consciousness, revealing the unknown power of her active subjectivity and presence. Whereas dramatic ghosts are typically subordinate reflections of the living characters onstage, Himiko is present and central. To enter into the world of *Tea*, therefore, is to experience an expressionist manifestation of her private consciousness. While Houston does not utilize the rhapsodic language, jarring emotional intensity, or severe abstraction of the traditional expressionist protagonist, she privileges the dramatic stature of Himiko by allowing her subjective perspective and invisible journey to dominate the action of the play. Houston's dramatic use of temporal and spatial fragmentation, shifting characters, and split action further reveals the ethereal quality of Himiko's ghostly existence and point of view.

That Himiko's earthly life was one of both abjection and objectification is made clear in the text. During her life in the community of international army families, she served as the convenient "Other" for the wives struggling to define their own identities in America. Her violent marriage to an abusive husband (who she eventually killed), her attempts to costume herself in a blonde wig and sunglasses, her sexual promiscuity and drunkenness after becoming a widow prompted community members to shun her. In fact, Atsuko, considered her nothing short of a foreigner:

> she came in a low cut dress and that yellow wig, walking like a Korean . . . So many things she did were not acceptable. If she acted like that in Japan, people would think she was . . . well, a prostitute. Something was not right inside her head. (172)

Himiko suffered the additional effects of severe objectification, a reduction of her subjective presence that made her seem less human to those around her. For instance, having been abandoned in her house, Teruko captures Himiko's inanimate quality in a descriptive memory that she offers to Atsuko, "Standing behind the frosty glass. She looked like she was made of wax" (168). Himiko's history as a dance-hall girl with the possible venture into prostitution, her unplanned pregnancy, her marriage to a physically abusive man who considered her a prize, the multiple references to her as a spectacle for others, all give evidence of a character who had been systematically dehumanized.

In contrast to her muted and neglected presence on earth, Himiko enjoys full expressionist centrality and agency in her death. This dramatic empowerment is demonstrated not only by the careful dramaturgical development of her suicide,[13] but in her given role as an all-seeing and all-judging narrative agent. Himiko's postmortem emergence as both a speaker of the hidden truths, and an enabler for dramatic action, is absolute and ironic. Her poignant running commentary during the "real life" tea ceremony illustrates her own understanding of the women's private interior lives and thoughts:

Chiz: Is this the first time you've ever had tea together?
Himiko: It is, isn't it, Setsuko-san?
Setsuko: I'm busy with my family. And I have so much sewing to do.
Himiko: What is your excuse, Atsuko-san?
Atsuko: I keep busy with the church.
Himiko: And Teruko?
Teruko: I try to visit everyone, but I like to play Bingo with my sugar pie. . .
Himiko: Everyone has an alibi for silence. (184)

Unlike the other characters in the play, and perhaps even the audience members, Himiko understands these alibis and the Japanese concept of *enryo* that demands their silence, and thus her stature within the dramatic performance rises. In this dramatic world, Houston does not allow spectators any mastery of knowledge over the characters as is commonly seen in realistic, well-made plays.[14] Here, Himiko is the all-knowing narrative force that both prompts and disseminates exposition; as the expressionist protagonist, she is the creative presence onstage.

The living characters are also subject to Himiko's newly empowered position, responding intuitively to her questions, suggestions, and spatial relationships. In this manner, Himiko invisibly guides the characters through the process of group reconciliation, the act that will release her soul from limbo and ensure the living characters' salvation as well. For instance, after Atsuko's unexpected emotional breakdown at the end of the play, the crisis moment of the play, Himiko steps forward and guides the character back to the group so that she may make amends. After the following spoken line, "Atsuko-san, stay. If you leave now, no one will rest," the stage directions read: "Himiko stands in front of Atsuko and, without touching her, helps her to stand and balance using her hands as delicate guides" (195).

Himiko's enabling power, however, is most strikingly demonstrated in her initiations of the non-realistic poetic choral odes, flashbacks, and fantasies that interrupt the realistically drawn action of the tea ceremony. The process of calling the women back to the past functions as a central motif in the play, and Himiko, who is both obsessed with and burdened by the past, serves as the flamboyant master of ceremony for these transports back in time and space. For example, upon hearing Atsuko's derogatory comments about her behavior at her husband's grave, Himiko rushes forward into the scene, causing the women to freeze in place in "real time." With a theatrical flair, Himiko transcends her earthbound identity and speaks in the voice of a male army military leader: the stage directions read that Himiko "defiantly calls them back into the past with a roll call, stamping her foot as she calls out each name" (172). A flashback scene follows in which the women watch Himiko pour beer on her husband's grave, an enactment of the women's shared history that stands in for the "real-time"living room discussion of the event.

The play's circular shape, peopled by characters that shift easily between time, space, and identities, reflects an unfixed and fluid space of representation, one that is without strict boundaries and meanings. Such a quality is certainly reflective of Himiko's ethereal state as a ghost, again highlighting the dominating force of her presence. Nevertheless, Houston's use of the shifting dramatic form is an embodiment of Himiko's real-life personal trauma with a racially marked and objectified body, and of her past desperate attempts to eschew her own corporeality. The desire to transcend her biological and social identity is seen most pointedly in her real and after-life donning of a blonde wig and sunglasses, elements that hide the distinguishing Asian features of eyes and hair. Her promiscuity, alcoholism, and suicide also give evidence of one who punished her body.

That Himiko's death ended her corporeal entrapment is clear, but her desire to transcend her biological and social identity is still an urgent aspect of her private subjective self. In the expressionist world of her interiority, this project is enacted to greater effect and darker irony. For instance, in one choral ode, Himiko transforms into an imaginary white male carnival barker, who teasingly welcomes the women to America. She says in a booming voice, with the gestures of a male persona:

Welcome, welcome to the Land of Milk and Honey, the Bible Belt . . . On behalf of the tourism bureau, we'd like to welcome you to Kansas, the Sunflower State. We know all about you people. We read the magazines. We saw the cartoon. We saw *Sayonara*. (185)

Himiko's enactment is full of dark irony, demonstrating her continued desire to struggle against the power structures and institutionalized racism that oppressed her in life.

The high point of Himiko's enactment of her racial and sexual opposites is certainly the choral ode in which she plays out her husband's violent attitudes toward herself. Explaining "his" attitude of ownership toward Himiko, she says, as her husband, "She crawls under my fist like an orphan beggin' for love and my knuckles come down like a magnet" (191). The "men" (played by their wives) are shocked by the cruelty of Himiko's husband and do not respond, the action pauses for a moment, and the choral ode suddenly shifts to new dramatic material. It is as if Himiko herself, as the dominating presence of the work, takes a breath to digest the reality of her past lived experience.

In the real world, Himiko's attempts to escape her identity were painfully unsuccessful, interpreted as signs of her mental instability. But in the unreal world of her interiority (i.e., the theatrical performance of *Tea*), her transformative acts are no longer unnatural. These repeated acts of transformation and performance as enacted by Himiko and the living characters simply become the rules by which the "game" is played. Houston thus uses the natural tools of theater – impersonation, role-playing, porous spatial and temporal boundaries – to allow for complex visions of Asian American identities to emerge. Himiko's impulse to cross identity boundaries is not only beneficial in leading the living characters toward their necessary self-disclosures and reconciliations, but also in broadening the vision of Asian American women onstage. This dual-edged project becomes most clear in the choral odes during which the characters' husbands and children are enacted. Through the performance space of Himiko's consciousness, each of the living women experiences brief moments in which the presumed layer of Asian American female identity is peeled away in order to expose possible alternative subjectivities lying beneath the surface. While the characters' (and actors') sexed and racially marked bodies remain unchanged, the interior subjective forces prove to be supple, sustaining, and expansive.

Through the creation of these non-realistic transformative moments, Houston has multiplied the signifying potential of the Asian American female identity onstage. The fact that the expression of these alternate identities has a positive and healing effect on the characters emphasizes the totalizing possibilities of Asian American female identity. Through the enactment of their husbands, children, and past selves, and in Himiko's case the spiritual embodiment of a live performance, the characters emerge whole, strengthened, and at peace. As Josephine Lee notes, Houston's use of character transformation celebrates rather than denigrates Asian American identity, suggesting the possibility for personal empowerment and liberation from racial and gender subaltern positions.[15]

Having healed through the many performed transformations, the living characters are prepared to enact the final portion of the tea ceremony, the event that releases Himiko's troubled, earthbound soul. In return, Himiko, who has also healed through her own transformative processes, releases the living characters from the totalizing web of her ghostly subjectivity. As she drinks from her imaginary cup, she utters the final word and judgment of the play, "perfect." The stage directions read that "the minute that word is uttered, the women pack up their things" and leave the stage (200). The final image is clear. When Himiko's consciousness releases itself, the world of the play - as seen through her eyes - ends. In this unreal character, Houston has created an Asian American identity that is not an object of the performance, but rather the ultimate embodiment of its theatrical presence.

FOB, by David Henry Hwang, offers another rich example of experimental character construction and development, one that not only inspires structural innovation but reflects a post-modernist vision of identity formation.[16] First performed in 1979, this short play is one of the earliest dramas to deconstruct the turbulent processes through which Asian American identities are created. Set in the familiar setting of a family-run Chinese restaurant, Dale, an affluent assimilationist Chinese American, and Steve, a recent, well-to-do Hong Kong immigrant, compete for the attention of Grace, a Chinese American who immigrated as a child under difficult social and economic conditions. By the end of the play, the audience is presented with two choices for Chinese American identity, either ethnic pride and solidarity as represented by the romance of Grace and Steve, or the lonely and rejected state of Dale.

While Hwang's preference for Grace and Steve's vision of Chinese American identity is clearly established in the text, his greater project is to explore the complex cultural, social, and historical factors that influence Chinese American life and ethnic identity. In direct contrast to the realistic milieu of the Chinese restaurant, Hwang applies what poet and dramatist Robert Lowell calls the "true unreal,"[17] representational techniques that reveal, rather than embody (as in the case of *Tea*), material truths and realities. The idea of the "true unreal" is playfully non-realistic in spirit, finding kinship in the work of the surrealists who, as J. L. Styan notes, believed that "only by seeking the 'inner reality' in the theatre's own basically unreal terms can drama begin to touch the real life, the 'outer reality' of its audience's world."[18] Theatrical experiments of the "true unreal" reach well beyond art for art's sake; these dramas posit a deliberate anti-realism that is revelatory of a direct, observable reality. As Lowell writes, "The true unreal is about something and eats from the abundance of reality."[19]

Hwang's "reality" is contemporary Chinese American life and identity formation. In order to explore this reality through the terms of the "true unreal," he purposely denies the coherent, readable characterology dictated by realist aesthetics. Throughout the play, Grace and Steve shift from their real-life selves into mythical and historic subjectivities that reveal cultural and historical influences. These often-surprising character transformations result in several different performance realities and lines of dramatic action, all of which collide in a chaotic, and often confusing, anti-reality in front of the audience. Unlike the realist aesthetics founded on the logical nature of social and material reality, the surrealist qualities of this work challenge the spectator's quest for stable meaning, easy identifications, and logical narrative. Here, Hwang presents characters that are theme-based and dramaturgically unstable, dramatic figures that exist in opposition to the recognizable, human mirrors articulated by Bermel in his realist paradigm, and assumed by Houston in her imaginative quest for character interiority in *Tea*.

Hwang's "game" of multiplicitous shifting characters is established in the very first scenes of the play. After Dale's prologue describing the negative qualities of the clumsy FOB (or, "fresh off the boat") stereotype, Steve, as his "natural self," enters the restaurant of Grace's family eager to buy a bing (a Chinese pancake). When a dispute emerges between Grace and Steve over whether or not the restaurant has this food item, Steve takes away a box of pastries she had been tying and announces that he is not a mere human customer but rather Gwan Gung, the immortal god of warriors, writers, and prostitutes. Oddly unphased by his announcement, Grace asks him to tell a story in order to prove his identity; while he becomes engrossed in his own story, she steals back the box he had stolen from her.

After Steve (as Gwan Gung) leaves in search of a bing at another restaurant, Grace transforms her previous "everyday" self into the identity of Fa Mu Lan, the archetypal woman warrior. While playing out this mythical alter ego of strength, she accidentally throws her cousin, Dale, to the floor, quickly recovering her original persona as "everyday" Grace upon realizing her error. With great comic timing, Steve returns to the scene, now transformed into a negative stereotype of an FOB; his clumsy words, movements, and interactions fuel Dale's insecurity over his own identity. For the rest of the play, Grace and Steve shift into the mythical Fa Mu Lan, Gwan Gung, and stereotyped FOB personas, playfully hiding their alter-egos from an unknowing Dale.

What is particularly interesting is the method by which Hwang roots his surrealistic dramaturgy in the revelatory agenda of Lowell's "true unreal." While the presence of Gwan Gung and Fa Mu Lan represents a collective consciousness among Chinese Americans, it also reveals the legacy of gender inequality in Grace and Dale's reality. In other words, Hwang uses surrealistic effects metatheatrically; these two non-realistic, mythological figures comment on the "real-world" of the play, and by extension, on the real-world of Chinese American culture as well. For instance, Gwan Gung (as played by Steve), is a male god figure, and as such he enjoys extreme privileges and freedoms; his principle activities appear to be disposing of villagers and immigrants for sport, and holding elaborate banquets. According to his first monologue, spoken in Grace's presence, the planned killing of villagers had become too tedious for the impatient god, so he decided to improvise. Donning a blindfold, he entered into the human realm swinging his sword wildly at whatever stands in his path, hoping that at least some good may be attained by his efforts. His violent spree resulted in the brutal killing of Fa Mu Lan's family, an act he does not feel responsible for given its arbitrary occurrence.

On the other hand, Fa Mu Lan (as played by Grace), is both mortal and female, and is therefore depicted as less powerful than Gwan Gung. Her displacement from war and prestige is emphasized with poetic flair; "for she is no goddess, but girl-girl who takes her father's place in battle. No goddess, but woman, warrior-woman" (14). The storyline of Fa Mu Lan's eventual revenge on Gwan Gung for the death of her family weaves in and out of the principal storyline of Steve and Dale's competition for Grace's favor, and culminates in a final battle scene that determines the drama's conclusion.

The legacy of preferential treatment by Chinese and Chinese American families for males has been a familiar theme in literature. Hwang's use of the mythical Fa Mu Lan/Gwan Gung conflict, therefore, reflects the material, real-world problems of gender difference between Grace and her cousin, Dale. Though their grandfather (called Gung Gung), was wealthy, Grace's mother and Dale's father (brother and sister) received widely disparate treatment as they sought to come to America. Dale's father came to America in luxury, while Grace's mother received no support and had to delay her arrival to the country (which resulted in Grace's language barrier and her subsequent estrangement from school). Without Gung Gung's help, Grace's family lives at a lower economic level than her cousin's. Dale revels in his father's early luxury:

> Dale: Well, Gung Gung was pretty rich back then, so Dad must've been a pretty disgusting ... one, too. You know, his first year, he spent like thirteen thousand dollars. And that was back 'round 1950.
> Grace: Well, Mom never got anything.
> Dale: That's probably 'cause women didn't get anything back then. (28)

Dale's cavalier attitude toward the unjust treatment of his aunt and cousin parallels Gwan Gung's guiltlessness over his arbitrary killing spree, a perspective that is clearly in line with a capitalist economic model unsympathetic to those who get left behind.[20] But even more important, Dale's gender privilege is integrated into the very form of the play, demonstrating Hwang's desire to reveal the discourses of power that underlie each character's lives. For instance, Dale's dramaturgically central role bookends the play with his "authoritative," direct audience addresses. He is also the main subject of humor in the play; with his extremely materialistic and racist attitudes, and inability to adapt to the more "correct" values, he pushes the play toward a comedy of character based on his own dysfunction. Dale's centrality is further enhanced by Grace and Steve's attempts to hide their mythical identities from him. This leads to arguably one of the most humorous moments in the play when the mythical battle of Gwan Gung and Fa Mu Lan crashes into Dale's "real" reality, a surrealistic event that leaves Dale aghast as to how to resolve the conflicting spheres of existence in front of him.

> Steve: I AM GWAN GUNG!
> Grace: And I am Fa Mu Lan.
> Dale: I'll be Chiang Kai-shek, how's that? (47)

Dale proves to be the real-world equivalent of a privileged Gwan Gung; he dominates conversations, refuses to either prepare for or clean up after the meal, and his desire to transform Steve (e.g., teaching him to disco so as to make him "normal") makes him god-like in his presumptuousness.

Hwang's surrealist inclusion of the mythological alter egos of Steve and Grace reflects the gender inequality in contemporary Chinese American life, while also offering a perspective on the potential mythical strength of an ethnic American community. But the presence of Chinese American archetypes is only one level of Hwang's investigation into Chinese American life and identity formation. Ultimately, Hwang appears to embrace the broader notion of a ruptured, multiplicitous Asian American identity, one that refuses singularity and essentialism. As scholars Lisa Lowe and Josephine Lee have theorized, the Asian American identity is highly diverse and different within itself, resistant to the notion of a monolithic Asian American identity. Given this post-modern perspective on Asian American identity, Lee questions the predominance of coherent realistically-drawn characters when the Asian American self is theorized to be, if not actually, "fragmented, discordant, and divided."[21]

Hwang answers Lee's question with his extended application of the "true unreal" to Steve's persona. Through the character of Steve, Hwang reveals the condition of a splintered and multiplicitous Asian American identity, one that is ruptured by the process of historical immigration. For while Dale is confined to one subjectivity, and Grace two, Steve, the recent immigrant from Hong Kong, carries with him (in addition to the Gwan Gung and FOB personae) the numerous, unnamed subjectivities of past immigrants. In a manner similar to his transformations into the other alter egos, Steve enacts a broad spectrum of historic Chinese immigrant experiences, opening yet another sphere of performance reality onstage. In a series of monologues, Steve changes into three nameless characters that are 1) in the midst of making the hopeful decision to come to America, 2) undergoing the interview process, and 3) struggling to survive in a new land. Just as the mythical gender asymmetry of Gwan Gung and Fa Mu Lan reveal a gender inequality rooted in cultural truth, these three splintered subjectivities are revelatory of certain historical truths of Chinese American life and identity. In these speeches, Hwang refers to some of the significant themes that characterize early Chinese immigration to America: the dreams of easy gold and instant riches envisioned by sojourners, the intensely rigorous interview process imposed by the American government, and the inevitability of performing the labor shunned by white Americans.

As presented by Hwang, these historically grounded alter-egos, emanating from the splintered persona of Steve, "eat from the abundance of reality." This unreal reality Hwang reveals is not simply historical in nature, it is also metatheatrical and ironic. Hwang's use of the "true unreal" is meant to expose the flawed thinking of Dale and Steve (and all Chinese Americans), who believe themselves insulated from the legacy of prejudice facing Chinese immigrants. As Josephine Lee points out, Dale certainly believes himself to be different from the foreign-born Steve, but Steve also assumes that his status as a well-to-do immigrant will distance him from past generations of Chinese immigration.[22] This assumption is proven incorrect: these historical subjectivities not only splinter his identity, but he, too, suffers from the historic legacy of being unwelcome and isolated in a new land. Steve, in the persona of Gwan Gung, articulates the gap between his prior expectations and the reality he has encountered:

> I have come here before many times. This time, I said I will have it easy. I will come as no ChinaMan before—on a plane, with money and rank. And there is no change. I am still treated like this? (47)

That Steve—as Gwan Gung, an FOB, and numerous immigrant identities—has suffered from prejudice and isolation is clear. Nevertheless, Hwang offers a panacea to this dilemma through the formulation of a positive, if not idealized, image of the Chinese American identity. This identity is based on the integration and acceptance of the multiple voices, perspectives, and stories that comprise the Chinese American experience, and is symbolized in this play by the romantic reconciliation of Steve and Grace in the ending moments of the play. Having been defeated as Gwan Gung by Fa Mu Lan in the final battle, Steve transforms into an historic immigrant subjectivity, one that humbly begs for food from an American housewife. Grace, as her "everyday" self, gives him the box with the bing, the food item he had desired at the beginning of the play. The two characters share an intimate moment as Steve (as an historic immigrant) eats the bing hungrily.

> Grace: Eat the bing. Hold it in your hands. Your hands . . . are beautiful.
> Lift it to your mouth. Your mouth . . . is beautiful.
> Bite it with your teeth. Your teeth . . . are beautiful. Crush it
> with your tongue. Your tongue . . . is beautiful. Slide it down
> your throat. Your throat is beautiful.
> Steve: Our hands are beautiful. (49)

Hwang's emphasis on the bodies of Steve and Grace during their reconciliation serves two distinct functions; on one hand, it recuperates the sensuality and humanity of Steve's body that had been distorted through his enactments of the Gwan Gung, FOB, and immigrant subjectivities. On the other hand, it reifies the multiple narratives and voices into the Chinese American body, creating a sense of wholeness of mind and body. Without a doubt, the body implies nature, an organic structure; its corporealness binds Steve into a realistic character with reality and realness. Steve, who had previously been depicted as an elusive, unreadable and splintered vessel of subjectivities (or, a surrealist dramatic figure), is now given full embodiment as a coherent, realistically drawn character, one that may be capable of dissolving the audience's aesthetic and emotional distances as alluded to in Bermel's character-centered realistic paradigm.

Therefore Hwang has illustrated a theoretical process by which a Chinese American identity may progress from a surrealistic whirlwind of splintered subjectivities to a final meaningful form. Dale's observation at the end of the play that Steve, who now speaks fluent American English, learned the language faster than anyone he had ever met possesses a pointed double meaning. While Steve has indeed gained coherence as a "flesh and blood" character by the end of the play, his ability to embody and articulate a new identity represents a broader and more diverse vision of an emerging Chinese American identity coming into focus.

In conclusion, it is important to note that Houston and Hwang's innovative aesthetics are grounded in motivating substance and argument, reflecting Szondi's rationale for the diversity of formal experimentation in the modern era. In effect, these two playwrights have explored the politics of form, specifically a politics of an emerging discourse on Asian American self-representation. Such an achievement challenges the critical tradition that values experimental plays primarily for their artistic effects, or in other words, for their allegiance to the art's for art sake movement. As Marc Robinson notes in his groundbreaking work on experimental theatre, *The Other American Drama*, "Too often . . . we limit our discussion of alternative writing to questions of form . . . and rarely venture into the foggier areas zones where one must reflect on how form embodies thought."[23]

In *Tea*, Houston delves beyond the limits of observable surface appearances to explore both the private interiorities of her characters and the empowering unreality of consciousness after death. In *FOB*, Hwang creates theme-based and multiplicitous characters in order to reveal certain truths of Chinese American life, history and identity formation. By allowing the meaning of their dramatic figures to emerge through non-realistic phenomena, Houston and Hwang have exposed the limitations of a representational model that posits truth in physical fact and appearance. Using expressionist and surrealist techniques, they not only confound the spectator's sense of mastery over the characters onstage, but also complicate the comforting process of audience-character identification promised by Bermel's realist paradigm. In these unreal dramas, it is the unreal character that is comforted and healed as it undergoes a theatrical process that recuperates power and self-definition.

In short, Houston and Hwang have created liberating spaces of contestation in which Asian American identities can shed the real-life burdens of objectification, stereotype, and essentialism. In these unusual dramatic worlds, an Asian American character can perform either the racial and gendered "Other," embody a live performance through her subjective force, or perhaps slip away into a host of identities, only to reemerge as a coherent persona by the end of the play. Identity now becomes less a "natural" material possession and more a process of active, playful and healing self-creation. As these two works demonstrate, formal experimentation offers Asian American theatre artists the ability to fully embrace the performative spirit of theatre, grounding the emerging voices of Asian America in a broader, more consciously artistic and political, aesthetic vision.

Notes

Chapter 1

1. For parallel beginnings of Asian American Studies and Asian American community activism, see Glenn Omatsu's "The 'Four Prisons' and the Movements of Liberation: Asian American Activism from the 1960s to the 1990s" in *Asian American Studies: A Reader*, ed. Jean Yu-Wen Shen Wu and Min Song (New Brunswick: Rutgers University Press, 2000). The convergent interest of Asian American literary criticism and Asian American political activism is announced in the centrality of the phrase "claiming America" or "reclaiming America" in both fields of discourse.

2. Consider the recurrence of key concepts in recent Asian American critical monographs: Lisa Lowe, *Immigrant Acts: On Asian American Cultural Politics* (Durham: Duke University Press, 1996); David Leiwei Li's *Imagining the Nation: Asian American Literature and Cultural Consent* (Stanford: Stanford University Press, 1998); Wendy Ho, *In Her Mother's House: The Politics of Asian American Mother-Daughter Writing* (Walnut Creek: AltaMira Press, 1999); Rachel C. Lee, *The Americas of Asian American Literature: Gendered Fictions of Nation and Transnation* (Princeton: Princeton University Press, 1999); Sheng-mei Ma, *The Deathly Embrace: Orientalism and Asian American Identity* (Minneapolis: University of Minnesota Press, 2000); Leslie Bow, *Betrayal and Other Acts of Subversion: Feminism, Sexual Politics, Asian American Women's Literature* (Princeton: Princeton University Press, 2001); Viet Thanh Nguyen, *Race and Resistance: Literature and Politics in Asian America* (New York: Oxford University Press, 2002); Morris Young, *Minor Re/Visions: Asian American Literacy Narratives As a Rhetoric of Citizenship* (Carbondale, IL: Southern Illinois University Press, 2004).

3. In centrally locating the aesthetic in the analysis of Asian American literature, this volume responds to, and expands upon, earlier Asian American literary criticism that invites a formal, figurative, and intertextual emphasis in the reading of Asian American literature. Identifying a lack of formal and figurative analysis in current Asian American criticism, King-Kok Cheung's *Articulate Silences: Hisaye Yamamoto, Maxine Hong Kingston, Joy Kogawa* (Ithaca and London: Cornell University Press, 1993) attends to the narrative strategies in Asian American writing by women. Cheung emphatically states that just as it is important to exercise historical and social perspectives in reading Asian American literature, "it is equally important not to drown Asian American texts in context" (14). Sau-ling Wong's *Reading Asian American Literature: From Necessity to Extravagance* (Princeton: Princeton University Press, 1993) likewise insists on the equal significance of "contexts" and "intertexts" in developing a reading strategy for Asian American literature. While historical knowledge is indispensable, an intertextual reading practice—the highlighting of "choice and praxis" (10)—heightens the way Asian American texts "build upon, allude to, refine, controvert, and resonate with each other" (12). Further calls for a heightened awareness of form in the analysis of Asian American literature have been voiced in Shirley Lim's "Assaying the Gold; or Contesting the Ground of Asian American Literature," *New Literary History* 24 (1993): 147–69 and "Reconstructing Asian-American Poetry: A Case for Ethnopoetics," *MELUS* 14.2 (1987): 51–63; Patricia Chu, *Assimilating Asians: Gendered Strategies of Authorship in Asian America* (Durham: Duke University Press, 2000); Rocío G. Davis, *Transcultural Reinventions: Asian American and Asian Canadian Short-Story Cycles* (Toronto: TSAR Publications, 2001).
4. George Levine, "Reclaiming the Aesthetic," in *Aesthetics and Ideology*, ed. George Levine (New Brunswick: Rutgers University Press, 1994): 1, 3.
5. Michaels' assertion, which appeared in *Gold Standard and the Logic of Naturalism: American Literature at the Turn of the Century* (Berkeley: University of California Press, 1987), has functioned as a pivotal declaration for those contesting the reading of literature for oppositional tendencies. In this critical topography, the category of the aesthetic is seen not as forging a relationship with material reality, much less commenting on it; all we can say about the aesthetic is that it is yet another manifestation of the dominant logic of the culture. For instance, Michaels argues, "if 'The Yellow Wallpaper' is for me an exemplary text, it is not because it criticizes or endorses the culture of consumption, but precisely because, in a rigorous, not to say obsessive, way, it *exemplifies* that culture" (27, original emphasis). Many critics have argued that Michaels's immanent historicism conceives the "space of culture" as an omnipresent and singular entity; see Brook Thomas, "Walter Benn Michaels and the New Historicism"; Fredric Jameson, "Immanence and Nominalism in Postmodern Theoretical Discourse" in *Postmodernism or, The Cultural Logic of Late Capitalism* (Durham: Duke University Press, 1991); and Cary Wolfe, "Antinomies of Liberalism: The Politics of 'Belief' and the Project of Americanist Criticism," in *Discovering Difference: Contemporary Essays in American Culture*, ed. Christoph K. Lohmann (Bloomington: Indiana University Press, 1993).
6. Levine, "Reclaiming the Aesthetic": 2.
7. Consider, too, Stephen Regan's "The Return of the Aesthetic," the introductory essay to *The Politics of Pleasure: Aesthetics and Cultural Theory* (Philadelphia: Open

University Press, 1992). Responding to the way "the study of aesthetics has been marginalized or simply ignored in the later twentieth century" (1), the collection aims to reappraise and invigorate the study of aesthetics in relation to the concepts of "pleasure" and "value." Another critical essay collection on the aesthetic and beauty is *Beauty and the Critic: Aesthetics in an Age of Cultural Studies* (Tuscaloosa, AL: University of Alabama Press, 1997), especially Christopher Beach's "Recuperating the Aesthetic: Contemporary Approaches and the Case of Adorno."

8. Some examples are Alan Singer and Allen Dunn, eds. *Literary Aesthetics: A Reader* (Oxford: Blackwell Publishers, 2000), Patrick Maynard and Susan Feagin, eds. *Aesthetics: Oxford Reader* (Oxford: Oxford University Press, 1998), and Gaut Berys and Dominic McIver Lopes, eds. *Routledge Companion to Aesthetics* (London: Routledge, 2002).

9. Emory Elliott, "Cultural Diversity and the Problem of Aesthetics" in *Aesthetics in a Multicultural Age*, eds. Emory Elliott, Louis Freitas Caton, Jeffrey Rhyne (Oxford University Press, 2002): 8.

10. Tracing the transformation of single concepts (such as "pleasure" or "ethics") within the concept of the aesthetic are aforementioned Regan's *Politics of Pleasure* and Dorota Glowacka and Stephen Boos, eds. *Between Ethics and Aesthetics: Crossing the Boundaries* (Albany, NY: State University of New York Press 2002).

11. This is the agenda of Michael Clark, ed. *Revenge of the Aesthetic: The Place of Literature in Theory Today* (Berkeley: University of California Press, 2000) whose title boldly declares the essay collection's recuperative aim of bolstering the place of the aesthetic against sociological and ideological approaches to literature. Mark Rasmussen, ed. *Renaissance Literature and Its Formal Engagements* (New York: Palgrave, 2000) contests the eclipsed role of formal studies in Renaissance literary studies. The recent publication of Deepika Bahri, *Native Intelligence: Aesthetics, Politics, and Postcolonial Literature* (Minneapolis: University of Minnesota Press, 2003) is another attempt at centralizing the aesthetics within the concerns of postcolonial literature. In individual essays, too, such as W.J.T Mitchell's "The Commitment to Form; or, Still Crazy after All These Years," *PMLA* 118.2 (2003): 321–5, there is a growing insistence that literary analysis recognize the usefulness of formal analysis.

12. Levine, "Reclaiming the Aesthetic": 10.

13. Elaine Kim, *Asian American Literature: Introduction to the Writing and Its Social Context* (Philadelphia: Temple University Press, 1982).

14. Raymond Williams, *Keyword: A Vocabulary of Culture and Society* (New York: Oxford University Press, 1976): 6.

15. Elliott, "Cultural Diversity and the Problem of Aesthetics": 10.

16. Elliott, "Cultural Diversity and the Problems of Aesthetics": 14; Elliott especially points to Andrew Delbanco's essay "The Decline and Fall of Literature" in the *New York Review of Books* (Fall 1999) as being exemplary of the connection between conservative politics and conservative deployment of the aesthetic.

17. Abdul R. JanMohamed and David Lloyd, eds. *The Nature and Context of Minority Discourse* (New York: Oxford University Press, 1991): 4.

18. Nathaniel Mackey, *Discrepant Engagement: Dissonance, Cross-Culturality, and Experimental Writing* (New York: Cambridge University Press, 1993): 18.

19. Mackey (284, original emphasis). Numerous critics of ethnic minority writing have challenged precisely such a divisive and delimiting critical paradigm. In addition to

the aforementioned work such as Bahri's, Timothy Yu challenges the ostensible "in-compatib[ility]" between the "formal innovation represented by Language poetry and the feminist and multicultural poetries" in "Form and Identity in Language Poetry and Asian American Poetry," *Contemporary Literature* 41.3 (2002): 423. See also Aldon Lynn Nielsen, *Black Chant: Languages of African-American Postmodernism* (New York: Cambridge University Press, 1997).

20. The increasing need to examine the uses of literature in interdisciplinary studies is articulated in *American Literary Studies: A Methodological Reader* (New York: New York University Press, 2003). As the editors Michael Elliott and Claudia Stokes ask in their introduction, "What Is Literary Method and Why Does It Matter?": "What can texts tell us about American culture or history? How can literary interpretative methods be adapted to other fields? What do literary texts evince?" (1).

21. Garrett Hongo, "Asian American Literature: Questions of Identity," *Amerasia Journal* 20.3 (1994): 4–5.

22. Augie Tam, ed. "Is there an Asian American Aesthetic?" in *Contemporary Asian America: A Multidisciplinary Reader*, eds. Min Zhou and James V. Gatewood. (New York: New York University Press): 627–35.

23. Of course, the wording of the question itself (the adjectival use of "an Asian American" used to modify the noun "aesthetic") invites a concern over the pre-scriptive and homogenizing nature of the definition. The anxiety revealed in the panel participants' responses usefully delineates the conflicting views over the use of the aesthetic as the unifying ground of Asian American literary coalition. While some of the participants reject the very concept of "an Asian American aesthetic" as an oppressive requirement of identity politics, some strongly support the concept as a strategic ground of artistic, intellectual, and political inquiry.

Chapter 2

1. See the introduction to this volume.

2. On aesthetics and subjectivity, see the introduction and chapter 1 of Terry Eagleton, *The Ideology of the Aesthetic* (Oxford: Blackwell, 1990). For discussions of the sep-aration of the aesthetic from political economy see John Guillory, *Cultural Capital: The Problem of Literary Canon Formation* (Chicago: University of Chicago Press, 1993), especially chapter 5, and Mary Poovey, "Aesthetics and Political Economy in the Eighteenth Century: The Place of Gender in the Social Constitution of Knowl-edge," *Aesthetics and Ideology*, ed. George Levine (New Brunswick, NJ: Rutgers University Press, 1994): 79–105.

3. Lois-Ann Yamanaka, *Saturday Night at the Pahala Theatre* (Honolulu: Bamboo Ridge Press, 1993), *Wild Meat and the Bully Burgers* (San Diego: Harcourt Brace & Company, 1997), and *Blu's Hanging* (New York: Bard, 1998). For a more detailed chronology of events, consult the appendix to Candace Fujikane, "Sweeping Racism under the Rug of 'Censorship': The Controversy over Lois-Ann Yamanaka's *Blu's Hanging*," *Amerasia* 26.2 (2000): 158–94. My understanding of the controversy owes a great deal to the important work of Fujikane, who was directly embroiled in the protests at the local level in Hawaiʻi. See also Candace Fujikane, "Reimagining

Development and the Local in Lois-Ann Yamanaka's *Saturday Night at the Pahala Theatre*," *Women in Hawaiʻi: Sites, Identities, and Voices*, ed. Joyce N. Chinen, Kathleen O. Kane and Ida Yoshinaga (Honolulu: University of Hawaiʻi Press, 1997): 40–61.

4. See Candace Fujikane, "Asian Settler Colonialism in Hawaiʻi," *Amerasia* 26.2 (2000): xv–xxii, and Jonathan Okamura, "Social Stratification," *Multicultural Hawaiʻi: The Fabric of a Multiethnic Society*, ed. Michael Haas (New York: Garland, 1998): 185–204.

5. One salient indication that the award committee read *Blu's Hanging* in a continental and national American context rather than within a local Hawaiian framework can be seen in their description of Yamanaka as a "native Hawaiian" writer, which is incorrect since Yamanaka is not native Hawaiian but local Japanese. Such a basic error reveals a marked lack of familiarity with the racial politics of communities in Hawaiʻi and illuminates the unequal circulation of knowledge that leads to disparate readings.

6. Statement from the Board of the AAAS, *AAAS Newsletter*, 15.2 (1998): 5.

7. "Response by the Fiction Award Committee," *AAAS Newsletter* 15.2 (1998): 7.

8. This is Bourdieu's term. The most extensive elaboration of cultural capital can be found in Pierre Bourdieu, *Distinction: A Social Critique of the Judgement of Taste*, trans. Richard Nice (Cambridge, MA: Harvard University Press, 1984), but the title essay, along with "The Market of Symbolic Goods," in Bourdieu, *The Field of Cultural Production: Essays on Art and Literature*, ed. Randal Johnson (New York: Columbia University Press, 1993), provides perhaps the best summary of the workings of capital in the cultural field. See also Bourdieu, *The Rules of Art: Genesis and Structure of the Literary Field*, trans. Susan Emanuel (Stanford: Stanford University Press, 1995).

9. John Okada, *No-No Boy* (Seattle: University of Washington Press, 1979), and Theresa Hak Kyung Cha, *Dictée* (Berkeley: University of California Press, 2001).

10. Hyun Yi Kang, Norma Alarcon, and Elaine H. Kim, eds., *Writing Self, Writing Nation: A Collection of Essays on Dictée by Theresa Hak Kyung Cha* (Berkeley: Third Woman Press, 1994).

11. Sau-ling Wong cautions against such a developmental narrative in "Denationalization Reconsidered: Asian American Cultural Criticism at a Theoretical Crossroads," *Amerasia* 21.1-2 (1995): 1–27, which is echoed by King-Kok Cheung in "Re-Viewing Asian American Literatures," *An Interethnic Companion to Asian American Literature* (Cambridge: Cambridge University Press, 1997), but the force of their warnings is directed against the turn to transnationalism rather than a theoretical formalism.

12. Frank Chin, Jeffrey Paul Chan, Lawson Fusao Inada, and Shawn Wong, eds., *Aiiieeeee!: An Anthology of Asian American Writers* (New York: Meridian, 1997).

13. Elaine H. Kim, Asian American Literature: An Introduction to the Writings and Their Social Context (Philadelphia: Temple University Press, 1982).

14. Sau-ling Wong, *Reading Asian American Literature: From Necessity to Extravagance* (Princeton: Princeton University Press, 1993): 9.

15. See Levine, Introduction to *Aesthetics and Ideology*.

16. See Bourdieu, "The Production of Belief: Contribution to an Economy of Symbolic Goods," and "The Historical Genesis of a Pure Aesthetic," in *Field of Cultural Production*.

17. In "Literary Criticism at the Edge of the Millenium; or, from Here to History," *Aesthetics and Ideology*: 40–53, Myra Jehlen notes that "this ideological formalism may be in danger of generating its own reductionism. Far from there being any need to argue the unity of form and content, it now seems rather that critics are in danger of ignoring the more explicit content of a work as superficial or even as misleading" (45).

18. Lisa Lowe, *Immigrant Acts: On Asian American Cultural Politics* (Durham, NC: Duke University Press, 1996): 31.

19. Lowe also includes readings of *No-No Boy* and *America Is in the Heart*, but her readings are of their formal disruptions, and not, as in the earlier vein, of their representational content (*Immigrant Acts*, 45–51).

20. The recent work of Elaine Kim offers an interesting perspective on the critical/political transformations in the field. See the Foreword to *Reading the Literatures of Asian America*, ed. Shirley Lim and Amy Ling (Philadelphia: Temple University Press, 1992): xi–xvii, and "Poised on the In-Between: A Korean American's Reflections on Theresa Hak-Kyung Cha's *Dictée*," *Writing Self, Writing Nation*: 3–30.

21. Shelley Wong, "Unnaming the Same: Theresa Hak Kyung Cha's *Dictée*," *Writing Self, Writing Nation*: 132.

22. Similarly, the primary aim of critical activity in Asian American literary studies shifted from establishing the autonomy of Asian American *literature* to establishing the autonomy of Asian American *literary studies*. In order for critics to acquire greater autonomy, though, power must be seized in part from the institution, but also from the community, and from writers.

23. One of the primary goals of the Third World Strike was to foster academic work that was not merely esoteric knowledge for the sake of knowledge ("art for art's sake") but knowledge that would serve the needs of the community. This led to an emphasis on social science research that could be used to influence policy decisions, for example. See William Wei, *The Asian American Movement* (Philadelphia: Temple University Press, 1993), and Lane Ryo Hirabayashi and Marilyn C. Alquizola, "Asian American Studies: Reevaluating for the 1990s," *The State of Asian America: Activism and Resistance in the 1990s*, ed. Karin Aguilar-San Juan (Boston: South End Press, 1994): 351–64.

24. Crystal Parikh, "Blue Hawai'i: Asian Hawaiian Cultural Production and Racial Melancholia," *Journal of Asian American Studies* 5.3 (2002): 200.

25. Ibid., 199.

26. For a similarly evasive account of the controversy, see Kandice Chuh, *Imagine Otherwise: On Asian Americanist Critique* (Durham, NC: Duke University Press, 2003). In her discussion of the book in relation to the protests, Chuh acknowledges the antiracist critique, but then declares that "Asian American studies must be able to also function along a logic of *and*, as in . . . racism *and* what else? In my reading, *Blu's Hanging* theorizes an alternative epistemological space through its articulation of the failures of the heteronormative family as a construct that secures the promises of 'home' as a space of fulfilled needs and safety" (142–3, original emphasis). The problem is that the *and*, instead of prompting an analysis of the connection between the text's racism and its "nonheteronormativity," functions instead to maintain the political and the theoretical readings in two discrete spaces. Just as in Parikh's article, the literary analysis of the text occupies an "alternative epistemological space" that

reproduces the division of the conflict into a material domain of political conflict and a literary theoretical domain of the idealization of Asian American culture. Contrast this with the very different account given by Viet Nguyen in *Race & Resistance: Literature & Politics in Asian America* (Oxford: Oxford University Press, 2002), 157–66, which is altogether more sensitive to the particular historical context surrounding the protests.

27. It is, it seems to me, the resistance of *Rolling the R's* to universalizing readings that provokes my students almost without exception to perceive it as not literature. These responses seem to be ratified by the considerable disparity in the success achieved by Yamanaka and Linmark. While this resistance to abstraction also characterizes Yamanaka's earlier work, the trajectory of her career, from Bamboo Ridge, the small local press in Hawaiʻi, to Farrar, Straus & Giroux, is reflected in the growing literariness of her output.

28. R. Zamora Linmark, *Rolling the R's* (New York: Kaya Production, 1995): 146.

29. Ibid., 148–9.

Chapter 3

1. Stuart Hall, "New Ethnicities," *Stuart Hall: Critical Dialogues in Cultural Studies*, ed. D. Morley and K. Chen (London and New York: Routledge, 1996), 441–449.

2. Meaghan Morris, "Banality in Cultural Studies," *Discourse: Journal for Theoretical Studies in Media and Culture* 10, no. 2 (1988), 3–29.

3. John Guillory, "Bourdieu's Refusal," in *Pierre Bourdieu: Fieldwork in Culture*, ed. N. Brown and I. Szeman (Lanham and Oxford: Rowman and Littlefield Publishers, Inc, 2000), 21.

4. Morris, "Banality in Cultural Studies," 15.

5. Viet Thanh Nguyen, *Race and Resistance: Literature and Politics in Asian America* (Oxford: Oxford University Press, 2002), 145.

6. See Eleanor Ty, *The Politics of the Visible in Asian North American Narratives*, (Toronto: University of Toronto Press, 2004); Eleanor Ty and Donald Goellnicht, eds, *Asian North American Identities: Beyond the Hyphen*, (Indiana: Indiana University Press, 2004); and Guy Beauregard, "What is at Stake in Comparative Analyses of Asian Canadian and Asian American Literary Studies," *Essays on Canadian Writing* 75 (2000), 217–39 for discussions of "Asian North American" as an inclusive category of analysis.

7. See Jeff Derksen, "Making Race Opaque: Fred Wah's Poetics of Opposition and Differentiation," *West Coast Line* 29 (1995–6), 63 for a discussion of the trivialization of Wah's racial difference in discussions of his avant-garde poetics.

8. See Jeff Derksen, "Unrecognizable Texts: From Multicultural to Antisystemic Writing," in *Telling it Slant: Avant-Garde Poetics of the 1990s*, ed. M. Wallace and S. Marks (Tuscaloosa and London: The University of Alabama Press, 2002), 145–60.

9. See Walter K. Lew, *Premonitions: The Kaya Anthology of New Asian North American Poetry* (New York: Kaya Productions, 1995) for examples of Asian American experimental work. Perhaps tellingly, many of the authors contained in the anthology have increased visibility *outside* the field of Asian American literary studies.

10. See *The L=A=N=G=U=A=G=E Book*, ed. Bruce Andrews and Charles Bernstein (Carbondale: Southern Illinois University Press, 1984); *The Politics of Poetic Form: Poetry and Public Policy*, ed. Bernstein (New York: Roof Press, 1990); and Ron Silliman, *The New Sentence* (New York: Roof Press, 1977) for an elaboration of these poetics.

11. Timothy Yu, "Identity in Language Poetry," *Contemporary Literature* 41, no. 3 (2000): 423, emphasis added.

12. Jeff Derksen, "Making Race Opaque: Fred Wah's Poetics of Opposition and Differentiation," *West Coast Line* 29 (1995–6), 63.

13. Ron Silliman, "Poetry and the Politics of the Subject," *Socialist Review*, XVIII, 3 [July–September 1988], 63.

14. See Guy Beauregard, "The Emergence of 'Asian Canadian Literature': Can Lit's Obscene Supplement?" *Essays on Canadian Writing* 67 (1999), 53–76, and Donald Goellnicht, "A Long Labour: The Protracted Brith of Asian Canadian Literature," *Essays on Canadian Writing* 72 (2000), 1–41.

15. Goellnicht "A Long Labour," 1.

16. A revised version is included in Miki's book *Broken Entries: Race Subjectivity Writing* (Toronto: The Mercury Press, 1998).

17. See Beauregard "What Is at Stake in Comparative Analyses of Asian Canadian and Asian American Literary Studies"

18. See Marie Lo's dissertation, "Fields of Recognition: Reading Asian Canadian Literature in Asian America," (University of California, Berkeley, 2001).

19. Roy Miki, "Altered States: Global Currents, the Spectral Nation, and the Production of 'Asian Canadian,'" *Journal of Canadian Studies* 35, no. 3 (2000), 58.

20. Roy Miki, "Can Asian Adian? Reading the Scenes of 'Asian Canadian,'" *West Coast Line* 34, no. 3 (2001), 73.

21. Ibid, 75.

22. See Frank Chin, Jeffery Paul Chan, Lawson Fusao Inada, and Shawn Wong, eds. Aiiieeee!: An Anthology of Asian-American Writers. (New York: Doubleday, 1975).

23. Pierre Bourdieu, *The Field of Cultural Production*, ed. Randal Johnson (New York: Columbia University Press, 1992), 2. Introduction by Randal Johnson.

24. Pierre Bourdieu and Loic Waquant explain that "a field is simultaneously a *space of conflict and competition*, the analogy here being with a battlefield, in which participants vie to establish monopoly over the species of capital effective in it—cultural authority in the artistic field, scientific authority in the scientific field, sacerdotal authority in the religious field, and so forth—and the power to decree the hierarchy and 'conversion rates' between all forms of authority in the field of power." See Pierre Bourdieu and Loic Waquant, *An Invitation to Reflexive Sociology* (Chicago: The University of Chicago Press, 1992), 17.

25. Pierre Bourdieu, *The Field of Cultural Production*, 38–39.

26. Nguyen, *Race and Resistance*, 144.

27. Antonio Gramsci, *Selections from the Prison Notebooks* (London: Lawrence and Wishart, 1973).

28. Juliana Chang, "Reading Asian American Poetry," *MELUS* 21, no.1 (2001): 85. See also Brian Kim Stefans, "Remote Parsee: An Alternative Grammar of Asian North American Poetry," in *Telling it Slant: Avant-Garde Poetics of the 1990s*, ed. M.

Wallace and S. Marks (Tuscaloosa and London: The University of Alabama Press, 2002) 43–75.

29. Bruce Andrews, "Poetry as Explanation, Poetry as Praxis," *The Politics of Poetic Form: Poetry and Public Policy*, ed Charles Bernstein, (New York: Roof Press, 1990), 23.

30. Ibid, 23

31. Ibid, 24

32. Ron Silliman, Carla Harryman, Lyn Hejinian, Steve Benson, Bob Perelman, Barrett Watten, "Aesthetic Tendency and the Politics of Poetry: A Manifesto," 19–20 (1988): 264.

33. Ibid, 270.

34. Ron Silliman, *The New Sentence*, (New York: Roof Press, 1977): 10.

35. Ibid, 17.

36. Pierre Bourdieu, "The Market of Symbolic Goods," *Poetics* 14 (1985): 14.

37. Ibid, 16.

38. Ibid, 16.

39. John Guillory, *Cultural Capital: The Problem of Literary Canon Formation* (Chicago and London: The University of Chicago Press, 1993), 329.

40. Ibid, 329.

41. Bourdieu, "The Market of Symbolic Goods," 23.

42. Guillory, *Cultural Capital*, 330.

43. See Gilles Deleuze and Felix Guattari, *A Thousand Plateaus* (Minneapolis: University of Minnesota Press, 1987).

44. Michael Greer, "Ideology and Theory in Recent Experimental Writing, or, the Naming of 'Language Poetry,'" *boundary 2* 16, no. 1 (1989), 344.

45. Jeff Derksen, "Globalism and the Role of the Cultural: Nation, 'Multiculturalism', and Articulated Locals," Diss, English, University of Calgary, (2000), 59.

46. Nichol, bp, "TRG: A Conversation with Fred Wah," Open Letter (1977), 49.

47. Ibid, 42.

48. Quoted in Wah, *Faking It: Poetics and Hybridity*, ed. S. Kamboureli, *The Writer as Critic*. (Edmonton: NeWest Press, 2000), 24.

49. Ibid, 24.

50. Derksen, "Unrecognizable Texts," 69.

51. Fred Wah, *Waiting for Saskatchewan* (Winnipeg: Turnstone Press, 1985), 4.

52. Fred Wah, *Alley Alley Home Free* (Red Deer: Red Deer College Press, 1992): 5.

53. Jeff Derksen, "Globalism and the Role of the Cultural: Nation, 'Multiculturalism', and Articulated Locals," Diss, English, University of Calgary, (2000): 177.

54. I would like to acknowledge the generous support of the Social Sciences and Humanities Research Council of Canada.

Chapter 4

1. John Lowe, "Monkey Kings and Mojo: Postmodern Ethnic Humor in Kingston, Reed, and Vizenor," *MELUS* 21, no. 4 (1996): 104.

2. Maxine Hong Kingston, *The Woman Warrior: Memoirs of a Girlhood among Ghosts* (New York: Picador, 1981): 13.

3. Maxine Hong Kingston, *Tripmaster Monkey* (New York: Vintage, 1987): 18. Hereafter cited parenthetically within the text.

4. Diane Simmons, *Maxine Hong Kingston* (New York: Twayne 1999): 145–6.

5. Gerald Vizenor, *Manifest Manners: Postindian Warriors of Survivance* (Hanover: Wesleyan University Press, 1994): 136.

6. Richard Fung, "Multiculturalism Reconsidered," in *Yellow Peril Reconsidered*, ed. Paul Wong (Vancouver: On Edge, 1990): 18.

7. Gerald Vizenor, *Fugitve Poses: Native American Scenes of Absence and Presence* (Lincoln, NE: University of Nebraska Press, 1998): 154.

8. Simmons, Maxine Hong Kingston: 15.

9. Maxine Hong Kingston, "Cultural Mis-Readings by American Reviewers," in *Asian and Western Writers in Dialogue: New Cultural Identities*, ed. Guy Amirthanayagam (London: Macmillan, 1982): 55.

10. Vizenor, *Manners*: 132.

11. Graham Huggan, *The Postcolonial Exotic: Marketing the Margins* (New York: Routledge, 2001).

12. Sämi Ludwig, "Celebrating Ourselves in the Other, Or: Who Controls the Conceptual Allusions in Kingston?" in *Asian American Literature in the International Context: Readings on Fiction, Poetry, and Performance*, eds. Rocío G. Davis and Sämi Ludwig (Hamburg: LIT, 2002): 49

13. Ibid., 52.

14. Vizenor, *Manners*: 128.

15. Dorothy Wang, "Undercover Asian: John Yau and the Politics of Self-Identification," in *Asian American Literature in the International Context: Readings on Fiction, Poetry, and Performance*, eds. Rocío Davis and Sämi Ludwig (Hamburg: LIT, 2002): 137.

16. Wang writes, "Yau speaks of the late 1970s and 1980s, the period before he came to be included in anthologies of Asian American writing (in the early 1990s), as one in which 'there was literally nobody sympathetic to me'" (136).

17. Elaine Kim, Asian American Literature: An Introduction to the Writings and Their Social Context (Philadelphia: Temple University Press, 1982): 22.

18. Lisa Lowe, *Immigrant Acts: On Asian American Cultural Politics* (Durham, NC: Duke University Press, 1996): 65.

19. Vizenor, *Manners*: 16.

20. The following passage signals Elaine Kim's own departure from didacticism. As she proposes, "[t]he cultural nationalist defenses we constructed were anti-assimilationist. But while they opposed official nationalisms, the Asian American identity they allowed for was fixed, closed, and narrowly defined . . . privileging race over gender and class . . . and constructing a hierarchy of authenticity to separate the 'real' from the 'fake'" (Elaine Kim, "Preface," in *Charlie Chan Is Dead: An Anthology of Contemporary Asian American Fiction*, ed. Jessica Hagedorn [New York: Penguin, 1993]: ix).

21. Simmons, Maxine Hong Kingston: 37.

22. Ibid., 38.

23. Ludwig, "Celebrating Ourselves in the Other": 37.

24. Elaine Kim, "Preface": ix.

25. Vijay Prashad, *Everybody Was Kung Fu Fighting: Afro-Asian Connections and the Myth of Cultural Purity* (Boston: Beacon, 2001).

Chapter 5

1. Marjorie Perloff, review of *Forbidden Entries*, by John Yau, *Boston Review* 22.3-4 (1997): 39.
2. Timothy Yu, "Form and Identity in Language Poetry and Asian AmericanPoetry," *Contemporary Literature* 41.3 (Fall 2000): 448.
3. Marjorie Perloff, *Poetry on and Off the Page: Essays for Emergent Occasions*(Evanston, IL: Northwestern University Press, 1998): 24.
4. Ibid., 28.
5. Ibid., 19.
6. Ibid., 28.
7. Juliana Chang, "Reading Asian American Poetry," *MELUS* 21.1(1996): 87.
8. Paul Gilroy, "British Cultural Studies and the Pitfalls of Identity," in *Black British Cultural Studies*, ed. Houston Baker et al. (Chicago: University of Chicago Press, 1996): 238.
9. George Uba, "Versions of Identity in Post-Activist Asian American Poetry," in *Reading the Literatures of Asian America*, ed. Shirley Geok-lin Lim and Amy Ling (Philadelphia: Temple University Press, 1992): 43.
10. Ibid., 33.
11. Ibid., 36.
12. John Yau, *Radiant Silhouette: New and Selected Work* (Santa Rosa: Black Sparrow Press, 1989): 18.
13. John Yau, *Sometimes* (New York: Sheep Meadow Press, 1979): 39.
14. Ibid., 44.
15. Yau, *Radiant Silhouette*: 171.
16. Ibid., 111.
17. Benedict Anderson, *Imagined Communities: Reflections of the Origin and Spread of Nationalism* (London: Verso, 1991): 145.
18. Louis Althusser, "Ideology and the Ideological State Apparatuses" in *Critical Theory Since 1965*, ed. Hazard Adams and Leroy Searle (Tallahassee: Florida State University Press, 1986):, 248.
19. Lisa Lowe, *Immigrant Acts: On Asian American Cultural Politics* (Durham, NC: Duke University Press, 1996): 103–4.
20. Yau, Radiant Silhouette: 112.
21. Lowe: 25.
22. Lauren Berlant, *The Queen of America Goes to Washington City: Essays on Sex and Citizenship* (Durham, NC: Duke University Press, 1997): 48.
23. Ibid., 4.
24. Perloff, review: 39.
25. Homi K. Bhabba, "The Other Question: Discourse, Discrimination and the Discourse of Colonialism" in *Black British Cultural Studies*, ed. Houston Baker et al. (Chicago, University of Chicago Press, 1996): 90.
26. I would like to express my gratitude to John Yau for permission to quote his poetry and, of course, for the poetry itself. My thanks also go to Steve Axelrod for his typically insightful and encouraging comments on early versions of this essay.

Chapter 6

1. Shyam Selvadurai, *Funny Boy* (Toronto: McClelland and Stuart Inc., 1997); Michael Ondaatje, *Anil's Ghost* (New York: Vintage, 2001). On the short-story cycle and *Funny Boy* as a example of the genre, see Rocío G. Davis, *Transcultural Reinventions: Asian American and Asian Canadian Short-Story Cycles* (Toronto: TSAR Publications, 2001): 1–26, 40–50. See also Timothy Dow Adams' review of *Funny Boy*, "Coming of Age."*Canadian Literature* 149 (Summer 1996): 112–3. I appreciate Davis' formal precision but prefer to emphasize the book's cohesiveness by reading it as a bildungsroman.

2. See Catherine Belsey, "Constructing the Subject: Deconstructing the Text," in *Feminist Criticism and Social Change: Sex, Class, and Race in Literature and Culture*, ed. Judith Newton and Deborah Rosenfelt (New York: Methuen, 1985): 45–64; Louis Althusser, *Lenin and Philosophy and Other Essays* (New York: Monthly Review Press, 1971): 127–86; and Roland Barthes, *S/Z: An Essay* (New York: Hill and Wang/Farrar, Straus, and Giroux, 1974).

3. In this sense Arjie and Diggy are descendents of Elizabeth and Jane Bennett, Jo and Meg March, or Maggie and Tom Tulliver. See Jane Austen, *Pride and Prejudice* (New York: W. W. Norton, 1993); Louisa May Alcott, *Little Women* (New York: W. W. Norton, 2004): 287; and George Eliot, *The Mill on the Floss* (Boston: Houghton Mifflin, 1961).

4. See Toril Moi, *Sexual/Textual Politics: Feminist Literary Theory* (London and New York: Methuen, 1985): 99–100.

5. See Kingsley M. de Silva, "Sri Lanka: History," *The Far East and Australasia 2003, 34th Edition* (London: Europa Publications/Taylor and Francis Group, 2003): 1328-31; and "Post-Independence Politics" in *Background Note: Sri Lanka*, (U.S. Department of State: Bureau of South Asian Affairs, August 2003 website): http://www.state.gov/r/pa/ei/bgn/5249pf.htm

6. See Nancy Armstrong, *Desire and Domestic Fiction: A Political History of the Novel* (New York: Oxford University Press, 1987); and Patricia P. Chu, *Assimilating Asians: Gendered Strategies of Authorship in Asian America* (Durham, NC: Duke University Press, 2000): 14–5.

7. See Lauren Berlant and Michael Warner, "Sex in Public," *Critical Inquiry* 24:2 (Winter 1998): 547–66. The authors argue that in our culture heterosexuality and the exclusion of homosexuality are implicit, not only in the discussion of sex itself, but also in our culture's use of "the love plot of intimacy and familialism" to signify membership in the society; "scenes of intimacy, coupling, and kinship" to signify community; and the use of "generational narrative and reproduction" to signify historic connections to the past and future. These practices bestow upon heterosexuality a sense of rightness and normalcy, which they call "heteronormativity." Berlant and Warner argue that heteronormativity pervades social and cultural forms and practices defining "nationality, the state, and the law; commerce; medicine; and education; as well as in the conventions and affects of narrativity, romance, and other protected spaces of culture" (553-54). While I find the concept of heteronormativity useful, my use of the term is meant more as a gesture than a finished argument. Neither *Funny Boy* nor *Anil's Ghost* reimagines public society as

a realm of liberated sexual activity, but both expend much energy challenging the grip of heteronormativity on their protagonists.

8. The novel is set three years after Sirissa's disappearance in 1989, but evokes a historical assassination that occurred in 1993. See Ondaatje: 184–5, 294, and de Silva: 1333–5.

9. On the nineteenth-century detective story's positivist assumptions see Belsey: 58–63. On the historical novel see Fredric Jameson, *The Political Unconscious: Narrative as a Social Symbolic Act* (Ithaca, NY: Cornell University Press, 1981) and Georges Lukacs, *The Historical Novel* (Lincoln, NE: University of Nebraska Press, 1962).

10. Speaking of the composition of *Anil's Ghost,* Ondaatje has explained, "The structure happens as the story unravels, with each discovery, . . . a sidebar or descant. . . . These things are discovered in the actual writing, and they're finessed later on." Later, he says he likes to multiply perspectives within a single scene, comparing the multiple, simultaneous streams of consciousness with cubism, a visual analogy to a modernist fiction aesthetic. The interview and earlier work like *The English Patient* suggest Ondaatje's preference for open-ended, non-linear novel composition. See Dave Weich, "Michael Ondaatje's Cubist Civil War," at http://powells.com/authors/ondaatje.html and Ondaatje, *The English Patient* (New York: Vintage-Random, 1993).

11. Lisa Lowe, *Immigrant Acts: On Asian American Cultural Politics* (Durham, NC: Duke University Press, 1996): 104–7.

12. Berlant and Warner, "Sex in Public": 553–4.

13. Chu, Assimilating Asians: 9–19.

14. This seems to combine the assassination of President Ramasinghe Premadasa of the UNP (May 1 1993) by a suicide bomber with a suicide bombing that killed Clement V. Gunaratna, Minister of Industrial Development, at a parade in the capital marking the country's first "War Heroes' Day." For more on the country's political history see De Silva (1329–38) and "Peace Process of Sri Lanka: The Official Website of the Sri Lankan Government's Secretariat" (http://www.peacinsrilanka.org/fullstory1.asp).

15. According to tradition, Ananda was the primary transmitter and interpreter of the Buddha's teachings after the death of the Buddha. Personal communication, Professor Divya Saksena.

Chapter 7

1. As Sue-Im Lee points out accurately in the Introduction, the problem of representing Asian American life using identity politics, ethnography, and immigration history as transparent criteria both for literary production and critical reception has been the norm. Most notably, the controversy (albeit misogynist) between the editors of *Aiiieeeee!* and Maxine Hong Kingston is a case in point. Using Elaine Kim's *Asian American Literature* (1982) to mark the point of departure, Lee writes, "the artistic and political modality with which Asian American literature entered the U.S. academia demonstrates, in a meta-critical sense, what Raymond Williams identified as the dual condition of 'representation': there 'is a possible degree of overlap between representative and representation in their political and artistic senses.'" That

is, Asian American literary criticism served as more than a second level "represen-tation" of the artistic endeavors of literary production. It fundamentally functioned as a discursive "representative" of Asian American subject positions. The case of the listed South Asian authors is more complicated. For one, their experiences re-flect the post-1965 Immigration Reform period, so they are further removed from the brutal exclusionary and racist treatment experienced of the early Chinese and Japanese Americans. For another, because of their facility with the English language (thanks to the British), they perform a neat substitutive maneuver by using post-colonial resistance sensibilities and diasporic angst sentiments to assimilate into a multicultural/Asian America. All this notwithstanding, the novels of these authors beg for a political, sociohistorical reading.

2. I have argued this facet of contemporary South Asian writing elsewhere, too, most recently in "Ethical Responsibility in Inter-subjective Space" forthcoming in *Cross Wires: Asian American Imaginations in National, Transnational, and Global Contexts*, eds. Shirley Geok-Lin Lim, et.al., Temple University Press. The principal argument for using ethics is also articulated in different ways by Peter Singer in *The Ethics of Globalization* (New Haven, CT: Yale University Press, 2002) and Amy Chua in *World on Fire: How Exporting Free Market Democracy Breeds Ethnic Hatred and Global Instability* (New York: Doubleday, 2001).

3. I thank the editors for bringing Emory Elliott's *Aesthetics in a Multicultural Age* to my attention. While many of the essays in his anthology engage in multidisciplinary and multicultural challenges to a Western, classical understanding of aesthetics, my examples are slightly different because I braid ethics with feminist criticism, and create another trajectory for analysis beyond identity politics in explaining the value and pleasures of the text.

4. This line of reasoning mirrors Lee's point in the "Introduction," wherein criti-cal discourses assume "ethnic" can only lead to a sociological or anthropological "aesthetic."

5. Richard Cohen, *Face to Face with Levinas* (Albany, NY: State University of New York Press, 1986): 27.

6. Glowacka Dorota and Stephen Boos, eds. *Between Ethics and Aesthetics: Crossing the Boundaries* (New York: State University of New York, 2001): 3.

7. Passage quoted by Vicky Bell in "Ethics and Feminism" in *Between Ethics and Aesthetics*, eds. Dorota and Boos (Albany, NY: State University of New York Press 2002): 159.

8. Ibid., 159.

9. Marjorie Stone, "Between Ethics and Anguish: Feminist Ethics, Feminist Aesthet-ics, and Representations of Infanticide" in *Between Ethics and Aesthetics*, eds. Dorota and Boos.

10. Stone situates her argument about feminist ethics in comparing slave infanticide in a little-known poem by Elizabeth Barrett Browning, "The Runaway Slave at Pilgrim's Point" and Toni Morrison's *Beloved*. I find her argument applicable to my South Asian authors because of her careful explanation and coupling of feminist aesthetics and ethics.

11. Stone, "Between Ethics and Anguish": 132.

12. Anita Rau Badami, *A Hero's Walk* (Chapel Hill, NC: Algonquin Books, 2001) and Jhumpa Lahiri, *The Interpreter of Maladies* (New York: Houghton Mifflin,

1999). Direct quotations from these books will be cited parenthetically within the text.

13. See, for example, Alicia Otano's *Speaking the Past: Child Perspective in the Asian American Bildungsroman* (Hamburg: LIT Verlag, 2004).

14. Lan Cao, *Monkey Bridge* (New York: Penguin, 1998); Christina Chiu, *Troublemaker and Other Saints* (New York: G. P. Putnam, 2001); and Lois Ann Yamanaka, *Blu's Hanging* (New York: Avon Books, 1997).

15. Stone, "Between Ethics and Anguish": 136–7.

16. Robin Fiori, et al., eds. *Recognition, Responsibility, and Rights* (Lanham, MD: Rowman & Littlefield, 2003): ix.

17. Misha Strauss, "The Role of Recognition in the Formation of Self-Understanding" in *Recognition, Responsibility, and Rights*, eds. Robin Fiori, et al. (Lanham, MD: Rowman & Littlefield, 2003): 47–8.

18. Zygmunt Bauman, *Liquid Modernity* (Cambridge, UK: Polity Press, 2000). Bauman in discussing the "forms of togetherness" writes, "I propose that the passage from the convention-ruled to the moral condition is not marked by the sudden numbness of the once voluble demand, nor by the dropping of conditions which once circumscribed responsibility, but by the appearance (or reappearance) of what the ethical legislation declares off-limits in the world of morality—namely of the emotional relationship to the Other. I also propose that the kind of emotion which colors the relationship is secondary, regarding the very emotionality of encounter which is primary—and decisive" (62).

19. Ibid., 30–1.

20. Michael Smith writes in *The Moral Problem* (Malden, MA: Blackwell, 1994) that moral problems become apparent when the impossibility of reconciling the objectivity of morality, the action-guided character of judgment, and the foundational subject or the Humean principle of motivation come together. My focus is on the distinction between absolute standards of morality and the fluidity of ethical impulses in the messiness of everyday reality.

21. Bauman: 146, original italics.

22. Bauman makes the distinction between uncritical liberalism and responsible community action in "On Communitarianism and Human Freedom: Or How to Square the Circle," *Theory, Culture and Society*, 13.2 (1996): 79–90.

23. Acknowledgment: I thank Gurudev and Rohin Rajan for their guidance, Orin Grossman for his support, and am grateful to Sue Im Lee and Rocío Davis for their vigilance in making me revise for precision and clarity. I also thank the anonymous readers from Temple University Press for their helpful suggestions.

Chapter 8

1. Hugh Kenner, *The Pound Era* (Berkeley: University of California Press, 1971): 230.
2. For a fuller discussion of Pound's lyric legacy in American poetry, see Robert Kern, *Orientalism, Modernism, and the American Poem* (Cambridge: Cambridge University Press, 1996).
3. Walter K. Lew, ed., *Premonitions: The Kaya Anthology of New Asian North American Poetry* (New York: Kaya Production, 1995).

4. Pound, "A Few Don'ts," in *Literary Essays of Ezra Pound*, edited by T. S. Eliot (New York: New Directions, 1968): 4. First published in *Poetry* 1, no. 6 (March 1913).
5. Pound, *A Memoir of Gaudier-Brzeska* (New York: New Directions, 1970; 1914): 80.
6. Ernest Fenollosa, *The chinese written character as a medium for poetry* (San Francisco: City Lights Books, 1968; 1918): 3. Hereafter cited parenthetically in the text.
7. Jacques Derrida, *Of Grammatology* (Baltimore: Johns Hopkins University Press, 1976): 92.
8. Kern discusses Emerson's and Fenollosa's shared assumption of "the complete correspondence between language and nature" (135).
9. Pound, *ABC of Reading* (New York: New Directions, 1960; 1914): 21.
10. Ibid., 21.
11. Ibid., 22.
12. This analysis does not take into account Asian poets in America in the first half of the twentieth century. Poets like Sadakichi Hartmann, Yone Noguchi, and José Garcia Villa were recognized by luminaries of High Modernism, and new scholarship in Asian American poetry considers these poets that predate the creation of Asian America. My reading considers a specific modernist legacy that activist Asian American poets avoided and one post-activist Asian American poet who grapples with it.
13. For an elaboration of this position of lyric, see Mark Jeffreys, "Ideologies of Lyric: A Problem of Genre in Contemporary Anglophone Poetics," *PMLA* 110:2 (March 1995): 196–205.
14. Quoted in Elaine H. Kim's *Asian American Literature: An Introduction to the Writings and their Social Context* (Philadelphia: Temple University Press, 1982): 235.
15. See George Uba, "Versions of Identity in Post-Activist Asian American Poetry," in *Reading the Literatures of Asian America*, eds. Shirley Lim and Amy Ling (Philadelphia: Temple University Press, 1992).
16. I would like to thank Zou Lin for pointing this out, and for translating the Chinese in "Symphonic Poem: 'Unfinished.'"
17. I would like to thank Sue-Im Lee for suggesting this return to the lyric "I."
18. See Blackmur's "The Masks of Ezra Pound," in *Language as Gesture* (New York: Harcourt, Brace and Co., 1935): 79–112.
19. From Hall's "Cultural Identity and Cinematic Representation," *Framework* 36 (1989): 72. Further, this emphasis on lyric's ability to forge human connections is presently being taken up by scholars interested in rereading the lyric. See, for example, Susan Stewart's *Poetry and the Fate of the Senses* (Chicago: University of Chicago Press, 2002) for a more philosophical account of lyric as a means of sharing human expression and Kirsten Silva Gruesz's *Ambassadors of Culture: The Transamerican Origins of Latino Writing* (Princeton, NJ: Princeton University Press, 2002) for a new examination of lyric as a lens for reading a minority community.

Chapter 9

1. Recent studies, like Susan Stanford Friedman's "Definitional Excursions: The Meanings of Modern/Modernity/Modernism," *Modernism/Modernity* 8.3 (2001): 493–513, explore the plural and contradictory definitions of modernism to describe it as less a critical category than a critical terrain for interrogation. While this contention

is certainly crucial to a needed reopening of the field through an interrogation of its criteria for inclusion and exclusion, I think a fairly univocal operative definition of the ethos and aesthetics of modernism as canonized by later criticism may still be obtained by resorting to the critical work of the 1970s and 1980s, that is, the decades when modernism was being reassessed from a postmodern point of view and subjected to a comparative and inquisitive glance. My list of relevant features of modernist aesthetics, therefore, while obviously cursory and incomplete, mirrors the kind of consensus that set the stage for subsequent reactions, as displayed for instance in Ihab Hassan's well-known chart of the differences between modernism and postmodernism; a similar, longer list can be found in Marjorie Perloff's overview on modernist studies. Thus defined in terms of overall aesthetic directions and assumptions rather than individual themes and formal strategies, writers like Stein and Hemingway, Fitzgerald and Faulkner, Anderson and Wolfe appear to belong to the same category and to have much in common with the "High Modernism" of the usual suspects Pound, Eliot, Joyce, and Woolf. From now on, when mentioning general characteristics of the modernist novel, I will be referring to the works of such critics as: Ihab Hassan, *The Dismemberment of Orpheus: Toward a Postmodern Literature* (2nd enlarged edition, Madison, WI: University of Wisconsin, 1982); David Lodge, "Modernism, Antimodernism and Postmodernism" and "Historicism and Literary History: Mapping the Modern Period," in *Working with Structuralism. Essays and Reviews on Nineteenth- and Twentieth-Century Literature* (London: Routledge and Kegan Paul, 1981); Brian McHale, *Constructing Postmodernism* (London and New York: Routledge, 1992); James M. Mellard, *The Exploded Form: The Modernist Novel in America* (Urbana, IL: University of Illinois Press, 1980); Marjorie Perloff, "Modernist Studies," in *Redrawing the Boundaries. The Transformation of English and American Literary Studies*, eds. Stephen Greenblatt and Giles Gunn (New York: Modern Language Association, 1992); William V. Spanos, "The Detective and the Boundary: Some Notes on the Postmodern Literary Imagination," *boundary 2* 1:1 (Fall 1972): 163–89; Alan Wilde, *Horizons of Assent: Modernism, Postmodernism, and the Ironic Imagination* (Baltimore and London: The Johns Hopkins University Press, 1981).

2. David Finkle, "Ng's Kickoff Scores Touchdown," *The New York Times*, 14 February 1993.

3. Elaine H. Kim, foreword to *Reading the Literatures of Asian America*, eds. Shirley Geok-lin Lim and Amy Ling (Philadelphia: Temple University Press, 1992): xii.

4. Fae Myenne Ng, *Bone* (New York: Hyperion, 1993): 3. Page numbers will henceforth be included parenthetically in the text.

5. Roland Barthes, *S/Z*, trans. Richard Miller (New York: Hill and Wang, 1974).

6. Lisa Lowe, *Immigrant Acts : On Asian American Cultural Politics* (Durham, NC and London: Duke University Press, 1996): 122.

7. On gossip as both destructive and therapeutic, expressing the contradictory quality of the Chinatown community, see Julie Sze, "Have You Heard? Gossip, Silence, and Community in *Bone*," *Hitting Critical Mass: A Journal of Asian American Cultural Criticism* 2:1 (Winter 1994), online edition, no pagination.

8. Author's statement during the public presentation of the Italian translation of *Bone* at Centro Studi Americani in Rome (June 30, 1999).

9. Sau-ling Cynthia Wong used a similar argument in her article to defend Maxine Hong Kingston from some of Chin's criticisms, contending that some of Kingston's

alleged falsifications of the Chinese words and stories in *The Woman Warrior* were in fact representative of the second generation's experience of their Chinese cultural heritage, confusedly perceived and mediated in ways difficult to assess: see Frank Chin, "Come All Ye Asian American Writers of the Real and the Fake," in *The Big Aiiieeeee! An Anthology of Chinese American and Japanese American Literature*, eds. Jeffery Paul Chan, Frank Chin, Lawson Fusao Inada, and Shawn Wong (New York: Meridian, 1991); and Sau-ling Cynthia Wong, "Autobiography as Guided Chinatown Tour? Maxine Hong Kingston's *The Woman Warrior* and the Chinese American Autobiographical Controversy," in *Multicultural Autobiography: American Lives*, ed. James Robert Payne (Knoxville, TN: University of Tennessee Press, 1992): 248–79.

10. For a more detailed analysis of the metaphors in *Bone*, see my "Letteratura e/o testimonianza: *Bone* e il canone asiaticoamericano," *Nuova Corrente* 47 (2000): 327–60.

11. On food and its implications in Asian American literature, see Sau-Ling Cynthia Wong, *Reading Asian American Literature. From Necessity to Extravagance* (Princeton, NJ: Princeton University Press, 1993).

12. See Finkle, "Ng's Kickoff Scores Touchdown."

13. See note 8.

14. "Blood and bones. The oldtimers believed that the blood came from the mother and the bones from the father" (104); "The oldtimers believe we have a heavenly weight, and that our fates can be divined by the weighing of our bones" (153).

15. "This is a very non-Confucian thing to do," Ng states in an interview: Matthew Kreitman, "Ng digs up the Bones of decades gone by," *Hong Kong Express*, May 1994. For a reading of Ona's suicide as an anti-patriarchal act, see Benjamin Perez, "Sisters," *Hitting Critical Mass: A Journal of Asian American Cultural Criticism* 2:1 (Winter 1994), online edition, no pagination.

16. See Susannah Hunnewell, "When the Old Began to Die," *The New York Times Book Review*, 7 February 1993. For a reading of the bone image as a metaphor for connectedness, see Jay Chuang, "Bone in *Bone*," *Hitting Critical Mass: A Journal of Asian American Cultural Criticism* 2:1 (Winter 1994), online edition, no pagination.

17. Thomas W. Kim, "'For a paper son, paper is blood': Subjectivation and Authenticity in Fae Myenne Ng's *Bone*," *MELUS* 24.4 (Winter 1999): 41–56.

18. On the construction of space in the novel and its connections with body politics, political economy, commodification, and individual socialization, see Frederick Luis Aldama, "Spatial Re-Imaginations in Fae Myenne Ng's Chinatown," *Hitting Critical Mass: A Journal of Asian American Cultural Criticism* 1.2 (Spring 1994), online edition, no pagination; Serena Fusco, "'Our Inside Story': BodySpaces in Fae Myenne Ng's Chinatown," *Igitur* 3 (2002), 129–44; David Leiwi Li, *Imagining the Nation: Asian American Literature and Cultural Consent* (Stanford, CA: Stanford University Press, 1998).

19. Stephen J. Greenblatt, "Learning to Curse: Aspects of Linguistic Colonialism in the Sixteenth Century," in *Learning to Curse: Essays in Early Modern Culture* (New York and London: Routledge, 1990).

20. See Kreitman, "Ng Digs up the Bones."

21. For a reading of Mason's confrontation with his cousin Dale as evidence of the inner diversity of the Chinese American community, see Li, *Imagining the Nation*.

22. I wish to thank my student Vincenzo Bavaro for pointing this out to me during a classroom discussion of *Bone*.

23. On neologism and cultural, linguistic, and gender binaries, see Diane C. LeBlanc, "Neologism as Oppositional Language in Fae Myenne Ng's *Bone*," *Rocky Mountain Review* (Spring 2000): 11–22.

Chapter 10

1. Sara Suleri, *Meatless Days* (Chicago: University of Chicago Press, 1987); Garrett Hongo, *Volcano: A Memoir of Hawai'i* (New York: Alfred A. Knopf, 1995); Maxine Hong Kingston, *The Woman Warrior: Memoir of a Girlhood Among Ghosts* (New York: Knopf, 1975); Michael Ondaatje, *Running in the Family* (New York: Penguin, 1982). See my *Transcultural Reinventions: Asian American and Asian Canadian Short-Story Cycles* (Toronto: TSAR, 2001) for a discussion of Suleri and Hongo.

2. Clark Blaise and Bharati Mukherjee, *Days and Nights in Calcutta* (1977. St. Paul, MN: Hungry Mind Press, 1995). All quotations from this edition will be cited parenthetically within the text.

3. G. Thomas Couser posits a continuum between "ethnographic autobiography, in which the writer outranks the generally anonymous subject, to celebrity autobiography, in which the famous subject outranks the generally anonymous writer.... At the very centre are those texts produced by partners who are true peers—for example, dual autobiographies, in which each partner contributes a separate narrative, and truly co-authored (rather than "as-told-to") autobiographies.... In these texts there is more than one subject, and the act of collaboration may itself be presented in the foreground of the narrative rather than confined to the background or to supplementary texts" ("Collaborative Autobiography," in *Encyclopedia of Life Writing: Autobiographical and Biographical Forms*, ed. Margaretta Jolly (London: Fitzroy Dearborn Publishers, 2001): Vol. 1, 222.

4. Jeanne Wakatsuki Houston and James D. Houston, *Farewell to Manzanar*. (1973. New York: Bantam, 1995).

5. In her introduction, Chan relates how she encountered Lee's text, and worked with the author to expand the material (*Quiet Odyssey: A Pioneer Korean Woman in America* [Seattle: University of Washington Press, 1990]). Other collaborative texts include Le Ly Hapslip's two volumes of her autobiography—*When Heaven and Earth Changed Places* (New York: Plume, 1990) and *Child of War, Woman of Peace* (New York: Anchor Books, 1993)—the first written with Jay Wurts, and the second with her son, James Hayslip. In *Child of War*, Hayslip speaks briefly about her processes of collaboration (300).

6. *The Girl from Purple Mountain: Love, Honor, War, and One Family's Journey from China to America* (New York: Thomas Dunne Books, 2001).

7. Paul John Eakin, in *How Our Lives Become Stories: Making Selves* (Ithaca, NY: Cornell University Press, 1999), highlights the relational component of life writing, which often intersects with collaboration in autobiography. In Asian American writing, the relational component limned in Kingston's text marks the development of subsequent auto/biographies—in Suleri's *Meatless Days* and Helie Lee's *Still Life*

with Rice (New York: Touchstone, 1996), for example—and this concern offers a renewed aesthetic that complicates the concept of the individuality and autonomy of the narrator.

8. I use the term "performative" as Sidonie Smith does in her work on autobiographical storytelling ("Performativity, Autobiographical Practice, Resistance," *A/b: Auto/Biography Studies* 10. [1995]: 18).

9. Sidonie Smith and Julia Watson, *Reading Autobiography: A Guide for Interpreting Narratives* (Minneapolis, MN: University of Minnesota Press, 2001): 149.

10. Susanna Egan, *Mirror Talk: Genres of Crisis in Contemporary Autobiography*, (Chapel Hill, NC: University of North Carolina Press, 1999): 7–8.

11. Albert E. Stone, "Collaboration in Contemporary American Autobiography," *Revue Francaise D'Etudes Americaines* 14 (May 1982): 164.

12. Egan, *Mirror Talk*: 9–10.

13. Barry Fruchter, "Bharati Mukherjee," in *Asian American Autobiographers: A Bio-Bibliographical Critical Sourcebook,* ed. Guiyou Huang (Westport, CT: Greenwood Press, 2001): 258.

14. Smith and Watson, *Reading Autobiography*: 94.

15. Pramila Venkateswaran, "Bharati Mukherjee as Autobiographer," in *Bharati Mukherjee: Critical Perspectives*, ed. Emmanuel S. Nelson (New York: Garland Publishing, 1993): 23–45; Anindyo Roy, "The Aesthetics of an (Un)Willing Immigrant: Bharati Mukherjee's *Days and Nights in Calcutta* and *Jasmine*," in *Bharati Mukherjee: Critical Perspectives*, ed. Emmanuel S. Nelson (New York: Garland Publishing, 1993): 127–41.

16. Fruchter, "Bharati Mukherjee": 258.

17. Venkateswaran, "Bharati Mukherjee as Autobiographer": 24.

18. Another point concerns the book's editorial history: *Days and Nights in Calcutta* was published first in the United States in 1977 (it was published in Canada in 1986, and reissued with a new prologue and epilogue in the United States in 1995), where Mukherjee's popularity outshines her husband, and where her position as an Asian American subject has made her the focus of critical interest. This editorial consideration, and the desire of Asian American scholars to engage in issues of immigrant and ethnic identity, have led to what I believe is still an unjustified emphasis on Mukherjee in U.S readings of this book.

19. Because my discussion centers primarily on Blaise and Mukherjee's formal and aesthethic project, I will not discuss the nuances of their positions on ethnicity and nationhood. For a discussion of these issues, see Egan.

20. Egan, *Mirror Talk*: 135.

21. Ibid., 141.

22. Smith and Watson, *Reading Autobiography*: 143.

23. Eakin, *How Our Lives Become Stories*: 139.

24. Ibid., 59.

25. Couser, "Collaborative Autobiography": 223.

26. In his 1995 prologue to the volume, Blaise acknowledges his naïve superiority, his "imperial confidence" that justified his perspective on his experience, and led to some misguided conclusions and predictions about India.

27. Egan, *Mirror Talk*: 138.

28. Roy, "The Aesthetics of an (Un)Willing Immigrant": 198.

29. Ibid., 128–9.

30. Egan, *Mirror Talk*: 136.
31. Fruchter, "Bharati Mukherjee": 262.
32. Stone, "Collaboration in Contemporary American Autobiography": 153.

Chapter 11

1. See Richard Mathews, *Fantasy: The Liberation of Imagination,* (New York: Routledge, 2002): 20f, for an overview of how fantasy came to be established as a tradition within English and American literary history in particular, separate and discrete from the development of realism in literature. Hereafter cited in text.
2. An easy example would be all the *Star Trek* series, which have interrogated the standard societal attitudes toward homosexuality, monogamy, and racism, to name a few obvious issues. It is not germane to my argument to distinguish between science fiction and fantasy; rather, I am focusing on the power of imaginative nonrealistic fiction to inspire cogent social critique.
3. C. S. Lewis, *The Horse and His Boy* (1954. New York: Collier, 1971).
4. J.R.R. Tolkien, *The Fellowship of the Ring. The Lord of the Rings*, Part One (1965. New York: Ballantine, 1983). Lewis and Tolkien were members of the Inklings, a Christian writing group, along with George Macdonald, Owen Barfield, and Charles Williams.
5. Raymond E. Feist, *Magician: Master* (1982. Toronto: Bantam, 1988).
6. Two examples of fantasy sequences that depict nonwhite characters on their covers are Ursula LeGuin's Earthsea Trilogy, such as *A Wizard of Earthsea* (1968. New York: Bantam, 1977), in which whites are explicitly presented as the barbarian minority, and books by Octavia Butler, an African American science fiction writer, whose characters are black. See, for example *Parable of the Sower* (1993. New York: Warner Books, 1995).
7. Anne McCaffrey, *Dragonsdawn.* (New York: Del Rey-Ballantine, 1988).
8. Like fantasy, Asian American literature has progressed through essentialist phases into a more multicultural, multivalenced paradigm. See David Leiwei Li, who usefully chronicles the history of approaches toward creating an Asian American mythos in *Imagining the Nation: Asian American Literature and Cultural Consent* (Stanford, CA: Stanford University Press, 1998).
9. Laurence Yep, "World Building," portion of "Another World? A Sampling of Remarks on Science Fiction and Fantasy," in *Innocence & Experience: Essays & Conversations on Children's Literature*, edited and compiled by Barbara Harrison and Gregory Maguire (New York: Lothrop, Lee & Shepard Books, 1987): 182.
10. Ibid., 184.
11. Ibid., 183.
12. Laurence Yep, "Introduction," in *Sweetwater,* (1973, New York: HarperCollins, 2004): xiii.
13. The first three titles are *Dragon of the Lost Sea* (New York: HarperTrophy-HarperCollins, 1982); *Dragon Steel* (New York: Harper & Row, 1985); and *Dragon Cauldron* (New York: HarperCollins, 1991).
14. See my forthcoming "Towards a Poetics of Asian American Fantasy: Laurence Yep's Construction of a Bicultural Mythology" in *The Lion and the Unicorn* (Sum. 2006) for further discussion of Yep's Asian Americanness in his works.

15. Accessed on 7/25/03 and 7/28/03.
16. kandladin, "One of the best fantasy books I have ever read," review of *Dragon of the Lost Sea*, by Laurence Yep, Amazon.com Customer Reviews, 13 December 2000, http://www.amazon.com.
17. la_solinas, review of *Dragon of the Lost Sea*, by Laurence Yep, Amazon.com Customer Reviews, 3 April 2000, http://www.amazon.com.
18. "A reader," "A little bland, especially if you're Chinese...", review of *Dragon of the Lost Sea*, by Laurence Yep, Amazon.com Customer Reviews, 13 August 2000, http://www.amazon.com. [NB: there are two reviews of this book, both anonymous, both given this same title, both written on the same date.]
19. An interesting comparison could be made between Yep's adaptation of Chinese mythology and the Myth-O-Mania series by Kate McMullan, which radically and irreverently recasts Greek myths. See, for example, *Have a Hot Time, Hades!* (New York: Volo Publishing, 2002).
20. Laurence Yep, *Child of the Owl* (New York: HarperTrophy-HarperCollins, 1977).
21. The great-greatgranddaughter of Otter in the Golden Mountain Chronicles.
22. *Child of the Owl* has been named an ALA Notable Book, and has won the *Boston Globe* Horn Book Award, *School Library Journal* Best Book Award, and Jane Addams Children's Book Award.
23. Compare Kate McMullan's series for intermediate readers, or the adult series edited by Ellen Datlow and Terry Windling commencing with *Snow White, Blood Red* (New York: Eos, 1993, reprint edition), or Robin McKinley's *Door in the Hedge* (New York: Berkley Books, 1981).
24. Yep's "Paying with Shadows" is forthcoming in the Summer 2006 special issue of *Lion and the Unicorn*, which also contains my other article on Yep.
25. Laurence Yep, *Child of the Owl*: 216–7. Hereafter cited in text.
26. T. H. White, *The Once and Future King* (1956, New York: Ace Books, 1987).
27. Mathews, *Fantasy*: 118, 127, 127.
28. Yep, "Introduction": xi.
29. David Henry Hwang's *M Butterfly* (New York: Penguin, 1994), for instance, ingeniously exposes the constructed nature of white, male, and European desire.
30. Cynthia Kadohata, *The Glass Mountains*, (Clarkston, GA: Borealis-White Wolf Publishing, 1995). Hereafter cited in text.
31. Yep, "Paying."
32. For a fascinating example of a writer innovatively blending Asian American literature with science fiction, see William F. Wu's short story, "Black Powder," in the anthology compiled by Yep from student work done in his creative writing courses: Laurence Yep, *American Dragons: Twenty-Five Asian American Voices* (New York: HarperTrophy-HarperCollins, 1993).

Chapter 12

1. Albert Bermel, *Contradictory Characters* (Evanston, IL: Northwestern University Press, 1973): 11.
2. Ibid., 11.
3. See Josephine Lee in *Performing Asian America: Race and Ethnicity on the Contemporary Stage* (Philadelphia: Temple University Press, 1997): Chapter 2.

4. Jinqi Ling writes, "Abdul JanMohamed and David Lloyd regard such lack of aesthetic playfulness in writings by American minority writers as one textual emblem of racial minorities' social deformation, as well as an 'expression and sublimation' of the indignities historically suffered by them," in *Narrating Nationalism* (New York: Oxford University Press, 1998): 22.

5. See James Moy, *Marginal Sights: Staging the Chinese in America* (Iowa City, IA: University of Iowa Press, 1993).

6. Lee, *Performing Asian America*: 41.

7. While Josephine Lee acknowledges the healing process experienced by Asian American spectators in a realist performance, I suggest that the same process can also occur among non-Asian American spectators. Many popular Asian American plays have been successfully produced in mainstream venues.

8. Peter Szondi, *Theories of the Modern Drama* (Minneapolis: University of Minnesota Press, 1987).

9. Lee, Performing Asian America: 35.

10. Velina Hasu Houston, *Tea, Unbroken Thread*, ed. Roberta Uno (Amherst, MA: University of Massachusetts Press, 1993). Hereafter cited parenthetically within the text.

11. As Teruko concludes towards the end of play, "But today we have all gone a little farther with each other than we have before" (195).

12. See Karen Shimakawa, *National Abjection: The Asian American Body Onstage* (Durham, NC: Duke University Press, 2002) for a discussion of the deconstruction of stereotypes in Houston's *Tea*.

13. Himiko's suicide is not only enacted in the opening moment of the play, but proves the catalyst that brings the four estranged women together. As Chizuye concludes, "We're here today because we hurt inside like we never have before. Because when the first of us goes so violently and it's all over the paper, it wakes us up" (195).

14. The exception here is that the audience members are aware of Himiko's presence while the living characters are not.

15. Lee, *Performing Asian America*: 203.

16. David Henry Hwang, *FOB and Other Plays* (New York: Penguin Books, 1990). Hereafter cited parenthetically in the text.

17. Robert Lowell, *Notebook* (New York: Farrar, Straus & Giroux, 1970): 262.

18. J.L. Styan, *Modern Drama in Theory and Practice II* (New York: Cambridge University Press, 1996): 110.

19. Lowell, *Notebook*: 262.

20. Josephine Lee emphasizes Dale and Steve's capitalist values; she also draws a parallel between Grace's lower class struggles and her psychological need for the Fa Mu Lan alter ego, *Performing Asian America*: 179.

21. Lee, *Performing Asian America*: 36.

22. Ibid., 182.

23. Marc Robinson, *The Other American Drama* (Cambridge: Cambridge University Press, 1995).

Notes on Contributors

Mita Banerjee is Professor and Chair of American Studies at the University of Siegen, Germany. Her publications include *The Chutneyfication of History: Salman Rushdie, Michael Ondaatje, Bharati Mukherjee and the Postcolonial Debate* (Heidelberg: Winter 2002) and *Racing the Century* (Heidelberg: Winter 2005). She recently has become interested in a diasporic Asian cultural studies that would provide ways for looking at the role of Asian characters in German popular culture. She is currently working on a postcolonial reading of the American Renaissance.

Mark Chiang holds a B.A. from Yale and a Ph.D. from the University of California-Berkeley. He is currently an Assistant Professor in the English Department at the University of Illinois at Chicago, where he teaches courses in Asian American literature and multiethnic American literature. The essay in this volume derives from a book in progress, entitled "Representing Asian America: Race and Cultural Capital," that examines the question of what constitutes the "political" within the academy.

Patricia P. Chu is Associate Professor of English at George Washington University. She is the author of *Assimilating Asians: Gendered Strategies of Authorship in Asian America* (Duke University Press, 2000) and a contributor to *Asian American Identities Beyond the Hyphen* (Indiana University Press); *One Hundred Years of Korean Literature* (Sigur Center, George Washington University); *A Resource Guide to Asian American Literature* (MLA); *Arizona Quarterly*; and *Diaspora: A Journal of Transnational Studies*. Her current research interests include women's autobiography, Asian American travel narratives, and engaged Buddhism.

Rocío G. Davis is Associate Professor of American and Postcolonial Literatures and Director of the Institute of Liberal Arts at the University of Navarra, Spain.. Her publications include *Transcultural Reinventions: Asian American and Asian Canadian Short Story Cycles* (TSAR, 2001); *Sites of Ethnicity: Europe and the Americas* (co-edited with William Boelhower and Carmen Birkle, Winter Verlag, 2004); *Asian American Literature in the International Context: Readings on Fiction, Poetry, and Performance* (co-edited with Sämi Ludwig, LIT Verlag, 2002); and *Tricks with a Glass: Writing Ethnicity in Canada* (co-edited with Rosalía Baena, Rodopi, 2000). She has recently edited a special issue of the journal *MELUS* on Filipino American literature, and is currently working on a book on Asian American autobiographies of childhood.

Iyko Day is a Ph.D. Candidate in the Department of Ethnic Studies at the University of California, Berkeley. She is completing a dissertation examining literature, film, and visual art entitled "Dialectics of Asian North America: Queering a Transnational Place."

Donatella Izzo is professor of American Literature at Università degli Studi di Napoli "L'Orientale," Italy. She has published books and essays on Henry James, on U.S. authors of the nineteenth and twentieth centuries, and on literary theory. Her most recent books are *Portraying the Lady: Technologies of Gender in the Short Stories of Henry James* (University of Nebraska Press, 2001) and *"Contact Zones":Rewriting Genre across the East-West Border* (edited with Elena Spandri; Liguori, 2003) and *America at Large. Americanistica transnazionale e nuova comparatistica*, edited with Giorgio Mariani, (Shake, 2004).

Kimberly M. Jew teaches theatre history and literature at Washington and Lee University in Lexington, VA. She received her Ph.D. from New York University where she focused on modern drama and American theatre. She has published in the *Dictionary of Literary Biography*, the *Encyclopedia of Multiethnic American Literature*, and *The Midwestern Modern Language Association Journal*. She has recently received a Mellon Fellowship to complete her monograph on the experimental theatre of Elmer Rice.

Sue-Im Lee is Assistant Professor of English at Temple University. Her teaching and research areas are contemporary U. S. fiction, Asian American literature, and formal innovative fiction. She is currently at work on a book project entitled *Vexing Community in Contemporary U.S. Fiction*.

Christina Mar is a Ph.D. candidate at the University of California, Riverside. She is currently at work on her dissertation, "Vexed Exchanges: Marriage and Mixed Race in the U.S. National Family," which interrogates the discourses of family and nation underwriting constructions of mixed race Asian American literature.

Josephine Nock-Hee Park is Assistant Professor of English and Asian American Studies at the University of Pennsylvania. She is presently at work on a study of the legacy of American Orientalism in Asian American poetry entitled *Apparitions of Asia: Modernism's Orient and Asian American Poetry*.

Gita Rajan is the named Jane Watson Irwin Visiting Endowed Chair at Hamilton College in Women's Studies for 2004–5, and 2005–6. She is also an Associate Professor of English at Fairfield University. She publishes and teaches in Asian American, South Asian and Victorian literatures, Gender and Visual Culture, and in Globalization Studies. She was an Andrew Mellon Fellow at the University of Pennsylvania, a Paul Mellon Fellow at Yale University's Center for British Art, and a Scholar-in-Residence at New York University. She has published widely in her areas of research, and is completing a book on feminist ethics, South Asian public intellectuals, and globalization. She has co-edited *New Cosmopolitanisms: South Asians in the U.S.* (forthcoming, Stanford U Press), *An Introduction to Cultural Studies: History, Theory, Practice; Postcolonial Theory and Changing Cultural Contexts;* and *English Postcoloniality: Literatures From Around the World.* She is the U.S. editor of *South Asian Popular Culture*, a peer-reviewed journal from Taylor & Francis, and served on the Board of Directors for ASIANetwork (2001–4) and is the U.S. Representative on the Board for Multi Ethnic Societies of Europe and the Americas (2004–8).

Celestine Woo is Assistant Professor of English at Fort Lewis College in Colorado. She received her doctorate from New York University. Her areas of specialty are Shakespeare, British Romanticism, Asian American literature, and children's/young adult literature. She is also a poet, dancer, and choreographer.

Index

Harryman, Carla, 43
Harry Potter series (Rowling), 173
Hawai'i, Filipinos in, 19–20, *See also Blu's Hanging* (Yamanaka)
Hejinian, Lyn, 43
Hemingway, Ernest, 144
A Hero's Walk (Badami), 11, 107, 109–13
heteronomy, 37, 45
heteronormativity, 93, 101, 102, 214n.7
Hinduism, 100, 165
history, 78, 142–43
home, 110, 111–12, 165, 171
homosexuality, 87–88, 89, 93
Hongo, Garrett, 8, 159
The Horse and His Boy (Lewis), 175
Houston, Jeanne Wakatsuki, 160
Houston, Velina Hasu: *Tea,* 13, 188, 189, 190–96, 197
Huggan, Graham, 64
humanism, 6, 117, 118
human rights paradigm, 93, 94–95, 97
Hunter College, 8
Hwang, David Henry: *FOB,* 13, 188, 189–90, 196–202

identification, 169, 188–89, 202
identity, 75, 78, 84, 135–36, 192; Asian American, 67, 69, 177, 180, 195–96, 199; bicultural, 176, 177, 180–81, 185, 186; Chinese American, 57, 61–62, 68, 70, 145, 153, 196, 200–201; cross-cultural, 147–48; formation of, 199–202; lyric "I," 38, 48, 134–35; national, 72–73; open-ended, 67, 69; performance of, 141, 165, 167, 168; racial, 2, 28, 36; temporality and, 140–42; transcendence of, 194, 195; working-class, 49–50
identity, ethnic, 196. *See also* ethnicity
identity politics, 30, 84; culture and, 25–26; disidentification and, 80, 83
ideogram. *See* Chinese ideogram
idiosyncratic, the, 57, 58
Imo, Momoko, 188
imagery, 144, 148
imagination, fantasy and, 174, 176, 178, 185
Imagism, 12, 124–26, 130–31, 135, 136; Orientalism and, 123, 124, 129, 130, 133
immigrants, 78–79, 83, 96, 183–84, 200, 201; assimilation and, 104, 143, 176; autobiographies of, 143, 165–66, 170–71, 172; Chinese, 50, 146, 153. *See also* emigration/exile
Inada, Lawson, 129

"In a Station of the Metro" (Pound), 125
India, 162. *See also Days and Nights in Calcutta* (Blaise & Mukherjee)
institutional legitimization, 23–24, 28, 29, 39
interiority, 191, 194, 195, 197, 202
Interpreter of Maladies (Lahiri), 107
irony, 166, 169, 194, 200
Ishi (Native American), 10, 60, 61, 63, 65
isotropy, 145
Izzo, Donatella, 12, 137, 228

Jaggar, Alison, 120
James, Henry, 140, 144
Jameson, Fredric, 143
JanMohamed, Abdul R., 6
Japanese Americans, 20, 21, 160
Jasmine (Mukherjee), 104
Jew, Kimberley, 13, 187, 228
Johnson, Randal, 40
Journal of Asian American Studies, 31
justice, 99, 100. *See also* human rights paradigm

Kadohata, Cynthia, 12–13, 173, 174–75, 182–85, 186
Kenner, Hugh, 123
Kerouac, Jack, 63–64
Kim, Elaine, 4–5, 26, 27, 67, 68, 212n.20
Kim, Thomas, 148
Kingston, Maxine Hong, 186; *The Woman Warrior,* 55, 56–57, 61–62, 63, 64, 67–68. *See also Tripmaster Monkey* (Kingston)
Kiyooka, Roy, 37
Kogawa, Joy, 39

Lahiri, Jhumpa, 11, 105, 107, 113–19
language, 42, 50, 127, 151–52; assimilation and, 79–80; denaturalization of, 81–82; English language, 126, 152, 155, 215n.1; ideal, 132; metaphoric, 144–49; translation and, 150, 151. *See also* Chinese ideogram
language poetry, 10–11, 38, 42–44, 47, 49–50, 74–75; subject in, 48, 73, 74, 75–78. *See also* Wah, Fred
Lee, Josephine, 195, 199, 200
Lee, Li-Young, 37
Lee, Mary Paik, 160
Lee, SKY, 39
Lee, Sue-Im, 1, 18, 27, 173, 176, 215n.1, 228
legitimacy, 23–24, 28, 29, 45